T0195504

RAND and the Information Evolution

A History in Essays and Vignettes

WILLIS H. WARE

Funding for the publication of this document was provided through a generous gift from Paul Baran, an alumnus of RAND, and support from RAND via its philanthropic donors and income from operations.

Library of Congress Cataloging-in-Publication Data

Ware, Willis H.
    RAND and the information evolution : a history in essays and vignettes / Willis H. Ware.
      p. cm.
    Includes bibliographical references.
    ISBN 978-0-8330-4513-3 (pbk. : alk. paper)
    1. Rand Corporation—History. 2. Information technology—Research—United States—History.
3. Computer science—Research—United States—History. 4. Military research—United States—History—
20th century. 5. Research institutes—United States—History—20th century. I. Title.

QA76.27.W37 2008
355'.070973—dc22

                                      2008029573

The RAND Corporation is a nonprofit research organization providing objective analysis and effective solutions that address the challenges facing the public and private sectors around the world. RAND's publications do not necessarily reflect the opinions of its research clients and sponsors.

RAND® is a registered trademark.

Book design by Eileen La Russo

Published 2008 by the RAND Corporation
1776 Main Street, P.O. Box 2138, Santa Monica, CA 90407-2138
1200 South Hayes Street, Arlington, VA 22202-5050
4570 Fifth Avenue, Suite 600, Pittsburgh, PA 15213-2665
RAND URL: http://www.rand.org/
To order RAND documents or to obtain additional information, contact
Distribution Services: Telephone: (310) 451-7002;
Fax: (310) 451-6915; Email: order@rand.org

Energy permits things to exist; information, to behave purposefully.

Willis Howard Ware, 1997
—The First Law of Information Primacy[1]

When the events and achievements in this document were unfolding, the centrality of information in the scheme of things was only vaguely recognized and little discussed. Today, the role of information in the affairs of society, of organizations, of countries, of the world, and of the individual is widely recognized, discussed, researched, and understood. In this document are the earliest beginnings of it in one organization: the RAND Corporation.

---

[1] The author was led to frame this thought in his consideration of protecting the infrastructure of the United States against threats of various kinds, in particular against deliberately invoked ones. This statement reflects his judgment of the priority of energy and information relative to other segments of the infrastructure. See Ware (1998).

Dedication

This work is my legacy to RAND.

It, with its people, created an unprecedented culture and environment in which I could develop a wonderful and distinguished career.

I dedicate this book to my family: my wife Floy; my daughters Deborah and Alison; my son David; their respective spouses Edwin Pinson, Thomas Manoli, and Astrid Erling; and my granddaughters Arielle and Victoria Manoli. Each has supported me in many ways throughout my 65-year career.

I also acknowledge the many scores of individuals—fellow RANDites, professional colleagues, personal friends, acquaintances—who collectively formed the milieu in which both my career and I were embedded, shaped, influenced, and evolved.

—Willis H. Ware

Willis H. Ware

Preface

This document began as a summary of the computer-science research of the RAND computer department, then morphed into a reasonably comprehensive professional memoir that records and describes achievements, organizational details, and activities of the RAND department that supplied the corporation with computing support and conducted a program of computer-science research. Variously named over the years, the department's life span paralleled the evolution and growth of a commercial computing industry and the concurrent rise of computer science as an accepted discipline in academia.

While the document describes the computer machinery that RAND researchers and staff used and the environment in which it operated, it provides no extensive coverage of the programming side of the department nor of the programmer cadre. The many projects that they have undertaken are so varied that it would not be possible to even catalog them, much less to discuss them in detail. A few individuals are mentioned by name, but there were hundreds of others, many of whom made significant and lasting software contributions. Likewise, there is no discussion of the many who kept the machines running, funneled punched cards and magnetic tapes into and out of equipment, kept printers loaded with reams of paper, punched endless IBM® cards, and generally made the computer shop run in an efficient and orderly manner. Theirs is a story unto itself.

The document's source materials are varied and include both published and unpublished material, including ephemera. For many topics discussed herein, the principal published RAND documents are cited. Others are available most readily by browsing the RAND online bookstore by author.[2] We have done our best to ensure correct and working references to any online material, but of course such materials can move or be deleted without notice at any time, thus rendering those references potentially irretrievable, with the concomitant loss of historical material. The department produced its share of RAND documents, and a small number of these are available online through RAND. Published documents are available through RAND as well. However, many activities (especially in the earlier days) were not documented at all, or their content and effect were reflected in letters, internal memoranda, personal notes, or personal files. Most of the latter have vanished over the years or rest in boxes stored in garages, attics, or unknown

---

[2] See RAND (2007e).

other places. For many subjects and projects, there are no known publications—formal or internal. There are only memories.

The department staff included no historian or archivist. Thanks to the efforts of the current RAND archivist, Vivian Arterbery, there is some material in the RAND corporate archives, access to which is open to qualified historians. The materials on which this work is based—e.g., email messages, documents, downloads—have been deposited with the RAND archivist and are available to accredited historians on request. A few personal collections of material or collections of RAND-published documents have been transferred to archives at the Smithsonian Institution (Jerome and Dorothy Lemelson Center for the Study of Invention and Innovation at the National Museum of American History in Washington, D.C.), the Computer History Museum (Santa Clara, California), or the Charles Babbage Institute Center for the History of Information Technology (University of Minnesota Institute of Technology, Minneapolis, Minnesota).

RAND, as well as a generous grant by Paul Baran, supported production and publication of this document.[3]

Comments and questions should be directed to the compiler and primary author: Willis H. Ware, RAND Corporation, 1776 Main Street, P.O. Box 2138, Santa Monica, CA 90407-2138, 310-393-0411 x6432, Willis_Ware@rand.org, http://www.rand.org.

---

[3] The entire initial manuscript was prepared in a simple ASCII editor running in a DOS window under Microsoft® Windows® 2000 Professional. It is named esp and is a PC/DOS-oriented version of e, a RAND editor. esp was written by William Rogers, a member of the RAND economics department, whose company (Software Resources) provided RAND unlimited use of it in exchange for being allowed to use e as a design model. The many DOS files were then transferred to Microsoft Word® files to be integrated into a single volume, revised, and edited.

Contents

Figures

Photographs

Tables

Acknowledgments

Many people participated in this effort as contributors, as providers of facts and history, as commentators and informal reviewers, and as sources of support for the endeavor. Contributors, for the most part, conducted their work by electronic communications, notably email. Unless otherwise indicated, the author of each section or subsection is Willis Ware. However, he made generous use of excerpts from email messages, from published RAND documents, and occasionally from documents supplied by former RAND researchers. Much material has come from his own memories or papers and notes.

Department alumni who participated are the following: William Frederick (Bill) Gunning, George W. Brown, Paul Armer, Robert H. (Bob) Anderson, James P. (Jimmy) Wong Jr., Irwin D. (Irv) Greenwald, Wesley S. (Wes) Melahn, William L. (Bill) Sibley, John Patrick (Pat) Haverty, Paul Baran, Mario L. Juncosa, Norman Zalmon (Norm) Shapiro, Raymond W. (Ray) Clewett, Roy Fry, G. Edward (Ed) Bryan, Edward Charles (Ed) DeLand, Gabriel F. (Gabe) Groner, Ivan L. Finkle, James (Jim) Babcock, John F. Matousek, Michael (Mike) Warshaw, Edward A. (Ed) Feigenbaum, Eileen Mockbee Martner, D. Tracy (Tracy) Rumford, Malcolm R. (Mal) Davis, Robert N. (Bob) Reinstedt, Joseph W. (Joe) Smith, R. L. (Larry) Clark, and Eugene H. (Gene) Jacobs.

Another notable participant was longtime department consultant and friend, Robert L. (Bob) Patrick.

Early text-processing staff were important sources of information: Lynn Anderson, Sue Payne, and Christine d'Arc Taylor.

Many important alumni were not available to contribute directly to this document. One of particular import and an articulate and skillful writer must be mentioned—John David Williams, theoretical astronomer. He was the insightful, charismatic leader of the mathematics division (and therefore, the early computer activities) who made many things possible through his persuasions. Another is Cecil B. Hastings, whose death preceded the beginning of this effort by only a few months. His 1955 *Approximations for Digital Computers* had an effect on the world of computing that most observers suspect Cecil never realized.

It would be derelict not to acknowledge the past contributions and support of the founding group of RAND and of the early analysts and managers. Especially important to the success and achievements of the RAND "computerniks" were Franklin Rudolf (Frank) Collbohm, RAND's first president, and Julius Richard (Dick, aka

Goldy) Goldstein, RAND's first vice president and, eventually, first senior vice president. Both supported anything that we wanted to do, and Frank, especially, espoused the most wonderful of any possible supportive philosophy: "If it's important to the Air Force [RAND's first client], go do it." It would also be remiss not to acknowledge two other corporate officers—namely Stephen Parrish (Steve) Jeffries (corporate secretary) and James Scott (Scott) King (treasurer). Both of them also were corporate friends of the computing activities and were supportive in many ways—even when requests were strange and unusual.

Past and present RAND folks who helped bring this project to fruition are the following:

- Michael D. Rich, executive vice president, who provided support and encouragement for an effort that took much longer than originally anticipated
- Robert H. Anderson, who merits a double and vigorous thanks because he not only initially suggested the document but also strongly supported its development and production
- Rick Eden, RAND's associate director of research quality assurance, who, with diligent attention, identified and resolved the myriad details that morph a completed manuscript into a polished, final book
- Vivian Arterbery, RAND corporate secretary and archivist
- Ann Horn, curator of the RAND archives, who searched repeatedly for old items requested
- Jane F. Ryan, director of RAND's publications department, who made many old documents available
- Walter T. Nelson of the RAND library, who scanned old documents into computer format and then into editable computer files, providing invaluable support in getting old materials online
- Lori Emadi of the RAND library, who helped locate articles in *RANDom News* and the *RAND Alumni Bulletin*
- Diane Baldwin, RAND staff photographer, who located the photographs and prepared them for use in the document
- Mary O'Halloran and Mark Brite of RAND human resources for confirming names and dates in RAND personnel records
- Larry Johnson, who provided various historical details
- Donn E. Williams, director of RAND facilities and services, for information regarding the history of RAND's early buildings
- Lisa Bernard, RAND editor, who helped greatly to ensure clarity and consistency in writing style while preserving the individual voices of the contributors
- Todd Duft, RAND production editor, who coordinated a complicated and unique production challenge
- Eileen La Russo, RAND graphic designer, whose design skills integrated the text and photographs so well

- Patrice Lester, who converted the many DOS files of the original manuscript to Microsoft Word files
- Terri Perkins, who responded promptly and reliably to administrative and secretarial requests
- Christopher Dirks, who moved the manuscript into the RAND draft template and kept it stable through many rounds of addition, deletion, reorganization, and revision.

Unfortunately, not all of the hundreds of people associated with computing at RAND can be included. The roster of individuals identified by name in this document is far from a complete one. Nonetheless, it is important to acknowledge that those not mentioned individually herein should know that they are also a part of the department story, and equally so.

Abbreviations

2-D	two dimensional
A	accumulator register
AAF	U.S. Army Air Forces
ACM	Association for Computing Machinery
ADC	Air Defense Center
AEC	U.S. Atomic Energy Commission
AFIPS	American Federation of Information Processing Societies
AFSB	Air Force Studies Board
AFSC	Air Force Specialty Code
AFWAL	Air Force Wright Aeronautical Laboratory
AI	artificial intelligence
ALS	Advanced Logistics System
ARPA	Advanced Research Projects Agency
ARPANET	Advanced Research Projects Agency Network
BASIC	Beginner's All-Purpose Symbolic Instruction Code
BBN	Bolt, Beranek, and Newman
boPET	biaxially oriented polyethylene terephthalate
BuAer	Bureau of Aeronautics
BuStan	Bureau of Standards
CACM	*Communications of the ACM*
Caltech	California Institute of Technology
CE	customer engineer
CINC	commander in chief
CO_2	carbon dioxide
CPEC	card-programmed electronic calculator
CPU	central processing unit
CR-LF	carriage return, line feed

CRC	cyclical redundancy check
CSD	Computer Sciences Department
CSD	Computer Services Department
DARPA	Defense Advanced Research Projects Agency
DC	direct current
DDR&E	director, defense research and engineering
DEC	Digital Equipment Corporation
DEW	distant early warning
DIA	Defense Intelligence Agency
DoD	U.S. Department of Defense
DODCI	Department of Defense Computer Institute
DSB	Defense Science Board
EAM	electric accounting machine
EDVAC	Electronic Discrete Variable Automatic Computer
ENIAC	Electronic Numerical Integrator and Computer
EPAM	elementary perceiving and memorizing
FFRDC	federally funded research and development center
FJCC	Fall Joint Computer Conference
FLOP	floating octal point
FOB	free on board
GCRC	general clinical-research center
GPS	general problem solver
I/O	input-output
IAS	Institute for Advanced Study
IDA	Institute for Defense Analysis
IEEE	Institute of Electrical and Electronics Engineers
IFIP	International Federation for Information Processing
IMDS	interactive map-display system
IPL	information-processing language
IRE	Institute of Radio Engineers
ISL	information-system laboratory
IT	information technology
JCC	Joint Computer Conference
JOHNNIAC	John von Neumann Numerical Integrator and Automatic Computer
JOSS	JOHNNIAC open-shop system

kVA	kilovolt amperes
LDS	legal-decisionmaking system
LSL	logistic simulation laboratory
LT	Logic Theorist
MH	mail handler
MIT	Massachusetts Institute of Technology
MOS	military occupational specialty code
MQ	multiplier-quotient register
MS	mail system
MTST	magnetic tape to Selectric typewriter
NAA	North American Aviation
NAD	numerical analysis department
NAE	National Academy of Engineering
NDRC	National Defense Research Committee
NIH	National Institutes of Health
NJCC	National Joint Computer Committee
NORAD	North American Aerospace Defense Command
NOSY	nonsystem
NOTS	Naval Ordnance Test Station
NSA	National Security Agency
OFP	operational flight program
ONR	Office of Naval Research
OS	operating system
PAL	programmer-alert light
PDP	programmed data processor
PGEC	Professional Group on Electronic Computers
PPSC	Privacy Protection Study Commission
PRC	Planning Research Corporation
PUSS	Parliamentary Under-Secretary of State
REAC	Reeves Electronic Analog Computer
RITA	RAND intelligent terminal agent
ROSIE	rule-oriented system for implementing expertise
ROSS	rule-oriented simulation system
RSAC	RAND strategy-assessment center
SAC	Strategic Air Command

SACAPDS	Secretary's Advisory Committee on Automated Personal Data Systems
SAGE	semiautomatic ground environment
SDC	System Development Corporation
SGI	Silicon Graphics
SJCC	Spring Joint Computer Conference
SPO	System Project Office
SRGP	statistical research group at Princeton University
SSN	social-security number
STP	system training program
SWAC	Standards Western Automatic Computer
SWIRL	simulating warfare in the ROSS language
TA	teaching assistant
TATR	tactical air-target recommender
TLC	transfer logic cell
tp	text processor
TRAC	the RAND analog computer
TSO	Timesharing Option
TWIRL	tactical warfare in the ROSS language
UCI	University of California, Irvine
UNIVAC	universal automatic computer
USAF	U.S. Air Force
USC	University of Southern California
USPHS	U.S. Public Health Service, Commissioned Corps
VAX	virtual address extension
WYSIWYG	what you see is what you get

CHAPTER ONE

Introduction

"So very difficult a matter it is to trace and find out the truth of anything in history."

—*Plutarch*, The Life of Pericles

Purpose and Scope

This document describes, in rough chronological order, the achievements of a RAND department that has been named progressively Math-II, the numerical analysis department, the Computer Sciences Department (CSD), and the information sciences department. The department's time span extended from the formation of Project RAND (predecessor to the RAND Corporation) in 1946 through 1990, when all discipline-oriented departments in RAND were dissolved in favor of a programmatic organization.

From its earliest inception throughout much of its existence, the department had two missions and was two-pronged organizationally. It not only provided computing and programming services to the corporation but also conducted research projects that today would be called computer science. However, as computing—in the largest sense—evolved and matured, so did the capability to exploit machines by the user base throughout RAND. Inevitably, the user community developed its own ability to program and utilize computers. Thus, over time, this led to a decline in the programming activities within the department.

In the department's later history, the services and programming functions split off administratively and organizationally and became a separate function within RAND. By that time, there was an extensive commercial computing industry, and RAND's computing support was based almost solely on market products. From its beginning through 1983, the department also included a small but excellent model shop with extensive mechanical and electronic capabilities.

Many of the efforts described herein were a search for new knowledge with regard to the sophisticated use and exploitation of computers. Others, however, were very much oriented to the application of computer technology to real-world studies and client problems associated with policy studies. A few addressed important collateral and less technical issues of infusing computers and their functional capabilities into an organization—for example, the proper management approach and techniques for software-development efforts.

In particular, through much of the department's history, there were ongoing and substantial interactions with RAND's principal client, the U.S. Air Force (USAF). Often, this would be via participation on advisory groups and committees; at other times, it was through individual contacts and personal relationships. Topics of the day included the overall management of computing technology throughout the USAF organizational structure,[1] computer-system acquisition for new applications, software-development issues in major programs (not only in ground-based database installations but also in real-time weapon-system applications), computer technology in aircraft avionics, and personnel training. At the time, such activities were spoken of as "helping the client"; today, they would likely be called policy studies.[2]

Beginning somewhat later, approximately 1959, there was also a very close and intense ongoing relationship with the Advanced Research Projects Agency (ARPA), which supported much of the computer-science research.

While many projects originated within the department, others originated in other departments as innovative and often edge-of-the-art utilization of programming technology and computing power. Projects originating within the department usually pushed the computer-science frontier. Those originating in other departments usually pushed the computer-application frontier. Both types of project have been important influences on the development and evolution of computer science and applications.

The department's timeline paralleled the evolution of the computer hardware and software industries and the concurrent widespread utilization of the technology in the private, academic, and government sectors. It was also a time of growth for the professional societies and user groups that supported and helped create the field. Many members of the department's staff were stalwart participants, leaders, and officers in the new organizations that were formed and in older ones that were reinvented: notably, the Institute of Radio Engineers (IRE) and its successor, the Institute of Electrical and Electronics Engineers (IEEE); the Association for Computing Machinery (ACM); and the American Institute of Electrical Engineers, which joined with the IRE to become the IEEE.[3]

Since this is a memoir of the computing activities at RAND that emphasizes the early days, many of RAND's most profound achievements are not included or mentioned. In particular, the mathematics department is not treated, although it and the computing activities were intimately involved during the development of (among other things) linear

---

[1] For example, see Drezner, Shulman, and Ware (1975).

[2] One such effort concerned the development phase of the USAF F-16 aircraft, which was among the first of the software-intensive and software-controlled vehicles. Hyman L. Shulman (of RAND's engineering department) and Willis Ware (of the Computer Sciences Department) periodically made joint visits to the USAF System Project Office (SPO) at Wright-Patterson Air Force Base, Ohio, the contractor (General Dynamics in Fort Worth, Texas), and various air-staff offices. They persuaded the SPO director that he needed a full-time software expert on his staff and acted as an informal liaison and review mechanism to help alert the SPO to threatening or impending software problems.

[3] For a fuller discussion of this aspect of department history, see the section on professional societies in Chapter Seven.

programming, dynamic programming, game theory, modeling, and simulation.[4] Nor is there any discussion of the extensive work of RAND in military logistics, nuclear physics and atomic weaponry, strategic doctrine and tactics, the international economics of many countries, or military weaponry and utilization.

This document does not attempt to fit all the achievements and contributions of the department into the progress of the external world, nor does it always attempt to assess their effect and importance. On the other hand, sometimes there are documents or memories that relate a particular achievement to the world outside or to a particular client. At other times, there is a positive indicator or indirect feedback that some aspect of the department's work had influence or a direct effect. When known, they are identified and included.

For example, many individuals in the computing department achieved national reputations for their work; many went on to larger and more-prominent positions in universities and the commercial world. Three individuals who were either RAND staff members or closely connected consultants became Nobel laureates: William F. Sharpe, Harry Max Markowitz, and Herbert Alexander (Herb) Simon.[5] Others were honored by the National Academy of Engineering (NAE): Paul Baran, Keith William Uncapher, and Willis Ware. Four others received the ACM A. M. Turing Award, the most prestigious award in computing science: Allen Newell and Herb Simon (1975), Ivan Sutherland (1988), and Ed Feigenbaum (1994).

In short, this document augments currently available histories of RAND by capturing and recording a part of the corporation's achievements that are not elsewhere chronicled in detail.

Organization of the Document

This document basically follows the chronology of events and projects in the department as they unfolded. The successive topics are often independent and may have little commonality. There is no story line or topic that threads them all together neatly, other than the department itself. Occasionally, topics are clustered with others of mutual relevance. Since a reader may well choose to pick any topic about which to read, the document is written so that each section and subsection can stand on its own and not require the reader to flip back and forth to other sections. To support this flexibility, there is a small amount of intentional repetition.

To provide context for the department's activities, the document begins with a brief history of the RAND Corporation. This is followed by an overview of the computer-related activities of the first 35 or so years of RAND's existence. Following the overview and keyed to it, there is a collection of individual topics of various kinds. The major

---

[4]   For a short history of RAND's contributions to mathematics, see Augenstein (1993).

[5]   Herbert Simon, now deceased, was a longtime member of the Carnegie Institute of Technology (now Carnegie Mellon University) faculty.

projects or groups of projects are discussed in a series of short essays. Other subsections describe smaller projects or relate lesser events, even simple incidents or happenings that, in retrospect, may seemingly have little import but that were significant at the time.

Finally, there are anecdotes, sometimes of an operational nature and sometimes of a personal nature. The point of including collateral events and anecdotes is in part to enrich the reader's understanding of the department; their inclusion also provides insight to the computing culture of the time, the personalities of people, the attitude of vendors of the day, the hardware and software state-of-art, and, occasionally, some policy matter that would later become important to the field at large or to an organization. The hope is to capture not only the essence of the achievements themselves but also the joie de vivre of those working so close to the edge of the state of the art of computing in its early years.

The reader who wants just a "once over lightly" should read Chapter Two, particularly the second major section, "RAND Contributions to the Development of Computing." It can serve as an executive summary of the major topics of the entire document.

CHAPTER TWO

The Department

Conceptually, RAND is a technique in synthesis whereby scientific knowledge and talents are brought to bear upon military problems to aid the Air Force in the formulation of plans and policies. The technique is multi-disciplinary. Diverse skills and professions are organized to function as a team. It is of general applicability and can be employed in the analysis and solution of almost any type of complex problem requiring a scientific approach.[1]

—H. Rowan Gaither Jr.
then chair of the board of trustees
RAND Corporation

The Genesis of RAND

RAND, the corporation, celebrates its 60th anniversary in 2008.[2] On May 14, 1948, Project RAND—an outgrowth of World War II—had separated from the Douglas Aircraft Company of Santa Monica, California, and became an independent, nonprofit organization. The new entity was chartered in the state of California to "further and promote scientific, educational, and charitable purposes for the public welfare and security of the United States."

Known initially as the RAND Corporation, it quickly developed a unique style of policy study, blending a scrupulous nonpartisanship posture with rigorous, fact-based analysis to tackle society's most pressing problems. Early on, these efforts focused on national-security questions, including nuclear and atomic issues. Later, the organization was renamed RAND, but, in 2003, it again became the RAND Corporation. By the

---

[1] This characterization of RAND's research methodology is from the front matter of a corporate brochure that was used for general informational purposes and recruiting. It is neither dated nor identified with a document number, but it was most likely produced in the early 1950s. Today, of course, the phrasing would have to be generalized to read, "brought to bear upon client problems to aid it—the client—in the formulation of plans and policies." The document is quite complete and contains fascinating data. For instance, the personnel manager was Cecil Weihe; the sabbatic vacation plan is described; a major surgical operation under the Ross-Loos Medical Group plan was $25, and a nighttime physician house call, $3.50.

[2] The story of RAND's origin has been written many times in many ways for many occasions. Rather than recreate a wholly new version, this present one is derived from a brief history of RAND (RAND, 2008a). The abbreviation *RAND* is derived from *research and development*. It was not long before pundits, used to thinking of engineering development as following scientific research, twisted the meaning to be "research and no development." The name would sometimes be confused with similar established corporate names (e.g., Ingersoll-Rand Company, Remington Rand, Sperry Rand); with another Rand Corporation that existed in Cleveland, Ohio; and even with entertainer Sally Rand. Occasionally, someone would ask, "Who is Mr. Rand?" The present corporate name—RAND Corporation—is protected by trademark.

mid- to late 1960s, it was bringing its trademark mode of empirical, nonpartisan, independent analysis to the study of urgent domestic social and economic problems as well. More recently, it has extended its scope of interest to international and foreign issues.

Over time, RAND assembled a unique corps of researchers, notable not only for individual skills but for interdisciplinary cooperation. Importantly, it also evolved a supporting culture that could sustain and nourish a diverse collection of personalities—many of them individually strong—while encouraging their collective team performance.

It was rare to find such a wide range of backgrounds within a single organization, and rarer still for them to collaborate routinely and effectively. At RAND, scientists and engineers, social scientists from many specialties, humanists, and members of the various professions collectively addressed the problems and concerns of society and its organizations locally and around the world.

The essence of RAND is the analytic examination of complex problems, be they technological, policy, mathematical, social, or some combination of these and possibly other aspects—and no matter how complicated. Over the years, the studies have become predominantly policy-based, typically with a mathematical or technological component. Thus, from the very beginning and continuing to the present, there has been an emphasis on methodology, techniques, and technology to achieve analytic solutions to even the most demanding and intricate issues of study.

The Need for a New Kind of Organization

World War II had demonstrated to U.S. military and policy planners the importance of technological research and development for success on the battlefield. It also highlighted the wide range of scientists and academics outside the defense establishment who made such development possible. Furthermore, as the war drew to a close, it became apparent that complete and permanent peace might not be guaranteed. Discussions among people in what was then the war department, the Office of Scientific Research and Development, and industry focused on the need for a private organization to connect military planning and operations to relevant research and development.

In a report to the secretary of war, commanding general of the U.S. Army Air Forces (AAF) H. H. [Hap] Arnold wrote,

> During this war the Army, Army Air Forces, and the Navy have made unprecedented use of scientific and industrial resources. The conclusion is inescapable that we have not yet established the balance necessary to [ensure] the continuance of teamwork among the military, other government agencies, industry, and the universities. Scientific planning must be years in advance of the actual research and development work.[3]

---

[3]   Arnold (undated).

From these interactions came the concept of a Project RAND.[4] In addition to General Arnold, key players were Edward L. Bowles of the Massachusetts Institute of Technology (MIT), a consultant to the secretary of war; Gen. Lauris Norstad, then assistant chief of Air Staff, Plans; MG Curtis LeMay; Donald Wills Douglas, president of Douglas Aircraft Company; Arthur Emmons Raymond, chief engineer at Douglas; and Frank Collbohm, Raymond's assistant. (During the war, Bowles had brought both Raymond and Collbohm to the Pentagon to work on a special project that analyzed ways to improve the B-29's bombing effectiveness.)

The Douglas Years

On October 1, 1945, Arnold, Bowles, Douglas, Raymond, and Collbohm met at Hamilton Field (later Hamilton Air Force Base), California, to set up Project RAND under a special contract to the Douglas Aircraft Company, then in Santa Monica, California. Project RAND commenced operations in December 1945, expending a total of $640 in its first month of operation. That same month, the new office of deputy chief of Air Staff for Research and Development, to which Project RAND would report, was officially established, with Major General LeMay as its first appointee. On March 2, 1946, a letter of contract was executed that put Project RAND under Frank Collbohm's direction in a separate area within the Douglas Aircraft plant, physically located at the municipal Cloverfield Airport in Santa Monica, California.[5]

In May 1946, the first RAND report appeared, *Preliminary Design of an Experimental World-Circling Spaceship*.[6] It concerned the potential design, performance, and possible use of "world-circling spaceships"—satellites, as they would now be called. A year later, Project RAND moved from the Douglas plant to a location in downtown Santa Monica at 4th Street and Broadway. The building had originally been the site of *The Evening Outlook*, a Santa Monica newspaper, but has long since been demolished for a commercial mall and parking structure.

---

[4]   There are several books and documents about RAND and its activities, including Bruce L. R. Smith (1966); RAND (1973); Ware (1976); Merton E. Davies and Harris (1988); Fred Kaplan (1991); Trachtenberg (1991); Hafner and Lyon (1996); Jardini (1996); and May (1998); Hounshell (1998); Light (1998); and Collins (2002).

There is also a group of partially completed but unpublished documents from a corporate history effort of 1988–1989. It was undertaken in connection with the RAND 40th-anniversary exhibit. Among other things, it contains a group of documents that examined the status and performance of federal contract research centers (also called federally funded research and development centers, or FFRDCs). See Jackson (1989a, 1989b, 1989c, 1989d).

[5]   The buildings and hangers in the southeast corner of Santa Monica that fronted on Ocean Boulevard and housed the Douglas Aircraft Company have long been demolished. The area was redeveloped as a contemporary industrial park, but the airport per se continues to function for light planes and corporate jets.

[6]   Clauser (1946). This document and its supporting analysis were completed in three weeks at the request of Major General LeMay. Consisting of 21 chapters, each was written by one or more authors. Some of the authors subsequently became well known in science and defense matters (e.g., Louis Ridenour, David Griggs); others joined RAND (e.g., James Lipp, Glenn Harold Peebles, Curtis Victor Sturdevant). The document has been republished.

By early 1948, Project RAND had grown to 200 staff members, including mathematicians, engineers, aerodynamicists, physicists, chemists, economists, and psychologists. Its second annual report noted that

> the complexity of the problems, and the rapid, if uneven, advances in the various fields call for coordination, balance, and cross-fertilization of effort. Coming from the laboratories of industry, the seminars of universities, and the offices of administration, the RAND staff is very conscious of this need for teamwork.[7]

An Independent, Private Nonprofit Organization

The arrangement with Douglas had its pluses and minuses for both parent and offspring. Among others was the reluctance of other companies to share their corporate secrets and plans with Douglas—a potential competitor. By late 1947, separation was being discussed. In February 1948, the chief of staff of the newly created USAF wrote a letter to Donald Douglas that approved the evolution of Project RAND into a nonprofit corporation, independent of the Douglas Aircraft Company. Horace Rowan Gaither, a prominent San Francisco attorney who later served as president and then as chair of the board of the Ford Foundation, was retained as legal counsel to determine the best means of setting up an independent RAND Corporation.

By May, arrangements had been made with the Pacific National Bank, the Wells Fargo Bank, and the Union Trust Co. for lines of credit, provided that additional capital or other assets could be secured from other sources.

On May 14, 1948, the RAND Corporation was incorporated as a nonprofit organization under the laws of the state of California. The articles of incorporation set forth RAND's purpose in language that was both remarkably brief and breathtakingly broad:

> To further and promote scientific, educational, and charitable purposes, all for the public welfare and security of the United States of America.[8]

The three signatories—Collbohm, Gaither, and Lawrence J. (Larry) Henderson Jr., RAND's associate director—together with eight other prominent individuals selected from academia and industry constituted RAND's original board of trustees. The other eight were Charles Dollard, president, Carnegie Corporation of New York; Lee Alvin DuBridge, president, California Institute of Technology; John A. Hutcheson, director, research laboratories, Westinghouse Electric Corporation; Alfred L. Loomis, scientist; Philip M. Morse, physicist, MIT; Frederick Franklin Stephan, professor of sociology and statistics and director, Office of Survey Research and Statistics, Princeton University; George D. Stoddard, president, University of Illinois; and Clyde E. Williams, director, Battelle Memorial Institute.

---

[7]   RAND (1948a).

[8]   RAND (1948b).

Informal discussions with representatives of the Ford Foundation led to an agreement at the end of July 1948 for an interest-free loan from the foundation and its guarantee of a private bank loan to RAND. A total of $1 million was secured for operating the new corporation. Four years later, an expansion of the foundation's loan enabled the establishment of a RAND-sponsored research program, which afforded the staff means to conduct small nonmilitary research projects. This marked the beginning of the diversification of RAND's agenda and was the first of many grants to RAND from the Ford Foundation to support important new research initiatives.

On November 1, 1948, the Project RAND contract was formally transferred from the Douglas Aircraft Company to the RAND Corporation.

The Nature of RAND's Contributions

Many of the highlights of RAND's early contributions to policymaking were summarized in a 1996 book commemorating the 50th anniversary of Project RAND, predecessor of the RAND Corporation.[9] In his doctoral dissertation examining RAND's early years and the broadening of its research agenda, historian David R. Jardini of Carnegie Mellon University compiled an exhaustive list of contributions by RAND researchers that went far beyond assistance to military decisionmakers.[10] They included significant achievements in space systems, the foundation for the U.S. space program and various fields of mathematics, and important contributions to digital computing and the branch of computer science known as artificial intelligence (AI).

Theories and tools for decisionmaking under uncertainty were created, and basic contributions were made to game theory, linear and dynamic programming, mathematical modeling and simulation, network theory, cost analysis, and, importantly, computing technology. Researcher Paul Baran's work on distributed communications, for example, undergirds today's Internet and helped provide the building blocks for it and World Wide Web technology.

Jardini singled out for special recognition the methodological approach called system analysis, whose objective was "to provide information to military decision-makers that would sharpen their judgment and provide the basis for more informed choices."[11] As RAND's agenda evolved, Jardini noted, "systems analysis served as the methodological basis for social policy planning and analysis across such disparate areas as urban decay, poverty, health care, education, and the efficient operation of municipal services such as police protection and fire fighting."[12]

---

[9]   RAND (1996).

[10] Jardini (1996).

[11] Jardini (1996, p. 13). In the taxonomy of today, the phrase *policy analysis* has come to replace *system analysis* as the top-level methodological label for analytic studies of policy issues. As such, RAND now regards itself to be a policy-analysis house and structures its doctrine and culture in that image.

[12] Jardini (1996, p. 13).

U.S. priorities have always shaped RAND's research agenda. With roots in the Cold War competition with the Soviet Union, the early defense-related agenda evolved—in concert with U.S. attention—to encompass such diverse subject areas as space, economic, social, and political affairs overseas and the direct role of government in social and economic problem-solving at home.

RAND Contributions to the Development of Computing

Project RAND—renamed Project AIR FORCE in 1978—has a historic record of achievement in the development of computing: RAND staff designed and built one of the earliest computers, developed an early online, interactive, terminal-based computer system, conceived the telecommunication technique that has become the basis for modern computer networks, and, very significantly, contributed to the evolution and substance of modern-day software technology.[13]

In the Beginning

When Project RAND began within the Douglas Aircraft Company, the automated tools of analysis were punched-card electric accounting machines (EAMs) and mechanical desktop calculators for numerical calculation and, for simulation, analog computers.

In 1948, Project RAND acquired an early model Reeves Electronic Analog Computer (REAC) and almost immediately made a number of significant improvements to it,[14] many of which were quickly absorbed by the tiny postwar analog computing industry. REAC[15] supported many of the early studies on missile trajectories, air-to-air combat maneuvers, and earth-to-moon orbits—the last far in advance of national attention to the subject.

Numerical calculations were carried out by hand, using large worksheets to organize the flow of the computational algorithm and its data, plus groups of people with Marchant, Friden, and Monroe calculators to do the arithmetic.[16]

The mechanized computational devices of the day were punched-card equipment—key punches, sorters, card punches, card readers, tabulators. The "problem solutions" of the time were evidenced in plugboards of various sizes, whose wiring sequenced events within the attached card device, numerous trays of 5,000 cards each, rows of file cabinets full of cards, paper printouts, and the rhythmic sounds of mechanical equipment at work.

---

[13] This overview is derived from an essay prepared by Willis Ware for a special publication honoring the 50th anniversary of the RAND–Air Force relationship (RAND, 1996). It has been supplemented by historical facts assembled from many sources, including extensive email interactions with RAND alumni. Much of this material is not elsewhere documented or published in a cohesive collection.

[14] Bill Gunning was the leader in this work.

[15] Individuals associated with the REAC include Edwin W. (Ed) Paxson Jr., Edward DeLand, Calvin Nissen, and Arnold Stifel Mengel.

[16] Many of the so-called calculator operators were, in fact, trained mathematicians. Among others would be Bernice B. Brown and Lucille Sollberg. Although the punched-card operation was centralized within the NAD of the mathematics division, the so-called hand calculators were distributed among the several other analytic departments.

As quickly as new models of equipment became available, Project RAND ordered them: the IBM 407 Accounting Machine, a cube-shaped "ice box" that stored ten 10-digit numbers; the IBM Card-Programmed Electronic Calculator (CPEC); the IBM 609 electronic calculator, and improved key punches.

Punched-card devices are programmed by making electrical connections among the parts through wiring on removable plugboards. Innovative RAND analysts[17] created large and complex plugboards in a continuing effort to create the most general-purpose calculating environment possible. The plugboards were the software of the day; the procedure writers, the programmers of the day.[18]

An Early Computing Success

Analytic demand for truly random numbers for modeling studies led to the construction of a special electronic mechanism to generate random numbers and punch them onto cards.[19] Eventually, this became the well-known *A Million Random Digits and 100,000 Normal Deviates* published in 1955. Still in demand, this collection has been available on magnetic tape, floppy disks, CD-ROM, and now online. The original book has recently been reprinted.[20]

The Move to Electronic Machines

The demand for solutions to complex analytic studies has always taxed, even outstripped, the computing power of the moment. In 1949, a team (John Williams, George Brown, and Bill Gunning) visited major potential vendors of electronic computers to assess their future intentions. As John Williams noted in a summary memo of the trip, "It was a dismal scene." There was no electronic-computer industry, nor were there plans anywhere for electronic machines.

Eminent mathematician John von Neumann, as a result of his wartime experiences, had initiated a project at the Institute for Advanced Study (IAS) in Princeton, New Jersey, to build a computer to his specifications. RAND opted, as did five other organizations, to piggyback on the work and build its own machine. With USAF encouragement and support, such a hardware project was commenced in the early 1950s in the basement of the building at 4th and Broadway in Santa Monica, RAND's first home away from Douglas.[21]

---

[17] Foremost among people associated with the punched-card operations would be Paul Armer (later to become the head of the NAD), John Donald (Don) Madden, Wes Melahn, Robert (Bob) Nash, and Julian J. (Goodie) Goodpasture.

[18] At one point, RAND persuaded IBM (the supplier of its punched-card equipment) to provide special double-sized plugboards to increase the number of steps that could be scheduled within a machine. When fully wired and with a protective cover in place, a large board could weigh 20–25 pounds.

[19] Bill Gunning and Cecil Hastings were the leaders in the project.

[20] RAND (2001).

[21] Individuals associated with the early phases of the RAND computer included Keith Uncapher, Louis Richard (Dick) Mockbee, Richard (Dick) Stahl, Bill Gunning, Roy Fry, Gardner E. Johnson, Mal Davis, Thomas O. (Tom) Ellis, Ray Clewett, and Willis Ware.

Significantly, the efforts in the several organizations associated with the "Princeton family of machines" were primarily hardware ones. At the time, there was little software research, but RAND inaugurated an internal series of symposia and lectures to acquaint its future users with this new device, including, importantly, discussion of technical and mathematical issues. The series commenced with the most basic of topics: the binary number system.[22]

When RAND moved into its building at 1700 Main Street in Santa Monica, the computer effort was well under way. A completed machine became operational in 1955, completely financed under the USAF contract, and named JOHNNIAC.[23]

The JOHNNIAC was intended from the beginning to be a production workhorse, not an R&D test bed or a tinkerer's toy. Accordingly, its presence stimulated an in-house educational and software-development effort to make the machine efficient and convenient for users.[24]

Software had to be built for things that users of contemporary desktop personal computers and workstations take for granted and largely do not even think about—e.g., software needed to start a machine on a problem, for managing databases, for managing memory resources, for handling peripherals (such as printers), for interfacing to the user. The modern desktop machine is a superb luxury compared to that of the early 1950s, not only in the hardware sense but also in the enormously varied and broad software base.

Each programming project was essentially a research effort to determine and develop appropriate mathematical methods and algorithms and then implement them in software.[25] The programmer had to handle every detail every time; memory had to be managed and efficiently conserved, punched cards had to be read in, the application had to punch cards and deliver output to the printer, the flow of computations had to be controlled, error bounds had to be estimated, and restart arrangements had to be provided in case of a hardware or software failure. There was never enough memory; machines were never fast enough; secondary storage devices—magnetic drums were a favorite of the day—were always too small. All of this led to very innovative and imaginative software development and clever tricks, as well as evolution of ingenious mathematical

---

[22] A lead contributor to these activities was Cecil Hastings, a mathematician by training. Other participants included Don Madden, Wes Melahn, and Paul Armer—each bringing a heritage of punched-card experience.

[23] Computers need names, and it was universally felt that it should be in honor of John von Neumann: the John von Neumann Numerical Integrator and Automatic Computer, or JOHNNIAC. When von Neumann heard of this, he modestly protested, but John Williams quickly overcame his reticence with this quip: "But, John, there are lots of things [i.e., restroom "johns"] in the world named after you, and you can't do anything about them."

[24] Early JOHNNIAC programmers, especially at the so-called system and utility levels, included Morton I. (Mort) Bernstein, John Clifford (Cliff) Shaw, Shirley L. Marks, and Leola Cutler.

[25] Early application-oriented programmers included Mort Bernstein, Don Madden, Wes Melahn, Irwin (Irv) Greenwald, Gene Jacobs, Cecil Hastings, and Oliver Gross. There apparently was a de facto decision (probably carrying over from the centralized punched-card operations) to keep the programming group for the electronic machine also centralized. This arrangement came to be called closed-shop programming but eventually gave way to an open-shop environment, with skilled programmers spread among several departments.

algorithms—all done under existing contracts with the USAF and also (by that time) the U.S. Atomic Energy Commission (AEC).

Calculation of mathematical functions was a trying problem in early computing, especially so because of scarce memory. The basic requirement led to the development of numerical approximations, published in a well-known book: *Approximations for Digital Computers*.[26] Paul Armer once estimated that the *Approximations* saved enough machine time and memory (measured in dollar value) to have financed Project RAND for 15 years.

Concurrently, internal software development produced a variety of tools—loaders, assemblers, print routines, special programming languages for small problems, binary-decimal and decimal-binary converters—which collectively simplified the task of the professional programming staff, which functioned in a closed-shop environment. This implied that the customer (the person with the problem) described his or her needs to a professional

Keith Uncapher at the console of the JOHNNIAC. A photograph of the computer's eponym, John von Neumann, hangs on the wall to the left.

---

[26] Hastings (1955).

programmer, who was then responsible for creating computer programs and code, managing the running of the programs, and delivering completed results to the customer.

The evolving mathematical demands of analytic studies led to the development of new approaches to problems and, importantly, to associated software that would perform the necessary calculations.

Among them were linear programming for optimization problems and the associated simplex method (and software) for calculation,[27] dynamic programming for sequential decisionmaking situations and its associated programs,[28] later the so-called information-processing languages,[29] which were the basis for subsequent AI and expert-system (rule-based) software,[30] the application of such techniques to important USAF problems (such as in logistics),[31] special languages (e.g., SIMSCRIPT®) for simulation and modeling[32] and matrix-based calculations. Significantly, RAND shared such software with the outside world, and its descendants are still in use. Some of it even became the basis of commercial companies.[33]

In the 1950s, there was little understanding of generalizing programming, and the notion of reusable software had not evolved except for collections of packages for commonly used calculations (called libraries) and so-called utilities, such as loaders, matrix arithmetic, printer control, scaling algorithms, and input-output (I/O) schemes.

The Middle Years

Concurrently with RAND's in-house effort, a commercial industry was developing, and, during the early 1950s, RAND had received (by a DC-6 air freighter) and installed serial number 11 of the IBM 701 Defense Calculator, as it had been initially called. It came with rudimentary programming-support tools, such as an assembler and a software library. While the concept of a monitor[34] to control the flow of problems through a computer had been suggested, an operating system (OS), as the term is now known and used, was not available.

The user protocol of the day called for the user to sign up for and take hands-on possession of a machine at a specified time and for a specified period. At the end of the assigned slot, the programmer would normally take away a printout and a memory dump (via a card deck) for examination at his or her desk. If the run were to crash or otherwise

---

[27] George Dantzig (not in the NAD), William (Bill) Orchard-Hays, and Leola Cutler.

[28] Richard (Dick) Bellman, Phillip (Phil) Wolfe, and Stuart (Stu) E. Dreyfus.

[29] The well-known team of "NSS" consisted of Allen Newell, Cliff Shaw, and Herbert Simon. Of these three, Shaw was at RAND; the other two, at Carnegie Mellon University.

[30] Fred M. Tonge and Ed Feigenbaum. Later, Bob Anderson, Henry A. Sowizral, Philip (Phil) Klahr, and Donald (Don) Waterman.

[31] Murray Geissler and Irving K. Cohen (neither in the computing department).

[32] Harry Markowitz.

[33] Computer Analysis Corporation, which became CACI.

[34] Ascribed to Bruce Moncreif, not of RAND.

behave peculiarly, the procedure was to provide the programmer with as much information as possible so that he or she could (ideally) identify—and repair—the fault.

A production (as opposed to a test or debug) run also had to include a "procedure sheet" to describe to the operator on duty how to conduct the run and what to do if it did not go as expected.

There was a minimum of standardization at the time. For example, the RAND 701 ran with at least four different assemblers and their associated software libraries; each had unique features of particular relevance for certain problems. The programmer would select the one best suited to the task at hand. To help minimize the inefficiency and inconvenience of this situation, RAND, together with other 701 users in the Southern California area, initiated a cooperative effort to produce common-use software[35] and participated vigorously in the Digital Computer Association, an early and local professional society.

Commercial machines evolved much more rapidly than it was feasible to upgrade the JOHNNIAC, which nonetheless was the basis of a continuing series of engineering advances, each making important contributions to the art of the time.[36] Among them were the first commercially produced magnetic core memory, which, for a while, was the largest in existence;[37] a transistor-based adder and logic which caused the JOHNNIAC to become a hybrid transistor–vacuum tube device; the first high-speed impact printer 140 columns wide (manufactured by Anderson-Nichols, an engineering contracting firm); and the first machine with extensive trouble-diagnostic capability from the operating console.

The JOHNNIAC Open-Shop System

Even though JOHNNIAC had been upgraded and improved as just noted, it fell behind the progress in the commercial fields, notably that of IBM. The decision not to add magnetic-tape units to the machine due to cost considerations effectively signaled the end of the machine's growth and tenure as a production vehicle. It was therefore turned to an R&D role for several projects.

Of particular importance was the JOHNNIAC open-shop system (JOSS®),[38] a specialized, remote-access, time-shared, JOHNNIAC-based software system that led the state of the art in putting tens of users concurrently in an interactive problem-solution environment on one machine. Initially, the system could support just 10 users scattered through the RAND buildings. Later, a production-engineered JOSS-2 was implemented

---

[35] This effort centered on Paul Armer, Irv Greenwald, Charles L. (Chuck) Baker, and John I. Derr. See Melahn (1956) and Baker (1956).

[36] These efforts centered on Keith Uncapher, Mal Davis, and Tom Ellis, supported by the electronic and mechanical shops.

[37] Its size was 4,096 40-bit words—large for its day but minuscule by contemporary standards. Other 4,096-word core memories currently in development were 36-bit word length.

[38] JOSS, or, as it was later renamed, JOSS-1, was conceived and functionally designed and its software implemented by Cliff Shaw and supported by engineers Tom Ellis and Mal Davis and the mechanical and electrical shops.

on a Digital Equipment Corporation (DEC) Programmed Data Processor (PDP)–6 machine. It supported not only 30 internal terminals but also a limited number of external ones within the USAF. Connectivity utilized dial-up commercial telephone circuits.[39]

The JOSS work came at a time when other organizations were also developing time-sharing remote-access systems, and it influenced some dozen or so of these other subsequent efforts elsewhere. A note in Cliff Shaw's own handwriting was posted on his door listing the other systems that (he believed) had been influenced by his JOSS work.[40]

There was also a JOSS-3, programmed by an IBM west coast facility, intended to run under IBM's OS/360 software. However, because RAND had trademarked the label *JOSS* and was reluctant to have it used by other organizations, the IBM version was never widely used.

Bob Anderson using the RAND tablet and videographic system.

The Tablet

JOHNNIAC also supported the initial development phase of the first operational digitizing tablet, a 10-inch–by–10-inch flat surface over which a free-pen stylus could be manually moved to put arbitrary hand motions digitally into a computer.[41] Later (under ARPA funding), a printed-circuit version was completed that was 36 inches by 36 inches. Under ARPA funding, approximately a dozen of the large models were made in house and supplied to various ARPA-funded research facilities.

Videographic System

As part of an ARPA-inspired interest in the human-machine symbiotic environment, RAND entered into a cooperative arrangement with an IBM facility at Los Altos, California, to develop a videographic system that would blend computer-produced digital information with television video images derived from a camera. The TV images were stored on a very large vertical magnetic disk, which was synchronized with the flow of information from a computer.[42]

With the technology of the day, it was a remarkable achievement to both store and synchronously display video and digital images on a single CRT display. What was dif-

---

[39] Chuck Baker led the JOSS-2 design team, which included Ed Bryan, Joe Smith, and Irv Greenwald.

[40] Reproduced in Chapter Six.

[41] This effort centered on Keith Uncapher, Tom Ellis, and Mal Davis, supported by the electronic and mechanical shops.

[42] The videographic effort also centered on the Uncapher/Ellis/Davis team.

ficult then would, with today's magnetic hard-drive technology and very sophisticated desktop-computer video cards that store images in digital form, be a rather straight-forward task.

A few—half dozen or so—videographic terminals were constructed that combined a tablet, a keyboard, a display, audio speaker and microphone, and flat work surface. The audio features were never exploited, but the video features, supported by the videographic systems, spawned several fascinating research projects.

One was the annotation of maps, a chore that military cartographers then did manu-ally. It was possible to display a map in video form and overlay it with typed annotations, arrows highlighting features, boxes, and circles to identify areas, and the other symbolic artifacts that were in use by cartographers. It was not necessary to save the final image for future use; rather, the sequence of user actions would be stored and used to reconstruct the desired combined image on demand.[43] Interestingly, this is the same technique that is embodied in the basic structure of the modern World Wide Web—namely, a site trans-mits to a local browser the "recipe" for constructing a page (e.g., fonts, format, colors) plus the "ingredients" (text, images). It does not transmit completed page displays.

Another project was the dictionary lookup of hand-drawn Chinese characters and words. The sequence in which the strokes of an ideograph are drawn indicates something about its meaning and was used by the software behind the videographic terminal to guide its dictionary search.[44]

Yet another project was BIOMOD, which used videographics to provide a graphical environment in which to construct biological models.[45]

The Later Years

By 1966, when JOHNNIAC was retired, a large commercial industry had evolved, and there was extensive software for every machine. RAND, as all other places, shifted entirely to commercial sources. Fortunately, many of the early Project RAND applications had been done on commercial machines and were exported to USAF organizations concerned with such issues as force planning, logistics research, basic research, and weapon effects and phenomenology. RAND's software was exported to the world at large also, notable the linear-programming simplex system, the various components for dynamic program-ming and game theory studies, and the SIMSCRIPT simulation language.

Within RAND, programming gradually became more and more application oriented (based on commercial software systems and languages) and less and less R&D in nature. Correspondingly, end users became more facile with programming languages and proce-dures, with the result that the closed shop transitioned into open-shop programming—the end users did their own.

---

[43] The principal researcher was Gabe Groner.

[44] The principal researcher was Gabe Groner.

[45] Ed DeLand and Thomas (Tom) L. Lincoln.

By its 50th anniversary, just before the turn of the millennium, RAND had become workstation based with everything networked in contemporary manner. Programming efforts today center on using commercial software (e.g., for statistical analysis, model building) and on developing applications with well-established, commercially available programming languages.

RAND and the USAF Computing Evolution

In this same interval of the 1950–1960s, the USAF was absorbing computer technology into its structure. Many RAND staffers supported and guided the USAF on policy and institutional matters. Among the last were assistance in establishing the career path for computer specialists (initially the 51xx Air Force Specialty Code [AFSC] series of career-path identifiers), software and programmatic issues of the Advanced Logistics System (ALS), participation in the USAF Scientific Advisory Board and its many studies, informal and quick support on project reviews and similar matters, design of the curriculum and actual instruction for the U.S. Department of Defense (DoD) Computer Institute, participation on formal study groups and committees sponsored by USAF headquarters, and advice and guidance on software aspects of weapon-system designs and procurement.[46]

Of particular impact was a major computer-resource management study conducted in 1974–1975 to advise the USAF on charting its long-term course for the acquisition, management, and operation of its computers, software, information systems, and related personnel.[47] Conducted directly for the USAF chief of staff, Gen. David Jones, it helped the USAF structure the oversight and management within the Air Staff and major commands of the new computing technology.

In the 1980s, USAF support—now conducted through the renamed Project AIR FORCE—continued its computer-science work with the development of programming languages tailored especially to battlefield and other military simulations and incorporating both rule-based and object-oriented constructs—such languages as the Rule-Oriented Simulation System (ROSS), Simulating Warfare in the ROSS Language (SWIRL), and Tactical Warfare in the ROSS Language (TWIRL).[48] By the 1990s, work for the USAF became directed largely to studies on force planning and utilization, logistics issues, personnel issues, and similar operational matters. Computer work became focused primarily on modeling and simulation, statistical analysis, database analysis, and similar support functions. Although a modest professional programming staff still existed, a great deal of the computer support was done directly by the research staff via a contemporary, fully networked workstation-and-server environment.

---

[46] Many individuals helped the USAF on a variety of matters. Among them were Paul Armer, Willis Ware, Keith Uncapher, Bob Patrick, James (Jim) D. Tupac, and Pat Haverty.

[47] See Drezner, Shulman, and Ware (1975) and Drezner et al. (1976).

[48] The development of ROSS, an English-like, object-oriented simulation language, SWIRL, and TWIRL is discussed in Chapter Six.

The Bottom Line

With primarily USAF funding, encouragement, and concurrence, but later also support from the AEC and ARPA, the computing cadre of Project RAND and the RAND Corporation

- helped lay the foundation for modern-day computing and the professional societies that support the field
- designed and built an outstanding computer for that time
- innovated much of the support software to facilitate programming and make computer usage efficient and convenient for all users
- pioneered the application of computer- and mathematics-based approaches to analytic studies
- was the first to exploit many mathematical techniques for real-world USAF (and others') problems
- evolved a close-knit in-house mathematical and computer-science staff to jointly handle increasingly complex problems, e.g., war games, simulations, battle models
- conducted a computer-science R&D effort focused on the needs of computer users and the real problems of the USAF and other clients
- developed the first online, interactive, terminal-based computer system to which a number of USAF users had remote access via telephone connections
- handed off these achievements to USAF centers as they materialized and developed
- helped USAF to move facilely into the emerging field of analytic studies based on extensive computing hardware and software as well as into a computer infrastructure for the operational and support forces
- handed off to the emerging discipline of computer science and to the computer users of the world much knowledge and intellectual advances to computer-based problem-solving—largely in the form of innovative and operational software packages, usually complete with relevant end-user documentation
- supported a wide range of RAND policy studies with computer-based know-how
- made significant contributions to important national policy issues, sometimes in a direct manner (e.g., information security, personal privacy), sometimes in a supporting role.

CHAPTER THREE

RAND's First Computer People

Who were the people who came first and helped shape the computing environment at the RAND Corporation? And, for that matter, in the evolving field of computing? The history of an organization is more than the sober presentation of such things as major accomplishments, key decisions, changes in corporate name, physical locations, and clients served.[1] While each is important in its own right, the people who made them happen have their own importance and place in history.[2]

A few organizations and various wartime relationships were of high relevance in building the initial Project RAND and later RAND Corporation staff. Predominantly, they were the Douglas Aircraft Company, Harvard University, MIT and its Radiation Laboratory, and Princeton University.

The Legacy of Wartime Collaboration

During World War II, many academics had become involved with various problems of the military. They were organized in many ways, but one of the significant groups was the war department's[3] National Defense Research Committee (NDRC),[4] which functioned under the Office of Scientific Research and Development and acted as a conduit to bring scientific, engineering, and academic personnel into contact with defense problems. Out of the personal relationships that the NDRC stimulated came a significant part of the initial cadre of the RAND research staff.[5]

---

[1] This particular sentence was prompted by a similar one from a document in the RAND archives (Bornet, 1962). The interview of Dick Mockbee is one of a series that Bornet undertook to capture the early history of some RAND people. Of this author's 18 documents in the RAND library, nine are interviews; two are about computer people. The Bornet collection is a fascinating source of information and, to some extent, the politics of early Project RAND and its transition from Douglas.

[2] Because this document concerns only the computer and information technology (IT) people of RAND, many important individuals associated with early RAND are not included.

[3] Now, of course, the U.S. Department of Defense.

[4] On the NDRC, see Bush (1970) and Stewart (1948, especially chapters 2 and 4).

[5] Many of the details in this discussion came from a personal interview of John Williams by Vaughn Bornet in 1962 (Bornet, 1969), an excellent, in-depth source of many details of early Project RAND. Another source is *John Williams—A Memoriam* (1964).

Arthur Raymond (vice president and chief engineer of Douglas Aircraft) and Frank Collbohm (his assistant and later assistant to Donald Douglas) had been brought into the war department by the secretary of war via his chief scientist and consultant Edward Bowles of MIT. They were wanted to help analyze the effectiveness of B-29 bombing campaigns and ballistic problems. Vannevar Bush (chair of the NDRC and also from MIT) provided analytic support via the NDRC/Applied Mathematics Panel. That panel happened to include John Williams, a theoretical astronomer from the University of Arizona who had been trained in the mathematics department of Princeton University and retained extensive ties there.

Early RAND Leaders

Most of RAND's early corporate leadership came from Douglas Aircraft. After the war, Donald Douglas approached the AAF in January 1946 with a plan for government and industry to work together on long-range strategic planning.[6] His action reflected the successful interactions during World War II between the national military establishment and commercial or private organizations. The proposal eventuated in the creation of Project RAND, which was contracted with the Douglas Aircraft Company in Santa Monica, California.[7]

Responsibility for the project was vested in Arthur Raymond who, at the time, was vice president of engineering, a position to which he rose after starting with Douglas as a metal worker. A graduate of Harvard University in 1920, he subsequently completed a master's degree in aeronautical engineering at MIT. After a lifetime career with Douglas, he retired in June 1960 and, among other things, became a consultant to the RAND Corporation.[8]

Raymond assigned the Project RAND directorship to Frank Collbohm, who, at the time, had become a special assistant to both Douglas and Raymond. Trained as an electrical engineer at the University of Wisconsin, he joined Douglas as an engineer in 1928. He became a leading flight-test pilot and engineer for the Douglas DC-1, DC-2, and DC-3 aircraft programs.[9] During World War II, he participated in several military projects for

---

[6] The available documentation is conflicting in regard to the genesis of a study organization. Some attribute the idea to Donald Douglas, as stated here, but others attribute it to General Arnold. In all likelihood, the idea arose from conversations among various individuals; the statement here could be interpreted as a response by Douglas to an AAF expression of interest.

[7] An unidentified item in the RAND archives but seemingly a draft brief obituary for Arthur Raymond credits him with the concept of the abbreviation *RAND* (from *research and development*), but Frank Collbohm's obituary in the *Los Angeles Times* credits it to General Arnold.

[8] From biographical material in the RAND archives and Smithsonian oral-history archives.

[9] As an indication of Collbohm's stature and reputation in the aircraft industry, the DC-3 is regarded as "one of the most influential aircraft in the history of aviation and is . . . ranked as one of the top-10 most important aircraft of all time" ("New Monument to Take Flight," 2004). It made air travel widely accessible and affordable to the public, as well as contributing to the AAF during World War II as the C-47. Beginning in 1935, some 13,000 of them were built—largely in the Santa Monica facility of the Douglas Company.

which he worked closely with MIT. In addition, he had an informal position in the Office of Scientific Research and Development of the war department and was a consultant to Secretary of War Robert Patterson. As a result of these relationships, he met many important people in applied-science fields—people who later would either join RAND, become a consultant to it, or become a pipeline for recruiting promising science and engineering graduates and, in some instances, their faculty. In particular, he met Edward Wells, the chief engineer of Boeing Aircraft Company. Raymond, Collbohm, and Wells together are credited with formulating the AAF program known as Project RAND.

In 1948, the project split from Douglas to become the RAND Corporation. The story goes that, after an unsuccessful search for presidential candidates, Frank Collbohm became RAND's founding president, a position he held through his retirement in 1967.[10]

To assist Collbohm in administering Project RAND, Dick Goldstein was appointed associate director (presumably chosen by Arthur Raymond, possibly with Collbohm's and Douglas's concurrence). Graduated from the University of Rochester as a mechanical engineer in 1932, he went on to attain a master's degree in mechanical and aeronautical engineering at the California Institute of Technology (Caltech) in 1934. Joining Douglas Aircraft in 1934 as research engineer, he became director of the Douglas Research Laboratory in 1946. In this regard, he would have been a natural candidate to provide leadership to the new Project RAND. When the RAND Corporation was formed, he became its associate director, a position that, in 1956, was renamed senior vice president and then executive vice president. He retired in January 1974.[11]

The third Douglas executive to join Project RAND was Scott King, whom Dick Goldstein persuaded to join RAND. Graduated with a B.A. in economics from Cornell University in 1939, he then received an M.B.A. from Harvard Business School. He joined Douglas in 1942, was in the U.S. Naval Reserve from 1944 to 1946, and was then assigned as contract administrator to Project RAND. Initially, he was the assistant treasurer for the RAND Corporation but became its treasurer in 1949, a position that he held until retirement in 1980.[12] He brought with him from Douglas Crawford Thompson, who became RAND's assistant treasurer.

The corporate secretary, Steve Jeffries was recruited from the Safeway grocery chain. Graduated from Pomona College and the University of Southern California with a degree in political science, he returned to Harvard Business School for an M.B.A. During World War II, he worked for Lockheed Overseas Corporation in Northern Ireland and later for MIT's radiation laboratory branch in Malvern, UK. Postwar, he

---

[10] From biographical material in the RAND archives plus obituaries in the *Los Angeles Times* (Oliver, 1990) and *The New York Times* ("F. R. Collbohm," 1990) and from Swain (undated). The latter's bibliography notes several books and documents in which information about RAND and Frank Collbohm can be found. It also mentions an oral history that Martin Collins and Joseph Tatarewicz conducted (1987).

[11] From biographical materials in the RAND archives—in particular, an unidentified biography dated January 1961 and a self-written biographical form dated June 30, 1970.

[12] From biographical materials in the RAND archives—in particular, a biography dated March 1972 that was apparently written for the board of trustees, plus a brief obituary in the October 1996 *RAND Items*.

returned to the radiation laboratory in Cambridge and then joined the Safeway Stores in labor relations.[13] One day, he received a phone call from Goldstein inviting him to join a company of which he had never heard—namely, RAND—which he joined in 1949.[14] Almost certainly, the link that brought him to RAND would have involved the people whom both he and RAND's management knew at MIT's radiation lab.

Project RAND decided to open an office near Washington, D.C., that would be the connecting link to the USAF and provide the final approval authority for briefings and documents delivered to the USAF. It would also handle administrative matters that might arise.

To run the Washington office, Larry Henderson was recruited in 1947. During the war, he had worked with the MIT radiation laboratory and with the secretary of war. This background was appropriate for the RAND assignment.[15]

Vada Mary Baldwin, who had been a secretary to Donald Douglas, was also assigned to Project RAND and transferred to the RAND Corporation when it formed. She held various secretarial positions, including that to Collbohm[16] and, later, to Paul Armer when he was head of the NAD.

Early Technical Staff

The first computerniks at RAND were of various disciplinary and work backgrounds. There were several threads of hiring: one thread of hires from Douglas, where Project RAND had first been situated; one from wartime relationships; one from university relationships; and one from recruiting. This section introduces key members of the early computing technical staff; where available, their own words describing their early work at RAND are provided.

The Douglas Thread

Arnold Mengel:[17] Arnold graduated from MIT as an electrical engineer in 1941 and then joined the U.S. Navy for the duration. He returned to MIT in 1945 to complete a master's degree also in electrical engineering, and then joined Project RAND in 1946. In 1948, he persuaded RAND to send him to Harvard, where he earned a master's degree in applied mathematics under Howard Aiken. Returning to RAND in 1949, he participated in

---

[13] From biographical material in the RAND archives; the corporate press obituary; obituary in the *Santa Monica (Calif.) Evening Outlook* for January 12, 1988; and an internal biography.

[14] From the October 1956 *RANDom News*, reprinted for internal System Development Corporation (SDC) use.

[15] Material in the Smithsonian oral histories.

[16] The secretarial assignment to Frank Collbohm is believed to be correct, although no documentary evidence has been discovered.

[17] Unless otherwise indicated, the words in these personal biovignettes are those of the individuals themselves transmitted via email to the author during the course of research for this document. In some cases, minor editing has been done or supplementary information from other sources has been added.

various studies, particularly those that involved modeling on the analog computer. From 1955 onward, he served in various administrative positions.[18]

Bill Gunning: Bill wrote of his early years at RAND:

> I was involved in a project to determine the temperature distribution in an aircraft windshield as it flew into icing conditions. We built an electronic model consisting of resistors, capacitors, switches, and sensors. This was a special case of the passive component model technique pushed to a very useful state by Gilbert McCann at Cal Tech. This sort of approach was used to predict the behavior of the electric power grid under transient stress conditions. Douglas bought one of the McCann type systems.

> Another example of the state of awareness of the Douglas flight-test lab people (who moved over to Project RAND) was the design, construction and use of a special purpose measurement/computation instrument that computed dynamic displacement based on signals from a collection of accelerometers which were mounted on a full size airplane that was subjected to drop tests in a giant hanger at Wright Field.

Arnold Mengel studied computing at Harvard University and was an initial user of the Reeves Electronic Analog Computer.

Dick Mockbee: Dick was originally with Douglas in the field testing of the Nike missile system. He heard about RAND through Bill Gunning, a close friend, while working on the random-number generator. He chose to join Project RAND because of personal friendships with Gunning and Dick Goldstein. He officially "moved over" in September 1948; his initial assignments were the random-number generator machine and later the installation of the REAC.

Don Madden: Don transferred to Project RAND before it left Douglas:

> My recollection of the 1940s is pretty hazy, especially the dates. I barely got my bachelor's degree before having to go into the Army in mid-43. In late-46 when I was getting out of the Army a friend at Douglas Aircraft told me that Douglas planned to do engineering calculations on punched cards machines. This sounded interesting to me so I took a job at Douglas in the Factory Tabulating Dept. The department had a room full of Remington-Rand punched card equipment.

---

[18] From biographical materials in the RAND archives: a brief biography (March 1972) prepared for a board meeting and a self-written biographical form that RAND assembled from its staff in June 1970.

The difficulty was that they never got to the engineering calculations. I grew impatient with the situation as 1947 wore on and looked around Douglas for some other position. I discovered something called Project RAND that seemed to be doing work that interested me. After interviews with several people (including John Williams), I was transferred to Project RAND in October or November of 47.

William P. Myers: William joined Project RAND from the "tab room" at Douglas. *Tab room* was a common name for the area that contained punched-card equipment—e.g., tabulators, key punches, card sorters.

Gan Baker and Gardner Johnson are thought to have come from Douglas, but the record is not clear.

The Wartime Thread

John Williams: John had accepted a position as chief statistician at the Naval Ordnance Test Station (NOTS) in Inyoken, California, after World War II, having decided to stop investigating meteor matters and continue work similar to what he had done during the war. Collbohm, who had become acquainted with Williams via the NDRC Mathematics Panel, phoned and persuaded the latter to join the new Project RAND effort at Douglas as chief of the mathematics division.

Williams, in turn, had persuaded two of his wartime staff to join him at NOTS: Cecil Hastings, who had gone to Brown University to be in charge of computing matters there, and Olaf Helmer, who had gone to Europe to instruct at a military university. As John put it,

> I had them all signed up for NOTS; when I changed horses myself, these poor fellows would have been orphans up there. And I wanted them with me. So I sent them telegrams saying that it was Project RAND and the Air Force that we were working for—and not the Naval Ordnance Test Station.[19]

Later, Williams was to observe that "Princeton University is a remarkable training ground for outstanding statisticians."

Ed Paxson: Ed was a skilled mathematician who was noted for his imaginative approach to solving problems. For example, in the late 1970s, when handheld calculators had become commonplace, he put together a package of programs for the HP-67/97 machines titled, *Hand Calculator Programs for Staff Officers*.[20] The package included many calculations—some very complex (military modeling and simulation, orbital mechanics), others very simple (mathematical functions, geographic calculations)—that military staff did in the normal course of their jobs.

---

[19] Bornet (1969, p. 15).

[20] Paxson (1978).

Frank Collbohm (left) and John Williams (center) listening to an explanation by George Dietrich

Cecil Hastings: During World War II, Cecil had been the leader in computing for the statistical research group at Princeton University (SRGP). John Williams headed one of its subgroups; he was trained as an astronomer and later joined RAND, initially as head of the mathematics division. Other members of the SRGP included Sam Wilkes, Fred Mosteller, Jimmy Savage, and Olaf Helmer; all were later to be a part of RAND, either as consultants or as resident staff. This chain of events was also the beginning of a long, productive relationship between John Williams, other mathematicians of RAND, and the mathematics groups at Princeton. RAND recruited many top-quality individuals via John Williams and his personal friendships.

At the time, the computing activities over which Cecil presided were, of course, primarily pen-and-paper processes supported by mechanical calculators.

In January 1994, Cecil wrote in a personal letter as follows:

> When the war ended, I went to Brown University and headed the Advanced Mechanics computing group. At the end of about a year, I got word from John

Williams that a Project RAND had begun at the Douglas Company in Santa Monica. I quit my job at Brown and rode the train to California. . . . Elaine (his wife) tells me that I acquired Mim Mack as secretary at the Douglas Company. Beth Ludwife and Yvonne Claeys already worked there. We acquired quite a number of the Douglas people.

Cecil died early in 2001 at the age of 81 from complications arising from Alzheimer's disease.

The University Thread

George Brown: Like many other mathematicians, George was a consultant to Project RAND in the summer of 1947. He joined Project RAND in the summer of 1948 as a Douglas employee. He then became chief of the NAD (also known as Math-II) within the mathematics division that John Williams headed. Brown had been at Princeton and shared these memories of John Williams:

> I can possibly add something about our early acquaintance (1938–39) with J. D. Williams when we had a bridge foursome at Princeton with Mosteller, [Alexander McFarlane (Alex)] Mood, [George] Brown, and Williams, all four graduate students of Sam [Wilkes]. That acquaintance led to Brown and Mood spending summer consulting at RAND (then still Douglas) just before the separation from Douglas and formation of RAND Corporation.

> I knew JDW from his year as a special student with Princeton's Math department, playing bridge regularly with John, Alex Mood, and Fred Mosteller. Probably at John's instigation Alex and I were invited to spend a month as consultants at RAND in the summer of 1947, together with many distinguished mathematicians and economists. I was immediately captivated by RAND's early work on Theory of Games. During the next academic year Alex and I were recruited by JDW for the Math Division at RAND and joined RAND, [and in the] summer of 1948, RAND [was] still under Douglas. My bio probably showed Macy's research Division my first job and an association with [John von Neumann] when I was at RCA Labs later. Just about the time of joining RAND or very soon after, I played a dual role, [in] the Math Division doing active research, and Chief of what was then the Numerical Analysis Department (NAD). NAD was busy doing work for other RAND divisions, as well [as] for itself, such as computer developments, Cecil's approximations, random number tables, etc.

Wes Melahn: Wes described how he came to RAND from Harvard to work on computer science:

> When I received my AB in Engineering Science and Applied Physics from Harvard University, Professor Howard Aiken was recruiting people for a new Masters degree program having to do with design and application of computers, computer science we would call it today. Aiken had just moved the Mark I into a new com-

puter building on campus and was busy "chomping out" books of Bessel functions and determined to prove that a complicated machine like the [Mark] I could be made to operate reliably.

I say "chomping out" because the computer was controlled by a program punched into a roll of IBM card stock, 80 columns wide and as long as needed. The huge sequencing device stepped ahead one line at a time sensing the 80 columns simultaneously. It was noisy and seemed to shake the whole building. I am not sure Professor Aiken ever conceded that an internally stored computer program was a good idea.

The Masters Degree program was new and sounded interesting; so I switched to it from Applied Mathematics that I had been planning to take.

Arnold Mengel had convinced the Project RAND people to send him to Harvard to participate in this program. We became friends and Arnold had good things to say about opportunities at Project RAND. Professor Fred Mosteller whom Howard Aiken had enlisted to teach the statistics courses in his program, also influenced my decision to go to work for Project RAND. Mosteller was a consultant to Project RAND and he found it to be a stimulating place.

Because I had been going to school around-the-calendar since completing four years of military service in WW II, he suggested it might be good for me to take a break and get some real world working experience before proceeding with more studies toward a PhD degree. As it turned out, my application was accepted and I went to work for Project RAND at Douglas Aircraft Company. I got lots of interesting and demanding real world experience, but I never found time to return to class at Harvard.

John Matousek: John described how he came to RAND from UCLA:

I was discharged from the US Army in March 1946 and entered UCLA that fall to complete my bachelor's degree in mathematics. I graduated in 1949 and continued on in graduate school specializing in mathematical statistics.

In my second year of graduate school, George Brown was one of my instructors. As I neared completion and began job hunting, George suggested that I interview at RAND. As I recall, I was interviewed by both Paul Armer and Don Madden and was offered a job in the Numerical Analysis Department as a procedure writer. I worked on many different projects in support of other RAND divisions. Only one I really remember was an atomic implosion study that had to be programmed to run on a computer at the Aberdeen Proving Ground—it wasn't the EDVAC [Electronic Discrete Variable Automatic Computer] but some similar name as I recall.

Had to program in base 16 machine language. For the numbers 10 thru 15 we used KSNJFL—we used the expression "King Sized Numbers Just For Laughs" to remember the sequence. Shortly thereafter, I was assigned to start preparing the simulated inputs for the then developing STP [the system training program] lab and worked on system training for both the manual and SAGE [semiautomatic ground environment] systems.

When we became System Development Corporation[21] in the spin-off in 1957, I continued with the system training programs. In 1961, I was asked to relocate to Lexington, MA to be program manager for the new 425L program—the NORAD [North American Aerospace Defense Command] Combat Operations Center to be built in Cheyenne Mountain [Air Force Station]. I spent three years in Lexington as program manager [and] moved to Colorado Springs in 1964 for the installation of the system in the computers in the mountain. Returned to Santa Monica in 1967 and held several different positions as VP for Applied Systems Div., Commercial Systems Div. and finally back to the old Air Defense Div. as many old timers were leaving in the wake of Wes's departure [as outgoing president] and George Mueller's arrival [as incoming president].

The Recruiting Thread

Paul Armer:[22] Paul graduated from UCLA as a meteorologist and served in that capacity during the war. In 1951, he succeeded George Brown as chief of the NAD in the mathematics division.

In his own words, here is how Paul made his way to RAND:

As a graduate, I went to [UCLA's] "Bureau of Occupations." After they interviewed me, they said, "Have we got the place for you!" I was told that it was a part of Douglas, which was looking for people with a mathematical background. [Project] RAND was the only prospect they presented to me. I told them I didn't want any others; if this one didn't work out I could always come back to them. I was interviewed at RAND by Cecil Hastings and introduced to George W. Brown. I started, I think, the next Monday. After a short time of running a desk calculator, I was offered the chance to learn about punched card machinery.

[Initially, the RAND contingent had been using the Douglas machines at its Santa Monica plant on second and third shifts.] I worked on swing shift in the machine room. [After Project RAND moved to its first corporate headquarters at 4th and Broadway in Santa Monica,] we got [our own machines,] and I worked the swing shift. The swing shift supervisor had a name like Fred Snipe; and the supervisor of the machine operation was Julian J. Goodpasture. Cecil was writing all the procedures for the machine room. At times on swing shift we would have wired up all the plug boards we had in advance for forthcoming steps. At that point, there was nothing for the operators to do other than take the cards out of machine "#A" for step "7" and put them into machine "#B" for step "8." Cecil was working very long

---

[21] For background on the SDC, see Baum (1981). For background on its predecessor—the system-development division of the RAND Corporation, see Chapter Two.

[22] On government forms that employees were required to complete as part of being processed for a security clearance, no question could be left unanswered. The instructions for middle initial were to enter *NMI* if the candidate had none. Some jokester began referring to Paul Armer as Paul NMI Armer.

hours (he averaged more than 80 hours per week) writing all the procedures that got carried out in the machine room.

So, one night when there was nothing for me to do, I went into Cecil's office and asked him why [he didn't] let me do some of the procedure writing for him. He agreed and a few weeks later he suggested that I move to day shift so that I could work face to face with the problem originators.

Roy Fry: Roy described how he came to RAND from North American Aviation (NAA):

My early interest in RAND was the [analog computer] REAC. I was working on the REAC at North American Aviation in Downey [California]. The drive from Santa Monica [to Downey] got to be too arduous (no freeways) so I was casting about for something closer. I believe it was the REAC people [at NAA] who suggested that RAND was looking for someone with REAC experience. So, I put

Paul Armer (left) passed the management baton to Willis Ware, who succeeded him as head of the Computer Sciences Department.

in an application and was accepted. After some time there, the JOHNNIAC was conceived, and I migrated to that project. The rest of my time at RAND for that session was on that program.

My second session at RAND was on [the JOHNNIAC project] . . . until I was recruited to take over the computer center and the mathematics department at the Atomics International division of North American.

Bill Sibley codeveloped the RAND videographic system and the RAND tablet.

Bill Sibley: Bill earned a degree at UCLA and came to RAND via the Lockheed company. He described it as a winding route:

I graduated from UCLA in mathematics. In fact, as I remember, I was a Teaching Assistant [TA] at the same time Gene Jacobs was a TA in the Math Dept. I got my Master's in math along with a California General Secondary Credential and eventually a Lifetime California Community College Instructors' Credential in math and computers.

While waiting for the Los Angeles City school system's hiring cycle—I was prepared to be the "Mr. Chips" of the LA secondary and community college system—I went to work for Lockheed in Burbank. It was mostly involved with flight test data reduction and engineering computing (punch card and IBM 701). If my memory serves me, Lockheed Burbank had the first IBM 701 on the West Coast. One of my lasting memories is extracting eigenvalues from large flutter matrices on IBM 604/519/sorter/collator equipment.

I worked with the RAND group who had left there to set up the Lockheed operation. I worked with Bob Bemer who had come from RAND with Julian Goodpasture and Bob [Bosak]. He and [Bosak] put together some truly magnificent IBM 407 boards. He was also instrumental in developing FLOP (Floating Octal Point) and I have a vague recollection that he or Bob invented the IBM 604 program step expander.

RAND sounded like the promised land so I applied in 1954 and started out working with Gene Jacobs.

Cliff Shaw: Cliff graduated from UCLA in mathematics and was initially an insurance actuary. During World War II, he was a navigator in the bomber fleet. According to some, Paul Armer interviewed him and was not impressed by his academic record, but, since people with programming and mathematical skills were hard to find, Armer hired him anyway.

There is a humorous story told about Cliff at the expense of programmers everywhere. After he had become a super world-class gold-star computer-science research programmer years later, his responses to a series of questions that a team of psychologists prepared to identify promising programmer candidates were used as a template to screen applicants. There was just one problem—namely, Shaw's skills were somewhat weak in writing. Thus—the anecdote concludes—a lot of people became good programmers but could not write program documentation at all well.

Gene Jacobs: Gene came to RAND after being a graduate student in mathematics at UCLA:

> George Brown was teaching part time at UCLA. The Bureau of Standards had a computer group on campus and I learned how to wire punch card plug boards.
>
> I asked Dr. Brown about RAND and he suggested I send in an application to the Math department, which I did. I was interviewed by Olaf Helmer, Paul Armer and Don Madden. I got an offer from RAND from the Numerical Analysis Department in the summer of 1951, probably because I already knew something about punch cards. I went to work for Paul Armer writing procedures.
>
> [I became] Don Madden's assistant. When Madden transferred to SDC in 1954, I became manager of Programming Services [at RAND].

Mort Bernstein: After graduating from the University of Pittsburgh with an M.S. in statistics, Mort first worked at the Pentagon on a University of Pittsburgh research project for the U.S. Army and then moved on to the Atlantic Research Corporation in Alexandria, Virginia. His widow, Maureen, provided the following information:

> In 1954, Mort found a notice in the Washington Post offering interviews for computer programming jobs at RAND in Santa Monica CA. So on a Sunday afternoon, after spending two hours with Paul Armer, Mort was convinced that he wanted to work at RAND. He told me Paul was one of the smartest, funniest people he had ever met. Earlier that year he had taken a government sponsored course taught by Grace Hopper (the someday Admiral Grace Hopper) who was even then a well respected and knowledgeable teacher of computer programming. That may have helped Mort get a job offer at RAND.

Ray Clewett: Ray related these memories of his first days at RAND in an article from the *RAND Alumni Bulletin*,[23] excerpted here:

> When I first came to RAND in 1951, it had graduated from an Air Force Project, to a non-profit Corporation, but it still had many characteristics of its original military beginnings. We worked out of an old two story poured concrete building

---

[23] Clewett (2002).

Ray Clewett was the chief machinist and head of the mechanical laboratory.

at the southwest corner of Fourth and Broadway in Santa Monica—the current location of the "Santa Monica Place" parking structure. The building was rather drab, and looked much like any of the other commercial buildings in the area. It had originally been the home of the Santa Monica Evening Outlook newspaper.

The RAND Corporation was not a very impressive establishment. There were no signs on the building, or other indications to show that the old newspaper office had become a "Top Secret" government research facility. The only identification was an unpretentious sign on the glass doors at the front of the building reading "The RAND Corporation" in small gold letters.

RAND was a new experience for me. Before coming to RAND, I had always worked in an aircraft factory, or a machine shop. Here I was working in a sophisticated office environment where everyone was clean, well educated, and very professional. At least half of the RAND staff had a Ph.D. degree. I had a high school diploma. At RAND, I worked in the Mathematics Department. In school I had barely passed my high school algebra classes.

Security was tight.[24] The entire building was a Classified Facility. For the first few months, until their Air Force Security Clearance came through, even new employees were escorted at all times (including to the Rest Rooms!). The building was patrolled by armed guards 24 hours a day and was never closed, or the doors locked. The guns the guards carried were not just for show. Twice each year each guard had to report to the Santa Monica Police Pistol Range to "Fire for Qualification." With my non-academic background, it was a little surprising that I would be hired by an organization as sophisticated as RAND. Fortunately, there were a number of factors involved that I knew nothing about.

For some time I had been dissatisfied with my job at Lear Avia, where I had been working, since leaving Douglas Aircraft at the end of the war. I had heard about RAND from a friend, who knew that another friend from Douglas, was now employed at RAND. I phoned that friend, and made an appointment for an interview.

I didn't find out until much later that my timing couldn't have been better. RAND was just starting construction of its new JOHNNIAC Computer. RAND wanted

---

[24] For many years, every member of the RAND guard force could recognize all employees and call them by name. Indeed, entry access to the building included one such guard recording names into a machine whose storage mechanism was a round plastic disc roughly 8 inches in diameter.

a more powerful computer for their Air Force research, and was just starting construction of the first electronic modules for one of these new machines.

RAND had planned to build its new machine in a small computer maintenance shop, where a small group [of] electronic engineers and technicians had been modifying RAND's old REAC computer. But they had no one to design, or tools to make, any mechanical parts. The original plan had been that any mechanical or metal parts they might need for the new machine, could be purchased, or made to order by outside vendors. Design and assembly had progressed to the point where it was becoming very clear that it was not going to be practical to depend on outside vendors to design and manufacture all the special mechanical parts that would be required. If they were going to build this new computer, they were going to need an in-house metal shop that could make parts for power supplies, electronic modules, fuse panels, mounting brackets, frame structure, and an external housing for the machine. I was hired to buy machinery, organize, and manage, a small machine shop that would be able to design and fabricate all the mechanical parts that would be needed to build JOHN-NIAC. JOHNNIAC was completed, and went into service at RAND in 1953. At about the same time IBM brought out their first commercial, "701 Main Frame Computer." JOHNNIAC was in continuous use at RAND from 1953 until 1966, when it was retired, and donated to the Los Angeles County Museum.

Keith Uncapher: Keith came to RAND after graduating from the California Polytechnic Institute (at San Luis Obispo) in mathematics. He wrote,

> My initial interview at RAND was prompted by the reputation RAND had at the time. In part the reputation came from my interview at Douglas. My interview at RAND was with Dr. George Brown and Paul Armer. At the time Paul told me that George wanted to hire me and if that didn't happen he wanted to hire me. I really wanted a hardware assignment and was hired and assigned to Bill Gunning. This was around July 4th 1950. I remain forever grateful to George Brown and Paul Armer for their faith in me. I still often remark to friends that the first twenty years at RAND I imagined was like going to work in Heaven each day. I truly believe RAND at the time was the most exciting place for an IT technologist or IT scientist to be in the US.

Keith Uncapher, trained as a mathematician at California Polytechnic Institute at San Luis Obispo, became a prominent electronics engineer.

Willis Ware: Willis came to RAND after moving from Princeton to southern California to work for NAA:

> I had met Gunning and maybe others when they visited the Institute for Advanced Study [IAS, in Princeton, New Jersey] to talk about our machine [for John von Neumann]. So when I came west in August 1951, it was

natural to retain the contact; also the local computer group met monthly on the UCLA campus in Harry Huskey's [wartime] temporary building—Institute for Numerical Analysis.

The JOHNNIAC was underway by 1952. Bill Gunning went skiing and broke his leg. RAND (namely George Brown) suddenly realized that RAND had all its JOHNNIAC eggs in one person and would be vulnerable if something more serious were to happen to Bill. Some insurance seemed like a valuable asset to have.

I had gotten disillusioned with the environment at North American Aviation to which I had come from IAS. I'm not sure how the link got established but I imagine that Bill/I talked about my coming to RAND. I filled out the paper work, had an interview with George Brown and was hired.[25]

Pat Haverty: Pat came to RAND in late December 1953 after being discharged from the Navy:

I was stationed at Arlington Hall where I was fortunate enough to be assigned to the newly arrived IBM 701. I had previously applied and was accepted at RAND in 1951 (Paul Armer and Don Madden interviewed me but elected to finish up my reserve commitment; I was in a Navy reserve unit specializing in cryptography). Both RAND and I were delighted to rejoin each other with 701 experience under my belt!!

Irv Greenwald: Like several others, Irv came to RAND from UCLA:

The Bureau of Occupations at UCLA sent me to RAND, which I had never heard of before. I was running out of GI Bill [benefits] and needed a job. I started in June of 1950 in the Outlook building.

Departmental Growth

The department grew quickly in size and in complexity, changing its name several times as it evolved.

An organization chart dated January 1, 1950 (Figure 3.1) shows the structure of the mathematics division and its groups. One, the NAD, already numbered 36: the electronics group (eight people) and the punched-card and hand-computing components (28 people).

By October 1, 1951, the NAD component had grown to 48 people and its laboratory group (formerly the electronics group) to 13. At that point, in line with John Williams' philosophy of maintaining extensive contacts throughout the mathematics community, the mathematics division had a roster of 65 consultants.

---

[25] Digby (2001). See also Digby (2005) and Ware (2005). See also LeLevier (2006) and Ware (2006).

By May 1, 1962, the NAD had become the Computer Sciences Department with a dozen discipline-oriented programming teams, a computer-operations group, a computer-system group (formerly the electronics group), a computer-system research group, a programming R&D group, and various administrative, staff, and special-assignment groups (Figure 3.2). The department maintained a roster of 32 consultants. Growth continued through the following years (Figures 3.3 through 3.7) at which point the department had attained its maximum size.

From its inception as the NAD, Paul Armer was its head. Somewhere between 1962 and 1964, he decided that he preferred to address issues other than administrative obligations. Accordingly, he arranged to exchange jobs with the associate head of engineering, Willis Ware, who then became head (see photo on page 31). Armer referred to the action as "the hat trick."

By the mid-1970s, the previously unified Computer Sciences Department—one part to conduct research and the other to provide computer services to the corporation—had split. Keith Uncapher and his group had left to form the Information Sciences Institute at the University of Southern California. The remnants of the research activity in the Computer Sciences Department were not organized into a specific group, although Bruce S. Borden organized a few of them into an information-system laboratory (ISL) to support the computer-science research. Later, Michael L. Wahrman, James D. Guyton, and James J. Gillogly successively became the heads of the ISL. The programming people and the machine-service people became the Computer Services Department (CSD), also called the RAND Computation Center.

The people who came earliest, the people listed in the organizational charts, those mentioned elsewhere in this document, and their colleagues who joined the department later, individually and collectively made the RAND computer-oriented department—whatever its name and organization—a force in the world, in the professional societies of the computing field, and in the RAND research program.

Figure 3.1. Personnel of the Mathematics Division, January 1, 1950

PERSONNEL OF THE MATHEMATICS DIVISION
J. D. Williams

1-1-50

Mathematics
O. Helmer

H. Ansoff
R. Belzer
N. Dalkey
M. Dresher
T. Edwards
O. Gross
E. Quade
J. Robinson
R. Snow
R. Specht
R. Wagner
    J. Edwards
    M. Langjahr

Statistics
A. Mood

B. Brown
T. Harris
J. Walsh
    R. Burns

Numerical Analysis
G. Brown
C. Hastings
        V. Baldwin
        L. Solberg

RAND Projects
H. Germond
B. Himes
M. McLaurie
    E. Chase

E. Paxson
V. Dudley
    R. McDermott

Hand Computing
P. Armer

E. Broderick
H. Hunter
H. MacGrath
E. Pond
W. Smith
J. Thompson

IBM
J. Goodpasture

R. Bemer
B. Chiapinelli
G. Kellman
J. MacIntosh
R. Middleton
D. Lindberg
B. Moats
E. Myer
W. Myers
R. Nash
R. Rumsey
F. Sipe
J. Van Paddenburg

Electronics
W. Gunning

G. Baker
B. Fry
G. Johnson
W. Melahn
R. Mengal
L. Mockbee
D. Slaughter

On leave of absence
J. McKinsey
L. Shapley

Procedures Staff
R. Bosak
J. Hall
J. Madden

Figure 3.2. Personnel of the NAD, May 1, 1962

5-1-62

P. Armer
W. H. Ware – Assoc. Dept. Head
R. H. Blechen – Admin. Asst.
R. N. Reinstedt – Spec. Asst.
F. J. Gruenberger

Staff

M. L. Juncosa   J. C. Shaw
M. E. Maron   N. Z. Shapiro
          P. Wolfe

Computer Systems Group

K. W. Uncapher
P. W. Baran
R. W. Clewett
L. J. Craig
M. R. Davis
E. C. DeLand
T. O. Ellis
L. R. Mockbee
I. D. Nehama
M. Warshaw
R.

Computer Systems Research Group

J. P. Haverty
B. A. Dawkins
D. R. Langfield
F. M. Tonge*

Applied Programming Group

J. D. Tupac
J. D. Babcock

Corporate Data Proc.
G. W. Armerding
W. L. Nadeau
T. Sawtelle

Math & CSD
J. I. Derr
G. B. Benedict
C. H. Bush
L. Cutler
R. J. Clasen
S. E. Dreyfus*
H. E. Kanter
B. Kotkin
M. L. Lind
S. L. Marks
A. B. Nelson
M. C. Prestrud
M. Selig
C. H. Smith
T. W. Ziehe

Economics
J. D. Little
G. Brown
R. J. Eggleton
E. M. Fairbrother
F. W. Finnegan, Jr.
B. Hausner
R. J. Hewitt
G. D. Johnson
A. H. Rosenthal
T. E. Wold

Engineering
W. L. Sibley
S. Belcher
B. W. Boehm
N. B. Brooks
J. L. Carlstedt
N. D. Cohen
D. T. Rumford

Physics
I. L. Finkle
N. Bilbreath
R. S. Grote
G. R. Levesque

Computer Operations Group

W. P. Myers
A. R. Acchi
J. T. Butler
K. Early
F. M. Horton
R. L. Kevershan
C. J. Kirchner
D. A. Lightfoot
C. M. Mason
H. Oku
B. N. Pepper**
H. L. Pierson
D. Price
E. K. Renner
J. M. Smith
B. Stone
B. C. Southard
K. J. Sweeney
B. Wattles
H. Weaver
C. L. Weihe
R. J. Young

Programming Research & Dev. Group

G. H. Mealy
M. I. Bernstein
G. E. Bryan
H. S. Kelly
J. W. Smith

Bethesda Office
C. L. Baker
D. A. Levine

Consultants

M. Balinski
F. S. Black
B. H. Bloom
D. G. Bobrow
S. Boehm
D. C. Cooper
R. A. Dupchak
G. W. Ernst
E. A. Feigenbaum
J. Feldman
B. F. Green, Jr.
C. Hastings, Jr.
J. Hausner
A. W. Holt
D. S. Hopp
K. E. Knight
R. K. Lindsay
D. D. McCracken
M. L. Minsky
A. Newell
H. Noguni
R. L. Patrick
A. J. Perlis
B. Raphael
J. J. Robinson
M. A. Shea
H. A. Simon
B. J. Stone
R. D. Tschirgi
T. A. VanWormer
M. B. Wolf

Administrative Personnel

Wade Holland**
Helen Snell
Vada Baldwin
Marie Chelidona
Dorothy Crabb
Annette Harrison
Arlene Leppek
Carol Moore
Helen Sadlon
Charlene Scherner
Nancy Sogaard
Lora Steele

*On leave of absence
**On military leave

Figure 3.3. Personnel of CSD, March 1964

March 1964

COMPUTER SCIENCES DEPARTMENT
W. H. Ware
P. Armer--Assoc. Dept. Head
R. H. Blechen--Admin. Ass't.

Senior Research Staff
M. L. Juncosa
M. E. Maron
N. Z. Shapiro
J. C. Shaw
P. Wolfe

Air Force Officer
Lt. Col. R. C. Alvestad

Department Assignments
C. L. Baker
G. E. Bryan
I. D. Greenwald
J. W. Smith
F. J. Gruenberger
J. P. Haverty
R. N. Reinstedt

Publications
W. B. Holland
L. Colbert

Research Assistance
B. C. Hammidt
R. Heirschfeldt
A. Paul
M. Westfall

Administrative Services
Helen Snell

Secretaries
Sherry Chester
Dorothy Crabb
Marie Grace
Jessie Gutteridge
Charlene Klink
Carol Moore
Joan Pederson
Helen Sadlon
Sharon Stalder
Edith Wolfe

Document Center
Vada Baldwin

Program Library
Lora Steele

Computer Systems
K. W. Uncapher
P. Baran
L. J. Craig
E. C. DeLand
T. O. Ellis
J. F. Heafner
G. D. Hornbuckle
W. L. Sibley
R. Turn
M. Warshaw
M. R. Davis
R. W. Clewett
G. W. Dietrich
G. N. Lucas
R. Stahl
R. I. Yoshimura
A. C. Lucero
F. E. McGee
N. B. Winston

Computing Services
J. D. Tupac

Systems
J. D. Babcock
B. Hausner
F. Valadez
R. A. Wagner

Programming

Economics
G. W. Armerding*
G. B. Benedict
G. D. Brown
M. Buchanan
C. H. Bush
R. J. Eggleton
F. W. Finnegan, Jr.
R. J. Moulenbelt
A. H. Rosenthal
R. J. Young

Special Assign.
B. W. Boehm
S. E. Dreyfus
D. R. Langfield
D. T. Rumford

Corporate Data Proc.
G. W. Armerding*
H. O. Oku
T. K. Sawtelle
T. E. Wold

Physics
I. L. Finkle
R. S. Grote
G. R. Levesque
H. L. Scantlin

ALDP
T. W. Ziehe
S. L. Marks
H. Noguni

Engineering
J. L. Carlstedt
S. Belcher
N. D. Cohen
M. Fujisaki
K. Harris
W. C. Hollis

Math & CSD
J. I. Derr
S. P. Azen
R. J. Clasen
L. Cutler
E. M. Fairbrother
N. L. Gilbreath
D. L. Hatch
A. B. Nelson

Operations
W. P. Myers
J. T. Butler
D. F. Caraway
T. C. Dorsey
K. L. Early
D. T. Gatley
S. Glaseman
R. L. Kevershan
C. J. Kirchner
D. R. Lahmeyer
D. A. Lightfoot
C. L. Mason
E. McCullough
B. N. Pepper
H. Pierson
E. K. Renner
M. A. Shea
B. C. Southard
B. F. Stone
E. Tolnai
C. L. Weihe

Consultants
M. Balinski
R. Balzer
B. H. Bloom
D. G. Bobrow
S. Boehm
G. B. Bradham
N. B. Brooks
D. D. Butler
R. W. Cottle
B. A. Dawkins
H. Dreyfus
R. A. Dupchak
G. W. Ernst
E. A. Feigenbaum
J. Feldman
B. Gordon
B. F. Green, Jr.
A. W. Holt
D. S. Hopp
G. Jaffray
K. E. Knight
R. K. Lindsay
J. D. Little
D. D. McCracken
D. M. McKay
M. L. Minsky
A. Newell
E. J. O'Connell, Jr.
R. L. Patrick
A. J. Perlis
B. Raphael
P. A. Reich
W. R. Reitman
J. J. Robinson
H. A. Simon
E. Stefferud
F. M. Tonge, Jr.
R. D. Tschirgl
L. Uhr
T. A. VanWormer
R. W. Watson
M. B. Wolf

*Dual Assignment

Figure 3.4. Personnel of CSD, May 15, 1966

5-15-66

W. H. Ware
P. Armer - Assoc. Dept. Head
R. H. Blechen - Admin. Ass't.

Senior Research Staff
M. L. Juncosa
M. E. Maron
N. Z. Shapiro
J. C. Shaw

Air Force Officer
Lt. Col. R. C. Alvestad

Department Assignments
C. L. Baker
G. E. Bryan
I. D. Greenwald
A. C. Lucero
J. W. Smith
J. P. Haverty
R. N. Reinstedt

Publications
J. T. Sturak
L. Colbert

Cybernetics Data Research
W. B. Holland
C. Exton
M. Westfall

Research Assistance
S. A. Harrison
R. M. Heirschfeldt
M. L. Rapp

Administrative Services
H. A. Snell

Secretaries
Sheila Banish   Laurie Harrington
Florence Bennett   Huldah McIver
Joan Berglund   Joan Pederson
Terri Cooper   Helen Sadlon
Dorothy Crabb   Charlotte West
Muriel Cullison   Lucy Wilson
Janet Dorrough

Computer Systems
K. W. Uncapher
P. Baran
L. J. Craig
E. C. DeLand
E. M. DuBois
T. O. Ellis
G. F. Groner
J. F. Heafner
G. D. Hornbuckle *
N. B. Reilly
W. L. Sibley
R. Turn

M. R. Davis
R. W. Clewett
G. W. Dietrich
G. N. Lucas
D. A. Malan
R. A. Matthews

R. I. Yoshimura
N. B. Winston

Document Control   Computer Program Librarian
Carol Moore   Pearl Leonhardt

Computing Services
J. D. Tupac

Programming

Special Assign.
S. E. Dreyfus*
J. L. Kuhns
D. R. Langfield
D. T. Rumford

Math/CSD
J. I. Derr
S. P. Azen
R. J. Clasen
N. D. Cohen
L. Cutler
N. L. Gilbreath
D. L. Hatch
G. Levitt

ALDP
T. W. Ziehe
P. A. Graves
S. L. Marks
H. A. Noguni
F. D. Valadez

Corporate Data Proc.
T. K. Sawtelle
R. J. Eggleton
H. O. Oku

Economics
I. L. Finkle
C. H. Bush
F. W. Finnegan, Jr.
D. Goldman
B. Hausner
R. J. Moulenbelt
A. H. Rosenthal
H. J. Shukiar
B. F. Stone
R. C. Villanueva
T. D. Wisniewski
R. J. Young

Engineering/Physics
B. W. Boehm
K. G. Brown
M. C. Fujisaki
K. Harris
R. H. Mayall
R. L. Mobley
A. B. Nelson
J. Rice
H. J. Richardson
J. E. Rieber

Systems & Operations
J. L. Carlstedt

Systems
G. D. Brown
E. M. Fairbrother
A. W. Frederick
H. L. Scantlin
T. E. Wold

Operations
W. P. Myers
R. L. Kevershan
W. H. Allen
R. K. Cook
R. J. Davis
K. L. Early
S. Glaseman
B. L. Holmes
J. R. Hurd
D. A. Lightfoot
R. E. McKenz
H. L. Pierson
C. K. Shult
C. D. Slepak
E. Tolnai
E. K. Renner
M. Bednarek
B. N. Dyer
P. C. Eastwood
B. C. Southard
C. L. Weihe
E. Yum

Consultants
N. S. Assali   E. A. Feigenbaum   G. E. Lindstrom   V. G. Ruhlig
M. Balinski   B. A. Gordon   M. A. Melkanoff   W. F. Sharpe
R. M. Balzer   F. J. Gruenberger E. G. Mesthene   H. A. Simon
G. G. Bloom   B. Hammidi   M. L. Minsky   P. L. Stephan
G. B. Bradham   A. W. Holt   A. Newell   F. M. Tonge, Jr.
N. B. Brooks   A. D. Inselberg   R. L. Patrick   R. A. Wagner
R. Cahn   R. W. Jonas   M. Penington   M. B. Wolf
R. A. DiPaoli   T. H. Kirschbaum   L. Rossi   S. B. Yuan
J. Economos   R. K. Lindsay   F. J. W. Roughton

*Leave of Absence

Figure 3.5. Personnel of CSD, May 15, 1968

5-15-68

COMPUTER SCIENCES DEPARTMENT

W. H. Ware

P. Armer - Assoc. Dept. Head

R. H. Blechen - Admin. Ass't.

Computer Services
J. P. Haverty
G. W. Armerding, Assoc.

Senior Research Staff
M. L. Juncosa
N. Z. Shapiro
J. C. Shaw

Department Assignments
M. L. Rapp
R. N. Reinstedt

Cybernetics Data Research
W. B. Holland
S. M Breit
P. J. Hays
D. J. McDonald
J. J. Schneider
M. Westfall
J. Economos

Computer Systems
K. W. Uncapher
R. M. Balzer
P. Baran
L. J. Craig**
E. C. DeLand**
T. O. Ellis
D. J. Farber
I. D. Greenwald
G. F. Groner
J. F. Heafner
W. H. Josephs
H. E. Petersen
W. L. Sibley
R. Turn

M. R. Davis
R. W. Clewett
G. W. Dietrich
J. Erskine
G. A. Herrick
G. N. Lucas
R. A. Matthews
R. I. Yoshimura

Computer Systems Analysis
B. W. Boehm
F. W. Blackwell
J. C. Clayton
J. A. Farquhar
K. Harris
V. R. Lamb

Video Graphics Proj.
G. W. Armerding
C. H. Bush
J. L. Carlstedt
G. Levitt

Special Assignments
N. D. Cohen
J. L. Kuhns
D. R. Langfield
G. R. Martins
D. T. Rumford
T. K. Sawtelle

Corporate Data Processing
E. M. Fairbrother
R. J. Eggleton
S. C. Hilfman
J. A. Jolissaint**
A. M. Maul
A. B. MacInnes

Applications Programming
I. L. Finkle

Math/Statistics/ Phys. Science
J. I. Derr
S. P. Azen
J. L. Casti
R. J. Clasen
L. Cutler
M. C. Fujisaki
R. H. Mayall
R. L. Mobley
A. B. Nelson

File Management Systems
T. D. Taft
F. W. Finnegan
D. T. Gatley
W. H. Hamilton
D. L. Hatch
H. Oku
R. J. Young

Simulation & Models
I. L. Finkle
B. Hausner*
L. A. Littleton
R. J. Moulenbelt
H. J. Shukiar
F. D. Valadez
R. C. Villanueva
T. D. Wisniewski

Staff Assignment
A. H. Rosenthal

Systems and Operations
T. E. Wold
W. P. Myers, Staff Ass't.

Systems
G. D. Brown
R. A. Berman
S. Glaseman
P. L. Love
J. E. Rieber

Program Librarian
Pearl Leonhardt

JOSS Support
R. L. Clark
A. C. Lucero
S. L. Marks

Operations
Day Shift
C. D. Slepak
W. N. Canillas
D. F. Caraway
J. R. Hurd
J. F. Kulp
D. A. Lightfoot
W. B. Montgomery
H. L. Pierson
M. T. Surlin
E. Tolnai

Night Shifts
W. H. Allen
D. L. Allen
R. K. Cook
R. J. Davis
B. C. Southard

Key Punch
E. K. Renner

First Shift
B. N. Dyer
P. C. Eastwood
M. A. Hartford
C. L. Weihe

Second Shift
Y. C. Holmes
E. Yum

Support Services
R. H. Blechen

Publications
J. T. Sturak
C. L. Fleming
R. A. Ladd

Research Assistance
S. A. Harrison**
R. M. Heirschfeldt

Administrative Services
H. A. Snell

Secretaries
Florence Bennett
Jerry Brenden
Dorothy Crabb
Janet Dorrough
Mary Harris
Skip Hendricks
Nona Lankford
Rosemary Rhoades
Helen Sinnis
Alice Stear

Intelligence Facility
Marilyn Corum

Document Control
Mary Jaynne Glaseman

Technical Typist
Joan Pederson

*Leave of Absence
**Part Time
Mo./Day - Start Time

Figure 3.6. Personnel of CSD, December 15, 1969

12-15-69

COMPUTER SCIENCES DEPARTMENT
W. H. Ware, Head
K. W. Uncapher, Assoc. Head   J. P. Haverty, Assoc. Head
E. J. Savage, Dept. Administrator

Senior Staff
M. L. Juncosa
N. Z. Shapiro
J. C. Shaw

Special Projects
J. L. Kuhns
M. L. Rapp
R. N. Reinstedt

Cybernetics
Data Research
W. B. Holland
P. J. Hays
J. B. Kelley
G. Rudins

Support Services
E. J. Savage

Administrative Services
H. A. Snell

Publications
J. T. Sturak
L. A. McDonald
L. L. Prusoff

Technical Typist
J. M. Pederson

Document Control
C. A. Taylor

Secretaries
Toni Clark
Dorothy Crabb
Helen Dodds
Ann Harper
Helen Sinnis
Alice Stear

* Part Time
** N. Y. Office

Computer Systems
K. W. Uncapher, Mgr.
T. O. Ellis, Assoc. Mgr.
R. H. Anderson
R. M. Balzer
R. A. Berman
I. R. Blackwell
R. C. Clark
E. C. DeLand
G. F. Groner
E. F. Harslem
J. F. Heafner
W. H. Josephs
R. A. Koster
H. E. Petersen
W. L. Sibley
R. Turn

M. R. Davis
H. E. Booth
R. W. Clewett
G. W. Dietrich
J. E. Erskine
O. E. Garza
G. A. Herrick
G. N. Lucas
R. A. Matthews
R. I. Yoshimura

Research Assistants
R. M. Heirschfeldt
J. E. Nakamura

Computer Systems Analysis
B. W. Boehm
T. E. Bell
F. W. Blackwell
J. C. Clayton
N. D. Cohen
J. A. Farquhar
K. Harris
R. S. Heiser
I. M. Iwashita
D. W. Kosy
R. A. Watson

Video Graphics Project
G. W. Armerding
R. L. Bisbey
C. H. Bush
J. L. Carlstedt

Special Assignments
J. Held**
D. R. Langfield
G. R. Martins
D. T. Runford
I. Shain
C. E. Shanesy**
S. Y. Su

Corporate Data Processing
E. M. Fairbrother
B. J. Cronk
R. J. Eggleton
A. L. Fox
J. L. Frederick
J. F. Gowen
J. P. Groves
K. V. Hamilton
J. A. Lockett
A. B. MacInnes
E. J. Rhodes
B. M. Steece
F. D. Valadez
V. M. Wharton
V. M. Wood

Rand Computation Center
J. P. Haverty, Mgr.
G. W. Armerding, Assoc. Mgr.

Applied Programming
T. E. Wold

Math/Statistics/Physical Science
J. I. Derr
L. Cutler
M. C. Fujisaki
K. J. Hall
R. H. Mayall
S. D. Oman
M. Roublow

Data Management Systems
G. Levitt
D. H. Stewart
T. D. Wisniewski
B. Yormark

Simulation & Models
H. J. Shukiar
M. B. Berman
G. M. Carter
M. J. Haley
L. L. Littleton
M. G. Samaniego

Data Management Services
T. K. Sawtelle
W. H. Allen
C. M. Dodd
F. M. Finnegan
K. D. Gorham
D. L. Hatch
C. N. Johnson
H. Oku
A. H. Rosenthal
R. J. Young

Climate Project
J. M. Clark
R. E. Hoffman
R. L. Mobley
A. B. Nelson

Intelligence Facility
P. T. Rumford
P. E. Brown*
M. Corum*
D. A. Lightfoot

Secretaries
Rosemary Rhoades
Jerry Brenden
Muriel Cullison
Skip Hendricks
Carol Hendrix
Susan Jackson
Gloria Smelser

Systems & Operations
G. D. Brown
W. P. Myers, Staff Ass't.

Systems
H. O. Casali
S. Glaseman
W. R. Hamilton
P. L. Love
R. D. Lutze
R. J. Moulenbelt
J. E. Rieber
A. C. Shetler
A. R. White

Operations
R. J. Davis

Day Shift
C. B. Angell
M. V. Byrne
J. S. Hackett
J. A. Hoepner
J. F. Kulp
A. L. Manuel
P. F. Nielsen
J. D. Rowe
J. J. Simac
B. C. Southard

Program Librarian
J. A. Saindon
M. H. Sammons

JOSS Support
A. C. Lucero
S. L. Marks

Keypunch
E. K. Renner

1st Shift
M. L. Bednarek*
L. I. DeLeon
B. N. Dyer
P. C. Eastwood
C. L. Weihe

2nd Shift
S. M. Shelton
Y. C. Shelton*
E. Yum

Night Shift
D. L. Allen
D. R. Campbell
W. J. Milligan
D. J. Montgomery
J. H. Pierce
M. P. Rush*
G. C. Williams*
A. M. Way
W. L. Zachary

Figure 3.7. Personnel of CSD, January 4, 1971

1-4-71

COMPUTER SCIENCES DEPARTMENT

W. H. Ware, Head

K. W. Uncapher, Associate Head   J. P. Haverty, Associate Head

R. N. Reinstedt, Deputy

H. A. Snell, Administrative Assistant

Senior Staff
M. L. Juncosa
N. Z. Shapiro
J. C. Shaw

Special Projects
M. L. Rapp

Cybernetics
Data Research
P. J. Hays
J. B. Kelley

Publications
. J. Horgan*
L. L. Prusoff
D. Sapriel

Technical Typist
J. M. Pederson

Document Control
P. E. Brown*
. H. Sammons*

Secretaries
Dorothy Crabb
Helen Dodds
Ann Harper
Helen Schroeder
Toni Sharp
Helen Sinnis

Computer Systems
K. W. Uncapher, Mgr.
T. O. Ellis, Assoc.
R. H. Anderson
R. M. Balzer
R. A. Berman
R. L. Clark
E. C. DeLand
G. F. Groner
E. F. Harslem
J. F. Heafner
W. H. Josephs
N. L. Sibley
R. Turn

M. R. Davis
H. E. Booth
R. W. Clewett
G. W. Dietrich
O. E. Garza
G. A. Herrick
N. A. Johnson
G. N. Lucas
R. A. Matthews
R. H. Parker
R. I. Yoshimura

Research Assistants
R. M. Heirschfeldt
J. E. Nakamura

Computer Systems Analysis
B. W. Boehm
T. E. Bell
F. W. Blackwell
N. D. Cohen
J. A. Farquhar
K. Harris
R. S. Heiser
I. M. Iwashita
D. W. Kosy
R. A. Watson

Special Projects
C. H. Bush
D. Hollingworth

Special Assignments
E. M. Fairbrother
D. R. Langfield
G. R. Martins
I. Nesbit
D. T. Rumford

Corporate Data Processing
T. E. Wold
P. K. Gowen
J. F. Groves
D. L. Hatch
R. S. Heiser**
J. A. Lockett
A. B. MacInnes
C. M. Wharton
V. M. Wood

Rand Computation Center, J. P. Haverty, Mgr.

Applied Programming
T. E. Wold

Math/Statistics/ Physical Science
J. I. Derr
L. Cutler
K. J. Hall
S. D. Oman
D. S. Pass
M. Roublow

Data Management Services
T. K. Sawtelle
C. M. Dodd
R. J. Eggleton
F. W. Finnegan
M. C. Fujisaki
C. N. Johnson
A. H. Rosenthal
R. J. Young

Data Management Systems
G. Levitt
D. H. Stewart
T. D. Wisniewski
B. Yormark

Simulations and Models
H. J. Shuklar
M. B. Berman
G. M. Carter
L. A. Littleton
M. G. Samaniego

Climate Project
J. M. Clark
R. E. Hoffman
R. L. Mobley
A. B. Nelson

Intelligence Facility
D. T. Rumford
P. E. Brown*
M. C. Corum*

Secretaries
Rosemary Rhoades
Jerry Brenden
Muriel Cullison
Skip Hendricks
Suzi Jackson
Ginny Kelsey
Gloria Smelser

N.Y. Rand Institute
D. T. Rumford
B. J. Hausner
J. Held
C. E. Shanesy

Systems & Operations
G. D. Brown
W. P. Myers, Staff Assistant

Systems
H. O. Casali
W. H. Allen
S. Glaseman
W. R. Hamilton
J. A. Hoepner
R. J. Moulenbelt
A. C. Shetler
R. F. von Buelow
A. R. White

Operations
R. J. Davis

1st shift
P. F. Nielsen
C. B. Angell
D. Ballantyne
J. S. Hackett
J. F. Kulp
A. L. Manuel
J. D. Rowe

2nd shift
D. L. Allen
D. R. Campbell
J. J. Simac
A. M. Way
G. C. Williams

3rd shift
J. H. Pierce
M. V. Byrne
W. L. Zachary

Production Control

1st shift
B. C. Southard

2nd shift
W. J. Milligan

Program Library
T. M. Allardice
M. H. Sammons*

JOSS Support
A. C. Lucero
S. L. Marks

Key Punch
E. K. Renner

1st shift
L. I. DeLeon
B. N. Dyer
C. L. Weihe

2nd shift
V. C. Shelton
E. Yum

---

* Part Time
** Temporary Assignment

CHAPTER FOUR

RAND's Early Computers

Mid–20th Century Computation

At its inception in 1946, RAND drew on the established techniques and methodology that various branches of science and engineering had evolved over the years. These were predominantly labor-intensive hand methods that depended on spreadsheets to organize the flow of a numeric solution and were supported by desktop mechanical machines that could do arithmetic (calculators) or by calculations involving mathematical functions (the slide rule). Three companies, producing machines under the trade names of Marchant, Friden, and Monroe, dominated the small industry producing desktop mechanical calculators. There were also specialized mechanical machines intended primarily for the financial industry of the time and the corresponding recordkeeping of businesses: e.g., the Felt and Tarrant Comptometer and other bookkeeping machines that Burroughs Corporation marketed.

RAND was also drawing on and contributing to the emerging analog and digital computing techniques and methodologies. A moderately advanced analog-computer art had started in mechanical form prior to World War II[1] and had been pushed during the war into an electronic manifestation.[2] Though there was a tiny commercial analog-computer industry, there was no commercial digital-computer industry when Project RAND was inaugurated. Prior to the war, Bell Telephone Laboratories had built some experimental digital machines; John Atanasoff had designed and built a small-scale digital computer at the University of Iowa; and the U.S. Army had funded the construction of the Electronic Numerical Integrator and Computer (ENIAC) at the Moore School of Electrical Engineering at the University of Pennsylvania. During the closing phase of World War II, the military services had become interested in simulating the full six-degree-of-freedom[3] flight of an aircraft and the U.S. Navy funded three major projects, all nicknamed after storms: Project Typhoon (analog) at the RCA Laboratories, Princeton, New Jersey; Project Cyclone (digital) at the Raytheon Company in Massachusetts; and Project Whirlwind (digital) at MIT.

---

[1] The mechanical differential analyzer that Vannevar Bush pioneered at MIT and replicated in a few other places, including the Moore School of Electrical Engineering at the University of Pennsylvania; the General Electric Company at Schenectady, New York; and the University of California, Los Angeles.

[2] Notably, a machine built by the Reeves Instrument Company to solve differential equations.

[3] The three spatial coordinates of the vehicle's center of gravity plus the vehicle's three angular coordinates with respect to its center of gravity.

Finally, there was a well-developed punched-card industry centered on IBM and Remington-Rand. IBM technology used rectangular holes in the punched cards; Remington-Rand, round holes. Thus, the two product lines were sometimes referred to as square-hole or round-hole equipment. The card formats were different, as was the encoding of alphabetic and numeric data on the card. An IBM card contained 80 alphanumeric characters; a Remington-Rand[4] card, 90.

From this mix, RAND's early use of computational equipment was the desktop calculators, the slide rule, and (of course) EAM punched-card machinery. In this last regard, RAND got started by using the card installation at Douglas Aircraft on the graveyard shift.

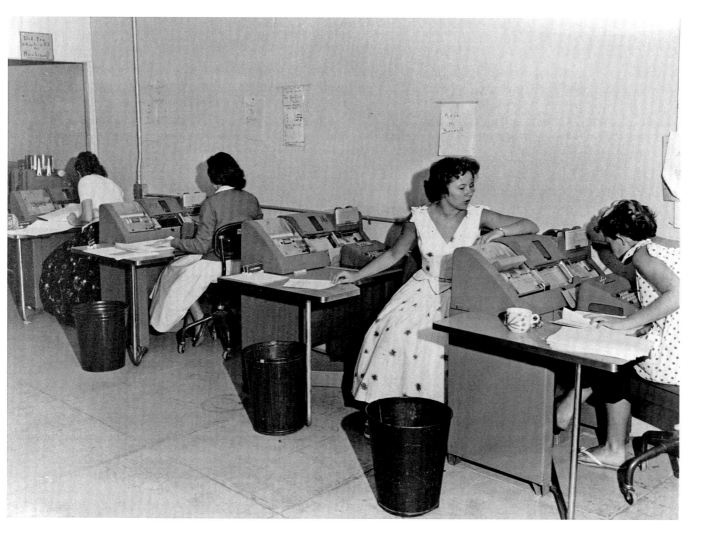

Keypunch operators created duplicate stacks of punched cards for each program, comparing them to ensure accuracy.

---

[4]   RAND had no relation to Remington-Rand (or, for that matter, Rand McNally).

Reeves Electronic Analog Computer

On his return from Harvard for an advanced degree, Arnold Mengel wrote a memorandum outlining his views on the acquisition of an analog computer.[5]

```
September 22, 1947
To:            E. W. Paxson
From:   A. S. Mengel
Subject:          ANALOGUE COMPUTERS


Purpose

This report will outline the information obtained during a brief
survey of the digital computer art. While only ONR [Office of Naval
Research] Special Devices Center and Reeves Instrument Company have
been visited, these contacts plus a survey of pertinent reports at
ONR have provided considerable information. Included in this report
will be a discussion of the Reeves Computer, a list of concerns work-
ing on analogue computers, and a list of sources of error in DC
[direct-current] operational circuits.


Summary

A modified version of the computer outlined in the pamphlet, "Reeves
Electronic Analogue Computer," can be obtained in three-five months
for about $24,000 f.o.b. [free on board.] It is recommended that such
a unit be obtained for RAND.


Reeves Computer

Two copies of the pamphlet mentioned above have been sent to you. As
outlined in our telephone conversation, the prices of the units (as
quoted by their vice-president, C. B. Dewey) are
    • Computer (with no DC amplifiers, power supply, etc.) C101
      $10,730.00
    • Servo Unit (10 servos and resolver) S101     $22,710.00
    • Recorder R101     $3,773.00

The servo unit cost can be cut by $3,500 by removing the resolver,
which requires complex modulating and demodulating equipment. The
chief engineer, H. D. Belock, and the project engineer, S. Godet,
agree with my opinion that 5 servos should be sufficient for use
with seven integrators. A servo unit with no resolver and five ser-
vos instead of ten, would cost $9,600, or a total cost for all three
units of $24,103. A conventional Brush recorder could be obtained for
about $1,000, but I doubt if the savings would be worth it, for their
recorder is much more convenient to use.

I think you are unduly concerned over the non-linear function poten-
tiometers, which I believe are described in Cyclone Report #2 and can
```

---

[5] Mengel (1947). The information in this section draws largely on Mengel and Melahn (1950).

be seen in the pamphlet in the picture under REAC servo Units heading (between cases 2 and 3). Although they now use rather elaborate cutting techniques, they previously set-up the potentioimeter drums by hand with an accuracy better than 2% and in a very short period of time.

They have had no experience with [integral] f(x,t)dx but offer two solutions. An additional unit using mechanical integration can be obtained or (as suggested by Bell Labs. to them) use your proposal of [integral]f(x,t) dx/dt dt. The computer uses no differentiating circuits because of the noise and hum troubles inherent with such DC operational amplifiers, but each servo has a tachometer which can be used for differentiating, so the above scheme is feasible.

Three models are in the process of being built for BuAer [Bureau of Aeronautics] and Dewey is now having a fourth one constructed along with them for us if we so desire, or for a floor model for themselves if we do not purchase it. He has been waiting for an excuse to build an extra model—we have given it to him and there is absolutely no obligation on our part at all.

Delivery on the computer and recorder can be made in three months, but five months will be required for the servo unit. A man can install the model and instruct a staff on operation at additional charge, but I don't feel instruction will be necessary as a maintenance and operation manual will be included.

I was quite impressed by the machine. Its flexibility, ease of setting parameters and initial conditions, the automatic balancing, nonlinear overload lights, etc. seem to be all that can be asked for. The method of mounting should make maintenance simply and quick. The diode limiters will be necessary for problems some of John Williams' group have, in which variable cannot go negative.

Analogue Computer Development Program

The following is a list of concerns involved in analogue computer developments (as outlined by Perry Crawford):
1. General Purpose
   a) M.I.T. (2), Moore School, G.E., A.P.G., UCLA (mechanical differential analyzers)
   b) Reeves Instrument Company
   c) George A. Philbrick [Researches], Boston, Mass. has a computer for sale, similar to [Gilbert] McCann's, but using DC operational amplifiers rather than TLC [transfer logic cell] circuits.
   d) M.I.T. Electrical Laboratories
   e) Columbia, [John R. Ragazinni] and [Frederick A. Russell]
2. Special Purpose
   a) Missile programs
      Reeves and RCA for the Navy
      A. C. Hall at M.I.T.—simulator tester for Navy

```
              Shranstad of BuStan [Bureau of Standards]
              Bell Laboratories—NIKE
              G. E.—tester—program now extinct
         b)   Franklin Institute for Navy . . .
              M.I.T. Instrument Lab. under [Robert C.] Seamans for AAF
         c)   Network Analyzers—many of which McCann's is a good example.
         d)   Raytheon has built small a model for linear equations up to
              fourth order.
         e)   Sperry has built one for themselves under [the guidance of]
              Harris [at Reeves] and have done research on electronic differ-
              ential analyzers as a subcontractor to Republic Aviation.
         f)   Simple models have been developed by G. E., Martin, Hughes,
              North American, Curtiss and others.


    Sources of Errors

    The primary sources of errors in DC operational circuits are:
    1. Finite input and output impedances
    2. Stray input voltages
    3. Changes in amplifier gain
    4. Capacitor leakage
    5. Finite amplifier gain
    6. Drift


    Number 5 was treated briefly in my previous letter to you. To expe-
    dite the delivery of this report, an analysis of the above effects
    will be discussed in a subsequent report, which will show that none
    of them (except possibly 6) contribute more than 0.2% error.


    Obviously, the errors can be reduced by use of short computing
    times, high gain, high leakage resistance, and long integrator time
    constant.
    There is usually a limit of about 2 minutes in computing time, since
    certain errors in DC analogue computers have a tendency to increase
    with time.6
```

Other than punched-card devices and mechanical calculators, there were no electronic devices that would support the calculations that RAND intended to pursue. The company did accept Mengel's recommendation, and a REAC arrived. An electronic analog computer was essentially an Erector Set whose pieces are electronic or electromechanical parts. The flow of the problem being solved was implemented in the pattern of interconnections among the basic parts. Thus, problem setup was detailed and tedious, requiring, among other things, teardown of the prior problem. The original REAC was not, in current parlance, user friendly.

Almost immediately, RAND made many improvements in the machine. The following sections describe the major ones.

---

[6]   Gunning and Mengel (1949).

Eddie Hatten at the console of the Reeves Electronic Analog Computer

Plug-Board Interconnections

Given its experience with the plug boards of punched-card electronic accounting machines, it was natural for RAND to imagine one as the problem-input device for the REAC. IBM was persuaded to make special boards and mounts—long and relatively narrow—that were large enough to accommodate all the connection points in the machine proper. Thus, problem setup consisted of plugging the appropriate wires into the board and mounting it in the holder. The problem-solver could concentrate on the problem instead of the machine's mechanisms. Thus, retaining the plugged-up boards could save problems, and simply inserting a new board could quickly change problems.

Chopper-Stabilized Amplifiers

In an electronic analog computer, the machine must be able to handle variables that do not change for long periods or that change very slowly. This implies that the operational amplifiers in the machine must have a frequency response down to 0 cycles per second— i.e., an input of 0 volts must produce an output of 0 volts. Unfortunately, electronic amplifiers of the day were not stable; a fixed input voltage would produce an output that varied uncontrollably over time as a result of thermal effects, stray electrical currents, and other effects. As Mengel noted in his memorandum, problem times of only a few minutes were feasible. The procedure was to balance all amplifiers—a tedious manual chore—and then quickly make the problem run.[7]

At the time, "the use of contact modulators (also called vibrators, converters, choppers) [were effective] as a means to stabilize d-c amplifiers . . . is well known."[8] Moreover, "the ingenious application of this technique to stabilize a wide-band feedback amplifier is believed to have been first used by A. W. Vance in connection with Project Typhoon"[9] and therefore called the "Vance drift correction system." All the amplifiers in RAND's REAC were accordingly modified[10] and problem-solution times of minutes to hours became feasible.

Arbitrary Function Input

This device consisted of a metallic cylinder roughly 8 inches in diameter and 15 inches long (the input drum—see photo, next page). There were fastenings for holding a piece of paper to the drum. The drum was driven by a servo motor angularly. Above it, in contact with the surface axially, was a linear resistor that could touch the surface. Thus, a voltage applied across the resistor would vary linearly from −100 volts at one end to the maximum of 100 volts at the other end.

The procedure for an arbitrary function input was as follows:

1. On a piece of 11-by-17-inch cross-section paper, plot the desired function with the independent axis along the 17-inch dimension.
2. Glue a piece of copper wire to the paper following the plot of the function.
3. Fasten the paper around the drum with the 17-inch dimension around the circumference.
4. Lower the linear resistor into contact with the wire on the drum surface.

The independent axis of the variable was then the angular position of the drum, and voltage on the wire (glued to the paper) would be the value of the function. As the problem demand rotated the drum back and forth, the wire voltage (through its contact with the linear resistor) varied according to the plot of the function.

These three major improvements together with upgraded potentiometers, a larger array of precision resistors and capacitors, elimination of stray ground currents between cabinets, and other changes made the REAC into a stable workhouse machine for a wide

---

[7] It is believed that one of the assignments for the newly hired Keith Uncapher was balancing the amplifiers prior to each problem run.

[8] Liston et al. (1946, p. 194).

[9] Serrell (1948).

[10] Mal Davis modified and maintained the amplifiers. He and Ed DeLand trained at UCLA on the mechanical differential analyzer.

The REAC used function-input drums (above) and problem-input boards (below).

array of scientific and engineering problems. Among them was the study of intercontinental ballistic missile (ICBM)–intercept schemes, modeling of human physiological and neural systems (e.g., the internal and external respiratory systems), aircraft and aerodynamic studies, nonlinear economics, transient hydraulics, Prandt-number heat studies, bang-bang–control systems, pharmaceutical-drug distribution in the human body, heat-transfer effects, and—well ahead of its time—exploration of the energy demands for earth-moon trajectories.

At one point, the REAC was refurbished and a small contest held to select a new name—the winner being simply TRAC, the RAND analog computer.

Eventually, the large, mainframe digital computers and their mathematical-modeling capability outran the REAC's ability. Moreover, RAND needed the REAC's space to accommodate an enlarged machine room for the digital equipment. Since the REAC was technically the property of the USAF, it was shipped in 1961 to the Air Academy at Colorado Springs for reinstallation and a few more years of productive work. It is believed that the machine later made its way to a small midwestern college and finally into the recycle bin.

While analog technology is still used in many places (e.g., as controllers for devices of many kinds), the large, general-purpose analog computer is a thing of the past.

As noted by Ed DeLand—father of RAND's REAC/TRAC for more than a decade,

> The difference between directly watching a highly instrumented (with sensors) real system operate [on an analog machine] vs. waiting while each individual piece and component [of the system is] calculated [on a digital machine] certainly [suggests that] it would be useful to have such a powerful tool now when simulations of complex systems in every field of endeavor are so common. The analog machine is now an anachronism, but it certainly was a brilliant invention and served [science and engineering] well.

Ed DeLand was known as the father of RAND's Reeves Electronic Analog Computer and as an innovative user.

The JOHNNIAC Digital Computer

In 1949 and 1950, RAND rented from IBM and operated a pair of CPECs and some 604s.[11] In 1950, a need for more computing power was felt, and the issue of larger and faster equipment arose. Should RAND attempt to build a machine for its needs or buy—and if buy, buy what?

The team of John Williams, George Brown, and Bill Gunning set out on a tour of the country to see what might be possible. They visited IBM at Poughkeepsie, the University of Illinois, the Moore School, and Eckert-Mauchly Computer Corporation. What they found was discouraging. Bill summed it up: "They were doing all kinds of tweaky things to circuits to make them work. It was all too whimsical." The only bright spot was the Princeton development at IAS, and thus it was that a working alliance between RAND and IAS came into being. RAND would build a machine patterned in the likeness of the Princeton one. So JOHNNIAC came from an illustrious ancestor—the so-called von Neumann machine developed at Princeton's IAS.[12]

---

[11] This section is a lightly modified version of a talk that Willis Ware gave at the decommissioning ceremony for the JOHNNIAC computer held at RAND on February 18, 1966. The talk was published (Ware, 1966). See also Gruenberger (1968), a very complete history of the project, including background material from von Neumann's original writing on the subject of the electronic computer.

[12] IAS is an independent organization situated in Princeton, New Jersey. It is not a part of Princeton University, though there are close collegial and research ties between them.

As part of his preparation for the trial to come, Bill spent three days a week working at UCLA on the Standards Western Automatic Computer (SWAC) machine being built there by BuStan. It is interesting to review a document of October 1950—from the same team of Brown, Gunning, and Williams to Frank Collbohm:

```
It is difficult at this stage to make sharp estimates of the sums
that will be needed during the fiscal years 1951 and 1952. The fol-
lowing, therefore, are deliberately conservative:

Total [estimated cost] 54,000 [FY51]; 63,000 [FY52]

In addition, the technicians, engineers, and programmers who will be
required for the project are currently available, with one exception:
we shall require a first-rate mechanical engineer for about 1 man-
year.

The personnel have been acquired and trained over the past three
years with this end in view. They have been occupied till now in
training activity and in design and construction work on other RAND
equipment, such as the random digit generator, the coverage machine
[Paxson's bombing simulator], the REAC, etc.

So far as operating personnel is concerned, we now have approxi-
mately the planned number. The actual total number needed to operate
the machines of Numerical Analysis may increase, say by two or three,
because of the recent improvements made in the REAC, which will be
much more voracious of problems than when originally obtained.
```

The total construction cost of the unnamed machine was estimated to be $150,000, with a construction period of two years.

Several of the decisions about JOHNNIAC were noteworthy for 1950:

- The design goal was to improve markedly the reliability of the Princeton machine. A minimum increase in reliability by a factor of 10 was to be achieved.
- Punched cards, not the teletypewriters of other machines of the day, were to be the JOHNNIAC's I/O media.
- The machine was to be designed as an operational equipment, not a laboratory experiment. It was intended to be used and to be maintained.
- The main store of the machine was to be the special electrostatic tube that Radio Corporation of America (RCA) developed under the name "selective electrostatic storage tube."

And so work commenced.

In 1952, Cecil Hastings reported as follows:

Discussions are in progress with regard to the console. Several schemes and meth-ods for entering numbers into the machine are being considered. Probably there will be an operator's console presenting to him only as much as he needs to play the machine, and a maintenance console [that] reveals the deepest secrets of the whole JOHNNIAC. No other machine can make this statement: Our console is human engineered.

JOHNNIAC will definitely be the most completely protected machine ever devised. The present plans for supervisory control will take care of the machine in event of voltage failure, refrigeration failure, fuse burnout, and all else. In addition to shutting down the machine, an alarm will be sounded and a tell-tale light will tell who do-ed it. The precise nature of this alarm is not yet settled; many diabolical devices, all directed toward the best interests of the operator, are being considered.

As is fairly evident to anyone who goes by the zoo,[13] the main frame for the JOHNNIAC is ready to receive registers. Bob Rumsey, who has been working with Mike Stobin to wire the filament transformers [that] supply power to heat vacuum tubes, has formed a private operation outside where he is holding down floor space vacated by IBM files. We promise to have this auxiliary activity (you might call it Rumsey's Rump Session) replaced by bona fide JOHNNIAC ventilation.

Gan Baker has been given the awesome responsibility of Chief Inspector. What this means in essence—we know where to point the finger—anything that goes wrong is, of course, Gan's fault. Under Gan's direction, the shop has produced all of the chassis of the adder, the digit resolver, the accumulator and the MQ [multiplier-quotient register].[14] Two memory registers are completed; two more will be completed in two weeks. Two clear and gate drivers have been completed. What all this adds up to is, that if Mike Stobin and Willis Ware who have been dealing with the ventilation engineers can come through with the ventilating equipment in time, it is very likely that we can have a smoke test of the arithmetic unit on the JOHNNIAC main frame in October [of 1952].

The goal of the test will be to connect the A [accumulator register] and MQ for end-around shifting (7.5 order)[15] and let the machine shift a set of digits all day while we hammer on the frame and wiggle wires. Applications for wire wigglers are now open.

What Cecil did not report, nor did anyone know at the time, was that RAND nearly built the proverbial "boat in a basement." Not until it was time to move JOHNNIAC's mainframe assembly from the old building to the one at 1700 Main Street (in Santa Monica—see

---

[13] The "zoo" was a special part of the basement in RAND's former building at 4th and Broadway in Santa Monica. Chicken wire set it off from the rest of the building, an arrangement having to do with security clearance and the necessity of keeping people separated.

[14] The MQ was the register holding the multiplier during multiplication or the quotient in division.

[15] All JOHNNIAC instructions—or "orders"—had a numerical designator. One of the machine's attributes was that its complete instruction repertoire could be typed on a single side of one sheet of paper. This aspect became a boastful inside joke in view of the voluminous user manuals for commercial machines of the time.

Chapter Five) did anyone appreciate that it would not go onto the elevator. The assembly was finally nudged up the elevator shaft but without use of the elevator. Concurrently with construction of the large machine, RAND was also building the so-called Junior version, a precise copy of one-fourth of the large one.

Early in 1953, all action moved into this building, and shortly thereafter, Junior was in operation as the engineering prototype to prove the designs. As John Williams proudly boasted in 1954, "During the time it was tested, something over a billion operations were carried out without a single error." Concurrently with the hardware activity, programmers-to-be conducted regular seminars. Sample problems were coded and analyzed, and gradually the difference between stored-program electronic computers and the previous card- and plug board–programmed machines came to be appreciated.

Among the important people at these seminars were Paul Armer, Bob Bosak, Robert (Bob) Bremer, Irv Greenwald, Jean Hall, Cecil Hastings, Gene Jacobs, Dave Langfield, Don Madden, John Matousek, Wes Melahn, Arnold Mengel, Ellis Myer, Bill Orchard-Hays, Bob Rumsey, Cliff Shaw, and Jack van Paddenberg.

All during JOHNNIAC construction, George Brown spent much of his time worrying about skiers (e.g., Bill Gunning) and airplane pilots (e.g., Roy Fry). George had visions of a large part of his project know-how winding up in the hospital.[16]

Early in the JOHNNIAC project, Bill Gunning decided that a "big switch" of some sort would be necessary to turn the power on or off to the machine. Accordingly, he asked Gardner Johnson to find something appropriate. Shortly, Johnson returned with a *huge* switch. It was one of the vertical switch-box controllers used in older trolley cars to handle the heavy current demand of the traction motors—the kind at which the motor operator stands and rotates a handle on the top. Needless to say, it exceeded Gunning's expectations. But it had come from a surplus shop, so discarding it was not financially painful.

JOHNNIAC became operational during the first half of 1953, and it computed its first prime number. Needless to say, during its earliest days of shakedown and operation, there was much maintenance and troubleshooting, and thereby unfolds another tale.

It had early been decided that the machine was to have a closed-cycle air-conditioning system. Cool—really, cold—air was to be pumped up the center of the frame, returned along the outside of the frame, and recooled in the basement. The air-conditioning installation designed for JOHNNIAC may never have an equal—lots of cold water to make cold air, duplication of equipment to give reliability, and a temperature-control system to end all. Most equipment items in the cooling system had a corresponding neighbor with which they could exchange jobs, and thus it was that there evolved a maze of plumbing and valves second to none. To keep the machine clean, a double set of filters was installed. Going all out, it was decided to use a filter called the Cambridge filter, guaranteed to take *everything* out of the air. However, these filters were never installed. Somehow, they stopped seeming necessary.

---

[16] It was this concern that led to Willis Ware joining RAND. His experience with construction and design of the von Neumann machine at IAS made him an ideal match.

When it came time to service the machine, someone had to open a door. It was like standing in the deep freeze, and everyone was soon wearing ski jackets—with hoods. The machine also acquired one of its early names—the Pneumoniac.

There is another noteworthy aspect of JOHNNIAC's early life having to do with the RCA Selectron tube. RCA regarded this tube, which was the machine's store (i.e., memory) at the time, as experimental, and thus guarantee did not cover it. However, at $800 each, it was a little hard not to argue with RCA about defective tubes. Many remember, especially Keith Uncapher, the long, almost-daily arguments about bad Selectron tubes; generally, Keith won his agreement to return the defective tube.

Later in 1953, a contract was let with the International Telemeter Corporation to produce a magnetic-core store for JOHNNIAC. This company was a venture into electronics by Paramount Pictures.[17]

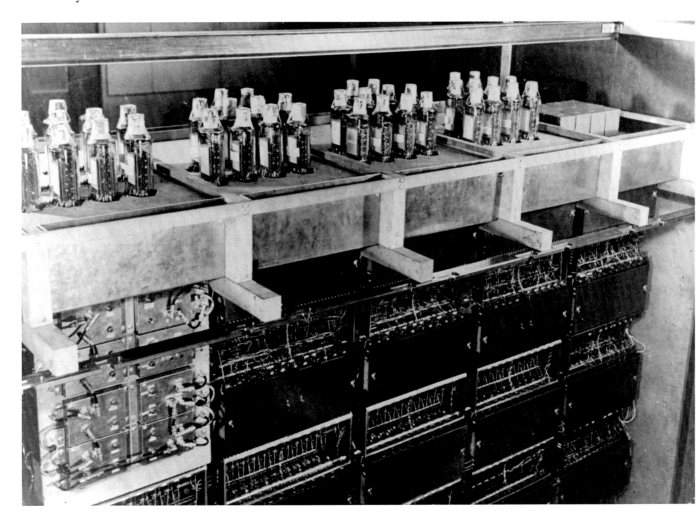

JOHNNIAC initially used a 256-word Selectron high-speed memory.

---

[17] Paramount's intention was to create a market and equipment for paid television. The contract with RAND was a way to retain the staff team of Bill Gunning (from RAND), Milton Rosenberg (from RCA, Princeton), and Raymond Stewart-Williams (from the UK) that Paramount had assembled.

At that time, core stores had been built only on an experimental basis at MIT. To maintain the reliability that had been designed into the rest of the machine, an extraordinarily detailed and tight specification was written for the work. It described a new level of design philosophy and required reliability, something at that time quite unfamiliar to the industrial world. For the next two years, the engineers at Telemeter found themselves boxed between RAND's engineering group, with its ever-present specification, and profit-minded Paramount Pictures.

Early in 1955, the Telemeter magnetic-core store was installed on JOHNNIAC. It was the first commercially available magnetic-core store, and, for a short while, it was the largest one in operation.[18] JOHNNIAC then settled into its computing load. In 1955, a 12,000-word magnetic drum was added. Inadvertently, RAND did some of the earliest research in running magnetic drums with the heads in contact with the surface, where they were not supposed to be. In 1954, an online printer had been added, and, in 1958, an improved model replaced it; the online plotter was also added in 1958. Finally, in 1963, a special piece of hardware called a magnetic targeted carrier (MTC) was added for the JOSS work.[19]

During JOHNNIAC's operational life, things occasionally happened to enliven the daily routine. For instance, in 1958, there was a small fire in one of the room–air-conditioning units. Damage was minor, but the high spots of the incident are best described in a memo from Keith Uncapher:

> There were no open flames and the damage was localized to the extent that the RAND people on hand could easily cope with the situation.
>
> So far, this incident sounds almost uneventful; however, the entire incident was plagued with unusual happenings [that] border on the humorous. For instance, while Frank McGee was operating a 10-lb. [carbon-dioxide, or CO_2] bottle, the flexible hose from the supply tank to the nozzle on the unit burst, disabling the unit. Another 5-lb unit, normally stored near the $1.2 [million JOHNNIAC] failed to operate, since it had lost its charge (or never had one!). By this time another 10-lb. unit was pressed into service until its hose also blew open.
>
> In parallel, Matt Miller was operating a 50-lb. [CO_2] cart unit from a ladder. It turns out that the nozzle of such a large unit builds up a large static electrical charge which accidentally was discharged through Matt Miller. This unbalanced Matt enough to tip the step-ladder on which he was standing, and Matt found himself on the floor.
>
> A replacement [person] then took the large nozzle in hand and proceeded to the top of the same stepladder. Upon reaching the next-to-the-top step the ladder broke in two pieces and once again, the nozzle and operator were airborne temporarily.

---

[18] Because of its 40-bit (vs. 36-bit) word length.

[19] Today, this device would be called a "swapping magnetic drum."

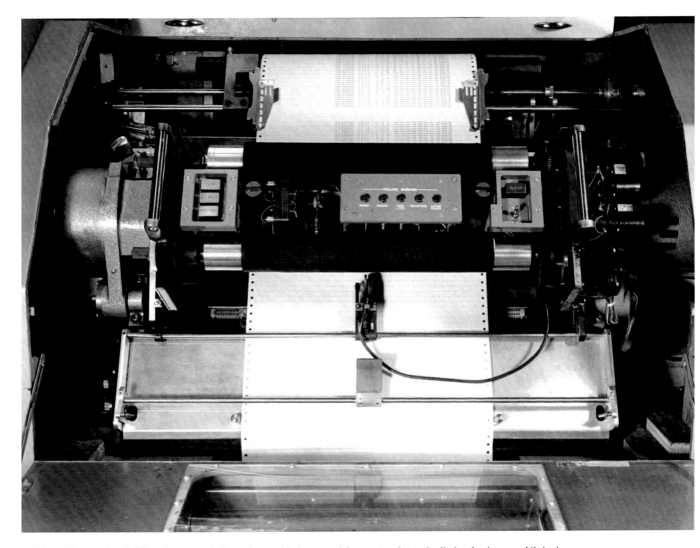

JOHNNIAC used a 140-column, rotating-drum, high-speed impact printer built by Anderson-Nichols.

By this time, it was discovered that the 50-lb. [CO_2] unit had developed a leak at the supply end of the hose. The tank valve was closed immediately and the unit was removed from the service. A more severe leak could have resulted in injury, since the entire tank probably would have discharged in seconds.

In light of the ever present possibility of fire, I should like to suggest that an immediate and extensive investigation of the [CO_2] units be made. One only need consider that 4 of 6 units failed during the incident reported herein, to realize the importance of the situation.

For much of its life, JOHNNIAC operated more than one shift. Its nighttime operations were under the control of the same people who operated the other computers.[20] On

_____

[20] Typically, these other machine runs were for corporate payroll.

lengthy computations, the operator would start the machine, switch off the room light, and go away—to come back later for the completed work. On many such occasions, it was noticed that machine errors were made, and, eventually, the story got around that JOHNNIAC was afraid of the dark.

So it turned out to be. On investigation, certain small neon tubes in the machine were found to be sensitive to light and required the presence of light for reliable operation. So a row of fluorescent lights was installed just inside the doors.

JOHNNIAC spanned an important period in the development of the computing field. During its 13 years and 50,000 hours of operation, perhaps 25,000 to 30,000 other computers have been built and installed; the industry has grown from nothing to $2 billion to $3 billion. For the time at which JOHNNIAC was built, it had many important features:

- a wonderfully complete instruction set with several innovations, such as the Display and the Hoot[21]
- a new order of reliability in performance—in early 1956, for example, it was consistently better than the IBM 701
- a sophisticated operating console with the ability to monitor every toggle in the machine and to execute instructions one by one or step by step
- complete marginal checking
- wired-in test routines for the store
- punched-card I/O
- the capability to measure, from one central place, the heater-cathode leakage of groups of tubes
- the only successful Selectron store ever built and operated
- the first commercial magnetic-core store
- the most skillfully engineered and operationally oriented machine of the Princeton family of machines
- the most protected machine ever built—no other machine can claim so many fuses, meters, and protective devices.

In the earliest days of 1954, most programming was done in machine language and in absolute octal. In 1955, Jules Schwartz wrote the first assembly routine for JOHNNIAC, and Cliff Shaw produced a revised assembler in 1956. Then came QUAD, an interpretive programming system, and SMAC, a small compiler.

Each was noted for being foolproof. The nonprofessional programmer could use these systems comfortably; the machine would report errors to him or her in great detail. There were other significant contributions to the programming art as well; among them were

---

[21] *Hoot* refers to a noise that the machine could make to signal the operator. In 1957, Mort Bernstein wrote an assembler so that he could program music to be played using the Hoot. The first song he programmed for the JOHNNIAC was "The Flight of the Bumblebee"; the assembler later became available to other staff (Mort Bernstein et al., 1998).

JOHNNIAC's end doors opened to reveal variable transformers (dials), "grasshopper" fuses (center panel), and meters (right panel) to monitor electrical currents.

items with such names as EASY FOX, CLEM, JBL-4, J-100, MORTRAN (by Mort Bernstein), and Load-and-Go.

In the late 1950s, the nature of JOHNNIAC's task changed. The rental equipment from IBM carried most of the computing load from the RAND staff. JOHNNIAC became a free good; its time was available for research use. The cost of operation was sufficiently low that one need not be concerned about using large amounts of machine time. Research consumed much of its time on the general questions of AI, and the initials *NSS* (Allen Newell, Cliff Shaw, and Herb Simon) came to be closely associated with JOHNNIAC. Newell, Shaw, and Simon used the machine extensively for research.

During this period came such achievements as the following:

- list structures, list-processing techniques, and their embodiment in such languages as IPL-2, -3, and -4
- chess-playing routines, such as CP-1 and -2
- theorem-proving routines, such as LT—the Logic Theorist
- the general problem solver—GPS
- the assembly-line balancer of Fred Tonge.

Subsequently, JOHNNIAC was the research tool that made possible two of RAND's high spots in computer research: the RAND tablet and JOSS (both described in Chapter Seven). The successful development of the RAND tablet came from the initial experiments on graphical I/O terminals that were done on JOHNNIAC. JOHNNIAC has made JOSS possible, an early system that provided each of its time-shared users with a typewriter connection from office to machine. Those who knew JOSS and perceived the friendliness of its help and reaction feel strongly that such systems represented one of the prominent ways of computing for the future.

JOHNNIAC was also the research tool that made possible a flowering of mathematical research at RAND. In his short history of RAND's contributions to mathematics, Bruno Augenstein made these observations:

> [D]uring the JOHNNIAC era an unprecedented symbiosis arose between the machine and RAND mathematics. The machine was pursued to allow computations on a large enough scale to test a number of mathematical applications notions; in turn, the presence of the machine inspired mathematicians to pose, formulate, and test mathematical applications concepts [that] would have been irrelevant and not pursuable in the absence of a machine of JOHNNIAC power.[22]

Certainly, it was fitting that a machine with JOHNNIAC's stature should have completed its career as a research vehicle, dedicated to improving and extending the technology and art that it helped inaugurate.

---

[22] Augenstein (1993, p. 6).

A small ceremony was held to turn off the machine. It was appropriate that Cliff Shaw, creator of JOSS, and Bill Gunning, chief engineer of JOHNNIAC's construction, had the honor. Cliff programmed JOSS so that it executed a 60-second countdown and then stopped the machine; Bill had the privilege of disconnecting the power on the final shutdown.

JOHNNIAC's "Obituary"

JOHNNIAC's demise was announced in a RAND press release from February 18, 1966, written by Shirley Marks in the style of a mock obituary:

Shirley Marks was a senior programmer.

```
                JOHNNIAC
                1953-1966


Friday, February 11, 1966, as it must to all
men—and machines—the end came to JOHNNIAC, mem-
ber of a distinguished family of computers known
as Princeton-type machines. This noble line of
electronic brains was sired by the human brain
of mathematician John von Neumann, for whom
JOHNNIAC was affectionately named.

The end came to JOHNNIAC in the same room at
The RAND Corporation in which, more than twelve
years earlier, its neons first flickered into
life. JOHNNIAC had entered a world [that] saw
the computer only as a mechanical extension of
man's hand on the keyboard of a desk calculator.
With the brashness of youth, with the knowledge
of its uniqueness, with the spirit of a pioneer,
JOHNNIAC has been credited with leading the way
to the modern concept of the computer as an
information processor—an electronic extension of
man's mind, helping him to design, to plan, to
judge, to decide, to learn.

As the end came, from nearby rooms was heard the busy chatter of
JOHNNIAC's sophisticated descendants. Absorbed in the wonder of their
mass-produced cores and graphic displays, of their systems and lan-
guages, they seemed unaware of the drama drawing to a close, of a
memory fading, a pulse unsteady. And finally, power failure; JOHNNIAC
had been unplugged.

Friday, February 18, 1966, final ceremonies were held for JOHNNIAC.
Many friends of the early days gathered, but not to grieve. There
were no flowers, only coffee, cake, and memories.

Enshrinement will be in the Los Angeles County Museum.
```

IBM Mainframes

Until minicomputers came into the commercial market, RAND was exclusively an IBM shop—the "big iron" mainframes and all ancillary equipment. At that time, everything was rented from IBM, but no records of details and dates have been discovered. Accordingly, the following listing has been compiled from the memories of several people, in particular, Ronald W. (Ron) Shell of RAND and Bob Patrick.[23] The computers are grouped into five categories (see Table 4.1): production machines in support of the corporation and its staff; R&D machines in support of the computer-science research projects; text-processor machines; special machines for either R&D or special corporate needs; and analog machines.

Bob Kevershan at the console of RAND's IBM 704

---

[23] Robert L. Patrick has a special place in the history of computing at RAND. At one point, Paul Armer tried to hire him for RAND. Patrick declined saying he wanted to be a consultant but that if it failed, he would join RAND. Armer signed him on as a consultant in 1959, a role he retained for 33 years. He was, so to speak, truly an "outside insider."

Table 4.1. Five Categories of Computers That RAND Used

Type	Description[a]
Production	Punched-card EAM. RAND had one or more of each of these: type 024 keypunch, type 082 sorter, type 402 tabulator, and type 407 tabulator cabled to a type 521 summary punch.
	IBM CPEC. Each had three ice-box storage units, each of which held ten 10-digit numbers.
	IBM 701. Originally named the defense calculator. Standard configuration was a card reader, a printer (a 407 without the counters), a 521 summary punch, a magnetic drum, four magnetic tapes, a central processing unit (CPU) with Williams Tube electrostatic storage of 2,048 36-bit words, and no standard OS software. The time was 1953.
	IBM 704. Rented in early 1956, this had the same architecture as that of a 701. The tapes were faster, the memory was magnetic core,[b] and up to 32,000 words were available.
	IBM 1401/7090.[c] These used tape coupled via manual exchange of magnetic tapes. The new wrinkle was the 1403 chain printer on the 1401. It provided excellent print quality, and the operator could change the chain cartridge. When a cartridge with both upper and lower cases was offered, primitive word processing became possible.
	IBM 7040/7044, loosely coupled via manual switching of tape units
	IBM 7040 operated as a stand-alone machine.
	Various IBM System 360 machines, from model 20 through model 65
	Various IBM System 370 machines, from model 158 through models 3032 and 3033 and ending with model 4381
	Various Sun machines
R&D	JOHNNIAC; also served as a production machine initially
	IBM 1620, used largely by Fred Gruenberger
	IBM 1130 as part of the videographic system
	DEC PDP-10 running under TENEX and DEC 20 running under TOPS-20
	DEC PDP-11/70 for graphics research and program development
	DEC PDP-6, host machine for JOSS-2 development; subsequently, a production machine at the personal, in-office level
Text processors	DEC PDP-11/45, initial text processor
	DEC PDP-11/70
	DEC virtual address extension (VAX)–11/780
	DEC VAX-11/785, final text processor
Special	Stromberg-Carlson 4060 tape-to–35-mm film for plotting
	DEC 2060
	Universal automatic computer (UNIVAC) in the early 1970s
	Data General Systems (two models: Nova and Eclipse) in the mid-1980s for CLINFO[d]
	Evans and Sutherland Picture System for graphics
	Silicon Graphics (SGI) for classified computing
	JOSS-3 on the IBM 370/158, where it was retired
Analog	REAC (later TRAC)

[a] Where two machines are listed, the first acted as problem-preparation input or output for the second.

[b] IBM's early magnetic-core units were very temperature sensitive. The following incident is accurate, although it may have pertained to the 7090's initial core memory rather than the 704's: The first ones immersed the core planes in tanks of temperature-controlled heated oil. The customer engineers had a special, movable hoist that lifted the plane from the tank. The first step in servicing a plane was to let it hang on the hoist until the oil dripped free. Air-cooled planes appeared very soon after the oil units.

[c] Generally, the IBM mainframes accepted input as card decks, magnetic tapes, or operator console-switch actions.

[d] CLINFO is discussed in Chapter Seven in the section on the RAND tablet, videographics, and related projects.

RAND was among the earliest institutions to place an IBM defense calculator—the machine to be later renamed the IBM 701—on order. In line with its policy of never accepting serial number 1 of any new machine, RAND placed its order for serial number 11.[24]

In the early 1950s, there was not yet much experience with shipping delicate electronic equipment by truck, especially over long distances through variable weather conditions. IBM chose to air freight the delivery. It was felt that in-transit shocks would be correspondingly less, and it had the advantage that the system would be installed and "on rental" a week or more sooner.

The 701 was RAND's first venture into the world of commercially produced electronic digital computers, and, as such, its delivery was a major event. On the day of expected arrival, a number of individuals drove to nearby Santa Monica's Cloverfield Airport to await the arrival.

On schedule, the air freighter approached touchdown but with one wing high. Accordingly, it bounced on one side of the landing gear before settling onto the runway. The watchers on the flight line flinched at the unexpected shock to the load.

The computer equipment was transferred to a truck and driven the few miles to the RAND facility. Fortunately, no in-transit damage had occurred and the IBM customer engineers and field personnel readily proceeded with installation.

Other Machinery

- RAND purchased the first commercially available license for UNIX®.
- The RAND tablet coupled with an IBM 1800 and videographic terminals supported early experimentation with commercially available PCs other than IBM—the Xerox Dolphin.
- RAND was an early adopter and innovator of port-contention devices (automatic line selector) to handle terminal connections to a central machine.
- RAND's first remote-access widely used terminal device was from Ann Arbor.
- RAND used the IBM MTST (magnetic tape to Selectric typewriter) for a period.
- RAND experimented with optical character reading on a custom device to scan 12-pitch Prestige Elite® typed material.
- RAND was an early customer of Sun Microsystems (Sun 1 machine).

---

[24] It was a policy of Paul Armer never to order the first of a new line of machines on the belief that early models off the production line would probably have mistakes and problems.

A Building for People with Computers

RAND's plans to integrate analog and digital computers into its examination of complex problems affected its design of a new building to accommodate its growth.

When RAND was considering construction of a new building, there was a lively debate about the "topology" that it should have. In particular, John Williams argued that the design should be such that it would encourage the random meeting of individuals because (he asserted that) such encounters and fortuitous conversations would encourage new and innovative ideas and solutions to client problems. He concluded that the pre-ferred footprint would be a more-or-less square of offices surrounding an open interior court. He would have preferred a one-floor structure, but, due to space limitations on the property, he reluctantly accepted the fact that a big enough structure for RAND needs would have to be a two-story structure.[1]

In September 1951,[2] RAND had purchased from the City of Santa Monica an unde-veloped property of approximately 8 acres[3] that, during World War II, had been the site for an anti-aircraft gun battery together with the temporary wooden barracks and support buildings for the military troops and officers.[4] At that time, the northern edge of the RAND site was a street (subsequently abandoned by the city) named Seaside Terrace that ran from Main Street (of Santa Monica) to Ocean Avenue. Between it and the present Santa Monica Freeway (Interstate 10) was a property that had provided rental sites for mobile homes dur-

---

[1] John Williams wrote a memorandum summarizing his views and recommendations (Williams, 1950).

[2] Donn Williams of RAND's facilities and services department provided the dates and other real-estate data.

[3] A fact sheet distributed at a communitywide open house in February 1953 states that the price of the site was $250,000 and a size of "8+ acres." Over the succeeding several decades, RAND acquired several adjoining properties along Ocean Avenue. In particular, in July 1958 and July 1960, it acquired an old trailer court and the intervening abandoned city street; together, they became the site for building 2 and the north parking lot. Eventually, the corpora-tion held approximately 15 acres. In November 1999, it sold 11.3 acres to the City of Santa Monica for $53 million and held the remaining 3.7 acres at the south end for the construction of a new headquarters building, which it occupied in the latter months of 2004. Robert E. Yoder, who was one of the first 25 people to transfer from Douglas Aircraft to the RAND Corporation, with which he remained for 40 years, either verified or provided some of these facts. Cecil Weihe was first on the list of transferees and had charge of the various service and support functions—e.g., dispensary, purchasing, travel. His first task was to move 25 people from the Douglas plant at Cloverfield Airport (at the eastern edge of Santa Monica) across town to a building formerly occupied by the local newspaper, *The Evening Outlook* (at 4th Street and Broadway in the downtown section at the western edge of town).

[4] The revetted and partially underground gun sites occupied roughly the part of the site on which RAND's building 1 was constructed.

ing World War II.[5] The initial RAND property was bounded on the east by Main Street, on the north by Seaside Terrace, and on the west and south by an alley that proceeded from Seaside Terrace south for several hundred feet and turned east onto Main Street.

A New Building and Campus

Conforming to the Williams argument, the building's design was based on a series of roughly square modules that were hollow in the center—creating patios—and surrounded on all four sides by two rows of offices separated by an interior aisle. In each module, one set of offices faced onto the patio; the second set, onto an exterior wall of the building or onto the patio of an adjoining module.

The initially constructed platform was a linear row of three juxtaposed and connected modules (running north/south) parallel to Santa Monica's Main Street and facing eastward toward the city hall. At the north end of the three linear modules was an additional module facing westward. At the south end, there was only a half module. The resulting design was thus U-shaped, with the open side facing west along the alley toward Ocean Avenue and the Pacific Ocean. Thus, there were originally four patios, numbered north to south 1 through 3 and the northwest one, 4. The building occupied the northerly half (roughly) of the site; a surface parking lot, the southerly part.

Following occupancy of the building in January 1953 and shortly thereafter, it was realized that there was no conference room that could accommodate large meetings. Accordingly, in 1955, a two-story, T-shaped wing filled in the open side of the U to complete the westerly perimeter. A large conference room was included in the basement (known simply as the main conference room, or "the main" for short),[6] and above it was a corresponding area that changed from being a large commons room into offices and back again several times over the years. With the addition of the T, two new patios were created (numbers 5 and 6) to bring the number to six, and the building became a complete rectangle.

Later, in 1957, the pressure for additional space led to a two-story, E-shaped addition at the south end of the building. It followed the same arrangement, with two stories of office space but also included a below-grade area for the library. Two more patios (7 and 8) emerged as a result of the addition, bringing the total to eight. The eight patios served many purposes—for social gatherings, for receptions and luncheons, and for informal discussions and lunches among staff members. For a brief period, the easterly patio just

---

[5]   The story is that an elderly Greek man, who signed the papers of sale with an X, owned this property, which became RAND's north parking lot and site for a five-story second building called building 2. Some of the larger mobile homes were parked at the very edge of the property such that their rear portions hung in midair out over the depressed roadway that ran through McClure Tunnel under Ocean Avenue to the Pacific Coast Highway and later became the Santa Monica Freeway (Interstate 10).

[6]   At that time, the RAND staff included an acoustic expert, Ludwig W. (Sep) Sepmeyer, whose advice was that, for optimum sound performance, the walls of the room must be tilted inward by 11 degrees from true vertical. His requirement carried forward to a second large conference room (the administrative conference room, called "the admin" for short). It became an inside quip that the tilt of the walls must be 11 degrees—not 10, not 12, only 11 would do.

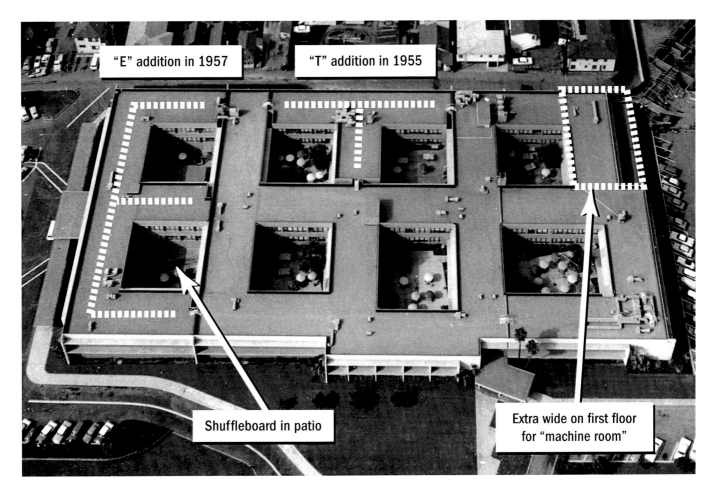

"E" addition in 1957

"T" addition in 1955

Shuffleboard in patio

Extra wide on first floor for "machine room"

RAND's headquarters at 1700 Main Street was constructed in stages, embodying John Williams' conception of a space networked to maximize chance encounters.

south of the main entrance (called patio 2) was converted to a golf putting green, and the southeasterly patio (called patio 3) had shuffleboard courts (visible in the photo above).[7]

There was discussion of incorporating a several-floor tower of office space—or possibly additional floors—to the E-shaped addition, but the idea was abandoned as not being really required. However, there was an unusual two-level feature. RAND undertook a research effort for the USAF Logistics Command that required the construction of a logistic simulation laboratory (LSL). This "Log Lab" structure was built (1978) in the southwest patio 7 of building 1. To achieve the necessary height, part of the structure was underground and part above ground level. The space was later used as an electronic laboratory for computer-science research and, eventually, by the library.[8]

---

[7] For an analysis of RAND's building as a seminal exemplar of architectural "mat discourse," see Kubo (2006). More-famous later examples include the Humanities and Social Sciences Center of the Freie Universität Berlin.

[8] RAND had prior experience using two-level structures as research laboratories. In a warehouse at 4th and Broadway in Santa Monica, RAND had innovated a group of techniques for training an organization as a whole at the system level (as opposed to skill training of individual components of the system), and, for this purpose, a two-floor facility was

Mathematician Ed Paxson (in foreground) and other staff on the putting green in one of the patios of the headquarters

Subjects in experiments in the lower level of the logistic simulation laboratory were observed from a balcony overhead (not shown).

To complete the story of the RAND-owned buildings prior to 2006, growing space needs led to the 1961 construction of a five-story building 2 with a Z-shaped floor plan, situated at the northwest corner of the campus and connected by walkways on both floors to the original building 1 at its northwest corner.[9]

Finally, in 1986, a temporary two-floor structure was added at the southwest corner of the building to complete the original RAND campus.

In 2006, all these buildings were demolished after RAND constructed a second new building on the site of what had been a large parking lot on the southern half of

---

required. The upper level was for the training officials and observers; the lower level, for the participants in the training exercise. This work culminated in the evolution and spin-off of the SDC for its work on behalf of the Air Defense Command of the USAF. More information regarding this laboratory and a photograph appear in Chapter Six.

[9] To hedge the possibility that such another two-level area like that in building 1 might again be needed for some future task, RAND's management was persuaded to construct the fifth floor of the Z-shaped building 2 with a double-height ceiling so that an upper deck could be constructed if needed. The dialog leading to this decision was between Willis Ware (of NAD) and Steve Jeffries (the corporate secretary). The feature was never used.

the campus. The northern half of the property, on which had stood the original three RAND-owned buildings, was sold to the City of Santa Monica.

The Machine Room

As RAND planned for the so-called new building (1700 Main Street) that would become its home after having been in a rented facility at 4th and Broadway in Santa Monica, it was a given that space for a variety of computer and calculating machines would have to be provided. Accordingly, the first floor and basement of the building's northwest corner was made much wider than the sides of the hollow rectangles that formed the footprint of the building everywhere else (see the aerial photo on p. 69).

At the time, the public saw RAND as an ultrasecret organization that worked for the federal government on military matters. As such, there was no desire or need to have the equipment in an exhibition installation that would allow the public to observe operations through windows.[10] In fact, a natural place to have put the machine room was underground beneath (what came to be) the north parking lot. To have done so would have incurred substantial additional cost, but there was also a genuine concern that the public might interpret such a move as RAND building a bomb shelter for its people because it knows something secret about the nature and likelihood of nuclear attack. The time in question was the early 1950s, when the threat of attacks from atomic weaponry was very real, and homeowners were building bomb shelters in back yards.

Two-Story Installation

RAND knew that it would be installing a variety of punched-card machinery, an electronic analog computer (the REAC) and its own custom-built digital computer (the JOHNNIAC). Since RAND built the latter machine for its own use, it could be designed as a single, large cabinet without extensive intercabling to other boxes.[11] It had been decided during the design of the building that the JOHNNIAC would be a two-story machine. Its electronics—central processor and memory—would be contained in a single cabinet suspended in a large (approximately 4 by 12 foot) hole in the floor.[12] Around it, on the first floor, would be ancillary equipment, such as card readers and punches, printers, console, test equipment, and storage cabinets. Beneath it, in the basement, would be power-supply equipment; ancillary devices, such as the magnetic drum; and air-chilling equipment.

---

[10] This is what IBM did to display an early 701 machine at its world headquarters in New York City. This machine was also made available to customers to use in preparation for the arrival and installation of their own computers.

[11] As noted earlier, the detailed design of the JOHNNIAC cabinetry was under the supervision of Ray Clewett, but Charles Eames Company, under contract with RAND, did the overall styling.

[12] During building planning, in anticipation that a second JOHNNIAC machine might be built, a second hole of similar size and displaced several feet to the east of the first hole was provided. However, it was floored over with a removable wooden structure and never utilized.

REAC Installation

The analog computer consisted of several cabinets with connecting cables. Since it was uncertain how the machine would be arranged or how it might be changed, in its area, a pattern of round holes with rectangular cover plates were cast into the floor as access holes for cableways between cabinets.

Raised-Floor Installation

When IBM introduced its first large-scale commercial machine—the IBM 701 patterned architecturally after the von Neumann machine being built at the IAS—it was packaged in many cabinets—e.g., the memory cabinet, the magnetic-tape cabinets, the central-processor cabinet. Such an arrangement facilitated the marketing of the machine and afforded flexibility in configuring the system to suit various customers' needs. However, the arrangement of multiple cabinets connected with cables also created problems. Since the interconnecting cables contained many conductors in an outer sheath, they were large in diameter. If simply laid on the floor between cabinets, they would be a risk to people walking around the

Cliff Shaw examining the installation of the JOHNNIAC

machine and an impediment to wheeled carts. Moreover, there was also the risk of damage to the cable itself and the detriment to the aesthetics of the installation.

At IBM's showcase installation of the machine behind large glass windows at its corporate headquarters in New York City, IBM displayed a solution to the cable problem: The various cabinets of the machine were placed on a raised floor high enough to provide room beneath for the cables that connected the various boxes together. Therefore, customers—as did RAND—generally adopted the IBM scheme of a raised floor. This arrangement of many cabinets connected by cables implied that the customer layout had to be furnished to IBM in advance of the delivery of the machine in order that cable lengths could be customized to the planned installation.

Commercial raised flooring was not available at that time, so RAND constructed its own design from wooden timbers.[13] The supporting piers were 12-inch cubes of treated lumber; they were generally arranged in a rectangular grid except for special places influenced by the arrangement and shape of computer cabinets. The lateral stringers between blocks were 4-inch by 6-inch treated material; the decking—cut to match the outlines of the stringer pattern of the overall floor—was 1.5-inch laminated plywood faced with commercial sheet flooring. Holes were cut in the decking as required to match the cable paths among cabinets.

Air Conditioning

In the two-story arrangement, a huge blower in the basement delivered chilled air into the center of the JOHNNIAC above (on the ground floor) and along its entire length. The air flowed upward through the center of the machine, where the heat of the 2,000 vacuum tubes was concentrated, was turned around in the top of the cabinet, and flowed downward between the outside of the electronics and the cabinet doors. It was then filtered (in the basement section), chilled, and recirculated in a closed loop.

To provide flexibility, it had been decided to provide all computer equipment with cooling from a central plant that produced chilled water that could be routed to water-to-air handlers wherever needed. This concentrated the equipment noise primarily in one room and provided operational efficiency.

In keeping with the design philosophy of the JOHNNIAC system, all components likely to fail—such as the refrigeration units to produce chilled water and the water pumps—were duplicated. Interpiping arrangements were provided so that connectivity among system components could be changed to permit removal of a failed unit for maintenance and repair. In addition, all equipment was sized to handle the total heat load so that component failures would not interfere with computer operations.

In the raised-floor arrangement, the first IBM machines were intended to discharge their heat load into the room and its air-cooling system. Commonly, a cabinet contained blowers, air filters, and intakes at the bottom and air discharges on the top surface. To

---

[13] Bob Bremer, the department's design drafter at the time, set the structural details of the floor design, and Ray Clewett oversaw its construction. Clewett also directed the activities of the mechanical shop and did the detailed mechanical design of many other things, notably RAND's JOHNNIAC computer.

accommodate the concentrated heat exiting cabinets, the room temperature had to be maintained quite low. It quickly became evident that this was an uncomfortable environment for operators and others who had to be in a chilly machine room.

Accordingly, when the IBM 704 replaced the IBM 701, it was decided to use the under-floor space as a big air plenum to deliver chilled air directly to each cabinet.[14] Similarly, the space above the ceiling was also a plenum to collect the exiting air from the many cabinets. Holes and grills were placed in the floor and in the ceiling to match each cabinet's position and its air intake and discharge. A separately controlled air system kept the room itself comfortable.

Since the punched-card equipment did not generate significant heat, there was no need for special treatment of its heat burden. It could be discharged into the room directly.

Configurations of the Machine Room

The configuration of the machine room as RAND moved into its new building is shown in the top diagram on the next page. Areas for both the REAC and the JOHNNIAC were set aside and special provisions made for them. Areas were also identified for an electrical laboratory, a mechanical laboratory, and a machine shop to support construction of the digital computer.[15] When it arrived later, the IBM 701 was installed as in the center-left diagram on the next page. Later, as new equipment came into place, the machine room was enlarged to become an L-shaped area. The IBM 704 was installed as in the center-right diagram. Eventually, as the amount of equipment increased, the keypunch area was moved out of the machine room, and later, the mechanical shop was relocated to the basement. The 1401/7090 was installed as in the bottom-left diagram and later, the 7044 as in the bottom-right diagram.

Open House

As RAND moved into its newly built headquarters in the fall of 1952, the management decided to host an open house for the public and local dignitaries. This action was sparked partly by the close relationship already existing between its officials[16] and vari-

---

[14] It is believed that this idea originated with RAND, although that view is based on memories, not on documentary evidence. Charles C. Porter, refrigeration engineer and representative of the Stanley Feuer Company (RAND's air-conditioning contractor at the time), may have suggested it to RAND.

[15] The electronic shop, supervised by Dick Mockbee, was at its peak during the construction of the JOHNNIAC machine and for some time thereafter. Gradually, as hardware projects completed and no new ones commenced, it attrited to zero. The mechanical shop, in addition to supporting JOHNNIAC and other hardware efforts, also supported the corporation in general with a variety of repairs and innovative solutions to minor problems. It essentially stopped operations with the retirement of Ray Clewett, who had been in charge of it from the beginning but retired in 1983. The equipment, most of which had been acquired from the "previously owned" market, was sold or retained for ongoing corporate use.

[16] Among others, the corporate secretary (Steve Jeffries), who was a member of the board of directors of the local Santa Monica Bank, and the corporate treasurer (Scott King), who held membership in local business-service organizations.

Figure 5.1 Early Configurations of the Machine Room

Initial Configuration of the Machine Room

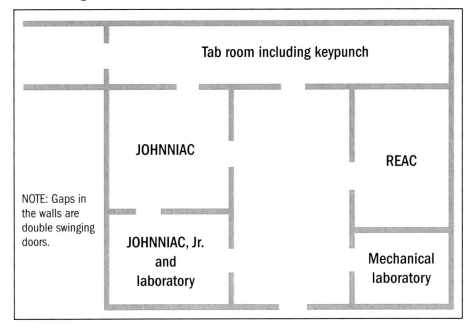

The Machine Room After the Arrival of the IBM 701

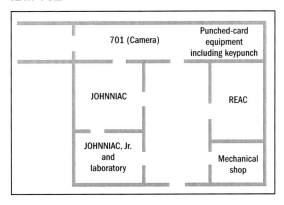

Configuration After the Addition of the IBM 704

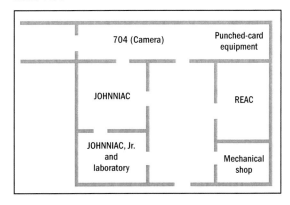

Configuration After the Addition of the 1401/7090

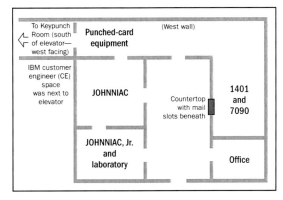

Configuration After the Addition of the 7040/7044

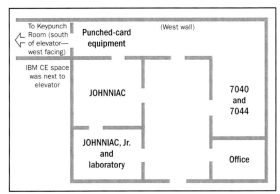

ous community organizations but also as a general "good-neighbor" move to dispel the locally held view of an ultrasecret organization whose activities might affect local residents negatively. Since RAND's mission was to perform analytic studies and its output would be reports and briefings, there was little to show except offices with furniture and related accoutrements; there would be no laboratories, physical things to demonstrate, or machinery in operation—except for its computing installation.

Accordingly, the NAD—as it was then named—was asked to organize a demonstration of its facilities. An open-house committee[17] was appointed, and, on Friday evening, February 13, 1953, and again on Sunday afternoon, February 15, the RAND facility and its people were on show to the public and invited guests.

Upon entering, guests were given a fact sheet below[18] that characterized the physical features of the structure and were directed toward the machine room with its collection of punched-card equipment, its analog computer, and the beginnings of RAND's self-built digital computer. A guest would register with a keypunch operator, who prepared an IBM card with the individual's name and birth date. Later on, this card would be used to print a personalized certificate welcoming the guest and acknowledging the occasion, and, at another station, the card was used to calculate the day of the week on which the person had been born. In addition, a guest could play tic-tac-toe against a computer, watch a card sorter manipulate colored card decks, or have a computer calculate, based on one's birth date, the day of the week on which one was born. In short, the demonstrations were the ones commonly used to show off a punched-card installation but supplemented by the opportunity to watch the analog computer draw various figures.

RAND Fact Sheet, February 13, 1953

1. The building is constructed or reinforced concrete throughout; it is entirely fire-resistant.
2. There are 115,000 square feet in the building, of which 15,000 square feet are basement space.
3. There are 365 offices in the building, plus 8 conference rooms, library commons room, etc.
4. Parking lot accommodates 320 cars.
5. Architect: H. Roy Kelley, F.A.I.A. (Fellow, Amer. Inst. of Arch.)
6. Building contractor: The William Simpson Construction Company
7. Landscaping: Evans and Reeves
8. Total cost: Approximately $1,650,000
9. Building financed by: Aetna Life Insurance Co.
10. Size of site: 8 acres plus

Douglas Aircraft, of course, was already well known in Santa Monica, but RAND was to become one of the largest employers in the city.

[17] Bob Nash, Willis Ware, and Don Madden.

[18] The surviving copies of this item are not annotated as to source. Probably, based on memories only, the NAD created it as part of its preparation. Undoubtedly, there would have been facts provided by various corporate offices.

Almost certainly, there were static displays of slide rules and calculators, possibly being demonstrated. Guests were more than likely ushered past the air-conditioning equipment and the huge motor generators in the basement—they were impressive and noisy machines.[19]

The open houses were a smashing success, and, on February 19, a memo from president Frank Collbohm noted NAD's contribution.

```
TO: Numerical Analysis Staff 19 February 1953
FROM: F. R. Collbohm M-748
SUBJECT: SHOW STEALING

At long last, the elite of Santa Monica now look upon RAND as an
electronic brain surrounded by miscellaneous care-takers. This is an
improvement over reputations we have had in the past!

Seriously, any one with eyes to see could not fail to be impressed
with the way you stole the show last Friday night and Sunday after-
noon. Your preliminary preparations, from setting up special problems
to converting yourselves into hucksters everyone, impressed your fel-
low workers no end. When we need a Sales Department, we will know
where to start recruiting. Thanks for a job well done.
```

Frank
F. R. Collbohm

The same day, the open-house committee, with its own memorandum, congratulated NAD members on their success.

```
To: Numerical Analysis Department 2-19-53
From: Bob Nash, Willis Ware, Don Madden M-730
Subject: Open House
Copies to: J. D. Williams, Central Files

We of the Open House Committee would like to express our appreciation
for the cooperation received from everyone in the department on mat-
ters concerning the Open House.

Both shows were overwhelmingly successful. Since every member of
Numerical Analysis effectively placed himself on a larger committee
to make certain that the project would be a success, our job was much
easier.
```

Bob   Don   Willis

I, too, would like to express my thanks to each and every one of you.
Paul Armer

---

[19] There were initially two motor-generator sets. The larger, rated at 312 kilovolt amperes (kVA), was intended to sup-ply all electronic equipment. The smaller one (150 kVA) was a backup unit to supply selected equipment.

Later Enhancements

The Camera

At the time of the IBM 701 and similar machines, the programmer generally "ran a problem" directly, sitting at the console and having sole custody of the entire machine and its resources. The early machines had no system-level software such as would be common today. Thus, when a program failed to execute properly, a programmer would do a "memory dump"[20] to the card punch or to the printer and jot down the patterns of the indicator lights[21] showing on the console; e.g., the memory location at which the program had halted the contents of registers. The programmer would then retire to his or her office with the original card deck, the aborted card deck and printout of memory, and notes to study the situation and search for programming or other errors. The next programmer (who had signed up for a time slot on the machine schedule) then took over the machine.

Eventually, computer-center managers realized that programmer resources could be more effectively used than having them sit at a console waiting for a problem result. Computer operators came into vogue, and the question became how to provide feedback to the programmer about the status of the program when it stopped. There evolved a de facto set of standards and procedures to direct the operator's handling of the program and any unusual situations. Typically, the programmer would provide the operator with a set of instructions, including what to do if the program did not perform properly; e.g., note the contents of specified memory locations, run other special diagnostic programs.

The memory dump and the status of indicated registers or memory locations were straightforward to provide, but how could the overall contents of the console display also be provided back to the programmer?

A camera! But it had to produce a picture that was detailed enough to portray the state of hundreds of tiny neon lamps on the console panel. An ordinary commercial camera would not do; it was not acceptable to wait for film processing and printing. A Polaroid® camera seemed to be an ideal answer, except that such cameras with long focal-length lenses[22] did not exist.

Thus, RAND built a special camera. A swing through the New York City camera stores yielded a vintage 14-inch (focal length) f4.5 (aperture) lens, a pneumatically operated shutter, and a Polaroid adapter intended to fit the press cameras of the time—typically

---

[20] There were colorful names for the process. One was to "Ex-Lax the memory," named after a popular laxative.

[21] The IBM 701 console displayed the 36 binary positions of the three arithmetic registers plus assorted other registers (e.g., instruction counter) and various status indicators. The state of any or all of them could be essential information for the programmer.

[22] To keep the space around the machine console clear of intruding objects, the camera had to be some feet to the rear of the operator and over his or her head but reachable. This suggested hanging it from the ceiling, but it also demanded a long focal-length lens to produce a large enough image.

a Graflex®.[23] Designed by Ray Clewett, the camera consisted of a light-tight plywood box roughly 18 inches on each side. Mounted on the front was the long focal-length lens and behind it, the shutter plane. Mounted on the back was the Polaroid adapter. Dangling from the front was a rubber tube and squeeze bulb to operate the shutter. The whole assembly was mounted on a pantograph arrangement that moved it from a storage position near the ceiling to the picture-taking position facing the console display.

The camera's dimensions and its position relative to the console were adjusted to yield an in-focus full-frame 4-inch by 5-inch Polaroid picture of the console display. Thus, the operator snapped a picture each time a program aborted and returned it along with a memory printout and card decks to the programmer.

As system software became available along with various diagnostic tools, the operator's actions became more and more routine. The need for the innovative tricks of the early days gradually disappeared.

Kevershan's Trough

As its computing needs changed and as various IBM models became available, RAND changed its installation to meet the demand and, concurrently, to keep costs within acceptable bounds. One such configuration utilized an IBM 704 as the main processing system but a minimal-configuration IBM 1401 to prepare input magnetic tapes for it and to receive output tapes from it. One might say that the 1401 acted as a card-to-tape device that prepared problems and stacked them on a tape for the 704. In the reverse direction, it acted as a tape-to-printer or -punch device to print or punch cards with results.

Many feet separated the two machines, and the machine operators soon tired of walking back and forth. Accordingly, a wooden trough was built between the operator stations; tapes in their protective covers could then be slid or rolled from machine to machine. The idea for the trough is attributed to Robert Kevershan, a machine operator for many years—thus the name.

Programmer-Alert Lights

As programmer-to-machine interaction became more and more routine, the process for submitting a problem became more procedural and less personalized.[24] The in-bound problem would be the delivery (to the machine room) of one or more card decks (or trays for large decks) plus written procedural instructions for inputting and running the problem. There would also be instructions indicating interim output that might occur and for handling unexpected stops, aborts, or crashes. Instructions for handling anomalous behavior were particularly important and directed the remedial actions that the operator was to take; e.g., run some diagnostic program, print out the contents of the memory, record the status of the control panel. Thus, a programmer might face several walking

---

[23] The author purchased these items during a business trip to New York and brought them back wrapped in clothing in a big carry-on briefcase.

[24] This was long before interactive remote-access time-sharing systems appeared and became commonplace.

trips daily from office to machine room, especially if the problem was in the debug or checkout phase. At the time, the RAND telephone system (provided by General Telephone Company through an on-premises mechanical switch) included a red light on each telephone handset that would illuminate when an incoming call had not been answered. It was a primitive form of the contemporary "call missed" feature.

Dick Mockbee, in charge of the electrical shop at the time, worked with a phone-company technician to divert the red lights to a more productive purpose. He decided to use them to notify programmers that their problem run had completed.[25] Accordingly, they became the programmer-alert light (PAL) system.[26]

As each job run completed, the machine operators would assemble output materials—punched cards, printout, notes, messages—and place them all in the programmer's individual mailbox at the service desk. The final action was to turn on the appropriate PAL to notify the person that work was ready for pickup.

On pickup of the materials, the programmer would then turn off his or her PAL.

[25] Eileen Mockbee Martner, Dick Mockbee's daughter, provided this fact.

[26] It is believed that the PAL system was installed when RAND received its IBM 7090 machine. At the same time, the machine room was completely overhauled. A long "service counter" was created to separate programmers (and others in the hallway) from the machines (on a raised floor) and their operators. Beneath the counter to the floor was a group of individual "programmer mailboxes" to receive completed outgoing work. Incoming work was delivered across the countertop.

CHAPTER SIX

Project Essays

A large number of major computer-science research projects were undertaken in the department over its lifetime. Generally, the computer-science research was dominated by hardware efforts in the early 1950s, progressed into mixed hardware and software efforts or software projects, and reached its peak in the 1960 and 1970s.[1] This chapter provides short essays on these projects in rough chronological order. Note that the first few projects were conducted when RAND was still in an EAM computing environment, before the advent of digital computing.

Also included are examples of support to RAND clients through fortuitous meetings, personal interactions, advisory participations, committee activities, and the like.[2]

Approximations

As electronic computers became essential tools for scientific and engineering calculations, hardware limitations (such as memory size and processing speed) restricted the complexity and quantity of computations (and, therefore, the size and nature of problems) that could be undertaken.[3] For electromechanical machines (i.e., punched-card based), relay and mechanical technology bounded the overall performance. For the earliest electronic machines (i.e., vacuum-tube technology), performance was significantly better, but there were still very real limitations on the size of problems that could be attempted. Programmers and users became very ingenious at extracting the maximum performance from whatever computing hardware was available.

The extensive and intensive use of tables of trigonometric, transcendental, and special functions and also nonelementary integrals that characterized the hand-calculating[4] era was not carried forward into the general-purpose digital-computing era because of the

---

[1] The timeline is based on one published in the *RAND Alumni Bulletin* (RAND, 2006, p. 1) but augmented by entries not included therein.

[2] For additional stories, see RAND (2006). There is slight duplication between material there and herein.

[3] Willis Ware wrote this subsection with contributions from Paul Armer, Bill Gunning, Mario Juncosa, and Jimmy Wong.

[4] *Hand calculation* (or its variations, such as desktop computing) is a categoric phrase for computational processes carried out by one or more individuals using mechanical desktop calculators, spreadsheets, and pencils. Sometimes, a part of a hand-calculation process might be carried out on punched-card equipment.

hardware limitations—notably, memory size—mentioned above. It became much more efficient in terms of computing time and memory to calculate each function or integral for each value of the argument needed but at the moment it was needed. With only arithmetic and logical operations available in a digital computer, functional values—or more precisely, approximations to them—had to be obtained by means of an appropriate algorithm. The issue, of course, had existed before the appearance of the electronic computer—namely, in the production of the tables used in hand- or desk-calculating procedures and in hand calculations. The matter also became relevant for built-in functions often included in certain special-purpose computers.

There are many possibilities for appropriate numerical processes: Among them are truncation of infinite series of special polynomials,[5] truncation of infinite series of special functions previously tabulated, Fourier series, truncation of infinite continued fractions, finite differencing, and other schemes. These approaches were all known and used in physical, astronomical, and other natural-science circles over many years, beginning in the late 18th century and extending through the mid-1950s. However, these methods had not become a part of standard college or university curricula in mathematics.

Consequently, in the late 1940s and very early 1950s, classically trained engineers and scientists, faced with immediate need for computed results from the newly developing computers, would base their thinking on their undergraduate calculus courses. Therefore, they would have a tendency to use truncated Taylor series. Unfortunately, many such series converge so slowly for values of the argument away from the center of the expansion that they prove to be unacceptable. Either the number of terms necessary to achieve a prescribed accuracy could lead to unacceptably long computer run times or the alternative of using only a few terms could yield intolerable errors. Moreover, when the function to be approximated had such features (in the argument's domain of interest) as a vertical slope, a cusp, an infinity, or a discontinuous derivative, truncated Taylor series and, more generally, polynomials are essentially useless.

The pressing requirement for guaranteed maximal error value combined with algorithms efficient in terms of minimal storage and numbers of arithmetic and logical operations[6] led Cecil Hastings to investigate a hand-

Cecil Hastings was the lead innovator of function approximations for use in digital computing.

---

[5]   For example, Chebyshev, Jacobi, Legendre, Laguerre, Hermite, Fourier, and others.

[6]   Efficiency was of particular importance in hand calculations. Indeed, the process of (long) division played a unique role in consideration of efficiency. Early desktop mechanical calculators often did not include automatic division, which implied that the operator had to step through the process manually, making the hand-executed process even more

tailored approach to constructing approximations for each specific function needed. The "tool box" consisted of such things as visual inspection of a plot of the target function to suggest insights to possible approximating functions, the use of polynomial Chebyshev methods that have minimum and maximum errors over an interval, and rational functions (the ratio of two polynomials whose coefficients were to be determined).

After creating some 75 such useful approximations and corresponding error bounds for 24 functions with the assistance of Jimmy Wong and Jeanne Hayward, RAND collected them into a book, *Approximations for Digital Computers*.[7] The introductory material in it described the processes—the tool box—for their derivation. The book proved to be a must-have item on every early numerical analyst's shelf. In part, this was because other available literature on numerical approximations tended to be much older and not attuned to the special needs of the emerging digital-computer environment. The RAND approximations filled an important void in the numerical world. The book quickly became known as the "RAND approximations," or sometimes the "Hastings approximations" after their originator. Prior to publication, the approximations were known to a limited community because each had been issued internally as an individual, brief, explanatory document, and some presentations to technical groups had been given.

There is no recorded history to establish the extent to which the RAND approximations were used in corporate computing installations, or their effect on the newly evolving mathematical field of numerical approximations. There was a general conviction that they had wide application and effect. Paul Armer once estimated that "Cecil's approximations [had] saved enough machine cycles [with their corresponding financial value] to underwrite RAND's Air Force project for fifteen years."

One military application is known and in part documented: namely, the on-board, integrated navigation-weapon control system (operational flight program [OFP]) developed in the mid- to late 1950s for the U.S. Navy's A-6 fighter-bomber aircraft.[8] The A-6 software was designed to run on a magnetic-drum machine.[9] Although the original programming team is not available, one can speculate why the approximations were

---

tedious and error prone. Moreover, division is the longest arithmetic operation in a digital computer. Consequently, numerical algorithms that minimized the number of divisions were much to be preferred.

[7]   Hastings (1955) ($4.00 at the time in hardback). Bob Bremer, a mechanical draftsman in the mathematics division, prepared the graphs in that publication. The story is that Cecil would hold a final draft drawing horizontally flat and sight along the curve. If the width of the line was not uniform to the eye, the job was done again.

Bremer subsequently did much of the design and drafting in connection with the building of the JOHNNIAC, and for other tasks associated with the RAND computing activities. He was succeeded by Nelson Lucas, who did the layout work (among other things) for the RAND Tablet.

[8]   This came to light in a brief mention of the application in a short note to an online electronic digest devoted to computer history. Further exchanges of electronic mail with William Earl Boebert (an early programmer and computer specialist) developed more details but in the context of "maintaining the software." In the military environment, maintenance implies not only correction of software aberrations—bugs—but also the addition of new operational features for the aircraft and its weapon systems.

[9]   The machine was formally known as the AN/ASQ 61 but was also nicknamed Diane.

likely to have been chosen.[10] To optimize a drum machine's performance, a technique called "minimum-latency programming" was often used.[11] As a consequence, the hardware nature of the machine imposed a time scale on the executing software. A Hastings approximation performs the same arithmetic steps independently of the argument and therefore executes in the same time for every argument. It fitted very neatly into the fixed and rigid time scale of a drum machine.

The other reason relates to the overall software architecture of the OFP, which must perform all of its tasks in a time table established by the aircraft, its activity (management of the flight path and weapon systems), and the crew's actions in the cockpit. In such a real-time environment, the computer-based system must keep up with things as they happen; there is no opportunity to "come back and take care of that later."[12]

Consequently, all required computational tasks typically were organized into a software loop that repeated endlessly and was tied to the rotational speed of the drum memory and also to the real-time activities of the aircraft and its crew. The fixed and known execution times of the approximations would have made them a natural choice to schedule events in the OFP architecture and meet the time demands of the operating environment.

The RAND approximations made profound contributions in many ways:

- They filled a void of major importance in the utilization of early electronic digital computers.
- They helped invigorate the nascent field of numerical analysis as a topic within mathematics curricula.
- They facilitated large-problem computations that would not otherwise have been feasible.
- They made possible some applications that would not have otherwise been possible.
- They contributed to effective error management in extended computations.

---

[10] The original design motivations are not known, but the probable rationale for choosing the approximations can be inferred from collateral knowledge of early airborne systems. The early A-6 software was produced at a time when the process for creating software was largely in the hands of the implementing programmers and commonly was poorly documented or if at all. Their decisions influenced other parts of the system as well as established the basic architecture of the program. The cost and complexity of redoing the software in subsequent years was not feasible for many reasons—e.g., financial requirements, operational impact, elapsed time to complete. Therefore, the initial architecture and design choices constrained all subsequent reprogramming in maintenance cycles—even though improved hardware and software techniques might have become available.

[11] This technique requires that successive instructions of the program be stored at selected (i.e., not sequential) circumferential locations on the drum so that the desired instruction would be under (or, at least, near) the magnetic readheads when it was needed.

[12] Interrupt-driven hardware architectures were not known when the flight software was initially implemented. Thus, the earliest OFPs would typically consist of a fixed sequence of computational tasks, each of which had to function in a given duration. The nature of each task when it executed was collect relevant data, check for cockpit inputs, do necessary calculations, and initiate necessary actions.

An operating system in the nature of contemporary ones (e.g., DOS, OS-360, UNIX, Linux, Windows) did not then exist and would not have been used with the relatively primitive computing hardware because of the burden on memory requirements and computing power. Rather, a simple job scheduler or master scheduler, which became increasingly complex as systems evolved, was the top-level authority in an executing OFP.

The relevance and usefulness of the approximations to the mathematical, analytic, and general computing community is reflected by a fifth printing in 1966, 11 years after initial publication. Some reviews after the second printing include the following:[13]

> This book is undoubtedly the book in the growing field of special function approximations. It is both a necessary reference book for all digital computer centers, and the best book now available that provides the beginner with an introduction to this interesting and difficult field.
>
> *—Journal of the Association for Computing Machinery*

> In a new method that combines judgment and intuition with formal mathematics, this set of approximations surpasses in simplicity, earlier approximations developed by conventional methods.
>
> *—Product Engineering*

> The computing world is greatly indebted to Hastings for this tour of his workshop.
>
> *—Science*

> In finding his approximations, the author relies partly upon scientific methods and partly upon artistic perceptions to obtain simple and elegant formulas. This makes this collection something unique and remarkable.
>
> *—American Scientist*

Random Digits and Normal Deviates

In 1955, the Free Press published an unusual volume from RAND that consisted wholly of two large tables that had been photoreproduced from an IBM 856 Cardatype printout: one table contained 1 million random digits and the other 100,000 Gaussian deviates.[14] The foreword of the book describes its origin and purpose:

> Early in the course of research at The RAND Corporation a demand arose for random numbers; these were needed to solve problems of various kinds by experimental probability procedures, which have come to be called Monte Carlo methods. Many of the applications required a large supply of random digits [or] normal deviates of high quality, and the tables [in this book] were produced to meet [such] requirements. The numbers have been used extensively by research workers

---

[13] These review excerpts are from the dust jacket of the fifth printing.

[14] Willis Ware wrote this subsection with contributions from Paul Armer, George Brown, Bill Gunning, Don Madden, and Alex Mood. The only known sources of information on the tables in *A Million Random Digits* are those included as a foreword and introduction within it, in a few scattered memories and recollections, in a few internal memoranda, in summaries attached to the book record entry in the RAND library data system and in the RAND publication index, and three formal but brief papers. The present discussion is based on these sources.

Bernice Brown, a mathematician, helped test the randomness of RAND's million random digits.

at RAND, and by many others, in the solution of a wide range of problems during the past seven years.[15]

[These tables] were a product of RAND's computing power (and patience). They have become a standard reference in engineering and econometrics textbooks and have been widely used in gaming and simulations that employ Monte Carlo trials. Still the largest known source of random digits and normal deviates, the work is routinely used by statisticians, physicists, polltakers, market analysts, lottery administrators, and quality control engineers.

On numerous RAND problems the largest existing table [prior to the effort that led to this book] would have had to be used many times over, with the consequent dangers of introducing unwanted correlations. The feasibility of working with as large a table as the present one resulted from developments in computing machinery [that] made possible the solving of very complicated distribution problems in a reasonable time by Monte Carlo methods.

The tables were constructed primarily for use with punched card machines. With the [development of] high-speed electronic computers, the storage of such tables is usually not practical [because of limited memory] and, in fact, much larger tables than the present one are often required. [Large-scale electronic] machines have caused research workers to turn to pseudo-random numbers [that] are computed by simple arithmetic processes directly by the machine as needed.

The random digits in this book were produced by re-randomization of a basic table generated by an electronic roulette wheel.[16] Briefly, a random frequency pulse source providing on the average about 100,000 pulses per second, was gated about once per second by a constant frequency pulse. Pulse standardization circuits passed the pulses through a 5-place binary counter. In principle the machine was a [32-pocket] roulette wheel [that] made, on the average, about 3000 revolutions per trial and produced one number per second. A binary-to-decimal converter was used [that] converted 20 of the 32 numbers (the other twelve were discarded) and retained only the final digit of two-digit numbers; this final digit was fed into an IBM punch to produce finally a punched card table of random digits.[17]

---

[15] The RAND tables remain useful for smaller-scale work and hand calculations; they are much used in agricultural research.

[16] For additional details, see Brown (1949).

[17] RAND (2001, foreword). From the preface: "The following persons participated in the production, testing, and preparation for publication of the tables of random digits and random normal deviates: Paul Armer, Ernest C. Bower,

Testing of the machine's output revealed certain biases in spite of careful electronic maintenance. Accordingly, additional processing of the tables was done to correct the shortfall.[18] Half of the 1 million digits were then used to construct the normal deviates.

The random-digit machine, given the technology of the time, would have been a vacuum-tube machine. The Douglas Aircraft Electrical Laboratory built it, and it was based on a variation of an idea that Cecil Hastings proposed. A gas-discharge voltage-regulator tube—a common tube widely used in regulated power supplies at the time—was the source of the random pulses.

The timeline for the production and testing of random digits is reported to have been as shown in Table 6.1.

Table 6.1. Timeline for Production and Testing of Random Digits

Date	Event
April 29, 1947	Production began
May 21, 1947	First half million completed
July 7, 1947	Full million completed
1948–1949	Randomness tests published

Since the transition of Project RAND to the RAND Corporation did not occur until November 1, 1948, but the organization had relocated to rented facilities in May 1947, it is not certain where the tables were completed, at the Douglas Aircraft facility or at the RAND Corporation facility at 4th and Broadway. A likely scenario is that the machine was

Mario Juncosa, a computational mathematician, provided mathematical support to the programming staff.

Bernice Brown, George W. Brown, Walter Frantz, Julian J. Goodpasture, William F. Gunning, Cecil Hastings, Olaf Helmer, Mario L. Juncosa, J. Donald Madden, Alex M. Mood, Robert T. Nash, John D. Williams. These tables were prepared in connection with analyses done for the United States Air Force."

The probable role of each in the project is as follows:

IBM processing and machine programming: Paul Armer, Goodie Goodpasture, Don Madden, and Bob Nash

Mathematicians and statisticians: George Brown, Cecil Hastings, Olaf Helmer, Mario Juncosa, and Alex Mood

Engineering (of the machine): Bill Gunning (from Douglas Flight Test Laboratory), Walter Frantz (Douglas Flight Test Laboratory), and Ernest Bower

Hand calculations and statistical testing: Bernice Brown and John Williams.

George Brown was responsible for the randomization processes needed to remove statistical biases from the original set of numbers. Bill Gunning and Walter Frantz did the engineering design and implementation of the roulette-wheel machine, assisted by Dick Mockbee and Ernest Bower.

[18] Bernice Brown (1948a, 1948b). Bernice described (1) the frequency test, (2) the poker test, (3) the serial test, and (4) the run test. It is unclear who suggested the poker test. It consisted of mapping groups of five digits in blocks of 5,000 into (kinds of) poker hands; e.g., bust, one pair, two pairs, three of a kind, full house, four of a kind, and five of a kind. The outcome was then compared to the corresponding statistical expectations of hands dealt from a poker deck. Don Madden performed the calculations for this test.

designed, built, debugged, and tested at the Douglas plant, was moved, and checked out again, and then produced the tables at the RAND facility. On the other hand, the dates could also support an alternative scenario, in which the first half million were produced at the Douglas plant and the second half at RAND.

There is no record of the disposition of the machine, but it was almost certainly moved from the Douglas facility to the RAND Corporation premises. Following completion of the tables, it presumably was dismantled or, perhaps, simply scrapped.

There are several anecdotes connected with the random digits, many of them because of the second part of its name—normal deviates—which (of course) refers to the Gaussian deviates of mathematical statistics. Among them are the following.

- A reference librarian catalogued the book under "abnormal psychology."
- A military officer asserted, "I wouldn't touch that with a 10 foot pole; I can't risk my clearance."
- A pundit proclaimed, "There is no such thing as a normal deviate."
- A Navy commander kept a copy with him while on submarine nuclear patrol duty and used selections from it to randomize the zigzag jinking in his evasive course navigation.

This book and its tables filled an important niche in numerical analysis at a time when the field was rapidly developing and Monte Carlo methods were a mainstay in certain kinds of analytic modeling. The evidence, in part, is that, in the first 15 years of its existence, the book had three printings and sold some 7,000 copies—a remarkable sales figure for a book containing a little bit of text and endless pages of tabulated numbers.

Because the demand for the book persisted, it was reprinted with an additional forward in the RAND paperback series in late 2001.[19]

The Bombing Simulator (aka Pinball Machine)

By the end of World War II, the Allied military forces had come to appreciate the effectiveness of strategic bombing of military and industrial targets.[20] It was natural, therefore, for this topic to be on Project RAND's interest list. Moreover, several of the staff had had experience with the subject as a result of their work for the war department during World War II.

Ed Paxson undertook to explore bombing effectiveness by designing and having built a machine which attempted to replicate the impact pattern and effects of large-scale

---

[19] RAND (2001).

[20] Ray Clewett, Bill Gunning, and Ed DeLand contributed to this subsection. This project dated from the earliest days of Project RAND while it was still under Douglas management and situated in the loft of the Douglas facility at Cloverfield Airport in Santa Monica. The most likely time period for it would have been 1946–1948. This window correlates well with the three individuals' memories about their employment dates with RAND and their conversations with Ed Paxson and the date (March 1, 1948) of the second annual report, which contains a brief description of this machine.

bombing drops, permitting the assessment of target consequences. Since the device used one collection of physical behaviors to emulate a second set that derived from the real world (i.e., the two sets of physical attributes are analogs of one another), in modern parlance, it would have been called a "physical analog computer." The machine had a variety of nicknames: Ed Paxson's machine, Paxson's machine, bomb simulator, Ed's machine, and pinball machine.

The Pinball Machine [21]

When a lot of bombs are tossed at a target a goodly number of them don't do a helluva lot of bad because either they miss the target or they hit where some other bombs have already wrecked the neighborhood. Our mathematicians are apparently unable to perceive the simple and obvious solution to this problem which consists merely of not dropping those bombs [that] are not going to be effective. They have tried to figure out how many bombs are wasted this silly way, but the going got too rough.

So they built a little machine to do the job, the said pinball machine. It lights lights, rings bells, and adds up your score automatically. And of course mathematicians like to use their fancier tricks however uncalled for they may be. For instance, they have squared the circle in this machine. This is an ancient old wheeze but still mildly spectacular; when one of their bombs explodes it devastates a perfect square. Fancier still is the device of using a steel ball to represent a city block in the target; this is known in the trade as sphering the block and requires a mean mathematician.

The most interesting feature of the machine is due to a slight misunderstanding of the general situation. I know you won't believe what I am about to reveal. But it's true, I swear. Go down to the basement and see. Just a little slip-up on a detail. This machine does not throw bombs at a target—it hurls targets at a bomb.

Since a lot of time had been spent on this contraption, a way had to be found to make it work; one of the guards luckily did so by the simple expedient of turning it upside down. Uncomfortable for the operator though. The thing has been churning merrily along for several months now and has dropped a total of 160,000 targets on a bomb. But the mathematics division lost interest in this game long ago, and nobody knows what happened to all those targets. Somebody ought to go have a look at the eight volumes of data. And rescue that poor operator; her feet are getting cold.

---

[21] This article appeared in RAND (1949). *RANDom News* was the periodic internal newsletter of the time. The article is unsigned, but Brownlee Haydon, who wrote a variety of materials for RAND and its officials, might have written it. The reference to "go down to the basement" indicates that the locale for the machine was the basement of RAND's facility at 4th and Broadway. There is some uncertainty in the historical record whether there had been more than one machine, but, on balance, it appears that only one design existed and was built.

RAND built a physical analog computer called the coverage machine that dropped thousands of ball bearings (targets) on bomb-pattern plates.

The Project RAND second annual report[22] contained a hand-drawn sketch of the machine together with a brief description. Key facts are as follows:

- It was built largely by a contract machine shop in West Los Angeles, California.

---

[22] RAND (1948a, pp. 28–29). This report is valuable reading in regard to the origin, aims, organization, and research interests of the time. It includes a list of consultants and subcontractors. Among other things, it reports on aerial refueling of bombing missions, and it speaks of system analysis as a research methodology. It also mentions and contains a picture of the RAND advisory council, whose members were aviation executives: J. H. Kindelberger, president, NAA; J. K. Northrop, president, Northrop Aircraft; C. L. Egtvedt, chair, Boeing Aircraft; Donald Douglas, president, Douglas Aircraft; and Arthur Raymond, vice president, Douglas Aircraft.

- The foundation main plate was a 0.5-inch-thick, 24-inch-square aluminum plate with a 4- to 5-inch–diameter cutout at the center. The foundation tabletop was somewhat larger than 24 inches and had a square hole in the center with a trap door covering it from below.
- A series of interchangeable "bomb pattern plates" fitted into the center opening; each had a unique set of holes of different shape, size, and arrangement. One of them had a 2-inch by 2-inch round-cornered square hole at its center.
- The interchangeable target plates—which were larger than the central square hold—were mounted in an arrangement along the right edge of the table. A plate was fastened to a drafter's parallel-motion device, which permitted it to be placed over the center square hole in various positions.
- The device used steel balls[23] approximately 0.0625 inch in diameter. A hopper suspended over the target plate in its right-edge position contained the balls. At the beginning of each bomb run, the holes in the target plate (which were large enough to allow balls to fall through) were filled from the hopper.
- The balls represented areas in the target that were to be bombed. The square hole in the center of the table represented the blast area of a bomb. After positioning the target plate, a trap door under the square blast-hole was electrically opened, and the balls from the target plate fell through. Thus comes the *RANDom News* quip about "throwing the target at the bomb."
- There was a "ball pump"—or "ball elevator"—that collected the balls that had dropped through the holes in the pattern plates and returned them to a hopper on the top side of the main plate.
- The number of balls that fell through was a measure of the damage done. A "centrifugal pump ejected the balls through a channel past a photo-cell [counter] and into a container. . . . An electronic counter kept score on the total damage done, the number of bombs dropped, and the number of times the problem had been run, using different aim points [i.e., the relative position of the target and blast plates]."[24]
- The count was recorded on punched cards: "About three seconds after counting finished, these data are automatically punched on a card by a standard IBM gang punch."
- The device spilled balls frequently; there were "balls all over the floor."
- The device wound up as so much scrap metal under a work bench.

For a simulated bomb run, the ball-filled target plate was moved over the square blast-area plate. The parallel-motion device kept things aligned properly; indicial marks on the tabletop indicated the relative positions of the plates and represented the target

---

[23] Among the stories that characterized the lore of early RAND was one to the effect that the Douglas–Project RAND purchasing agent had gotten used to strange requests. Among those requests was one for 10,000 steel balls.

[24] It is not known who designed the scoring mechanism; perhaps it was someone from the Douglas Flight Test Laboratory or some Douglas employee who would later join Project RAND. One possibility is Gardner Johnson, who could not be located for an interview. He later was a part of the engineering group that created the JOHNNIAC digital computer.

area's position relative to the bomb drop. The damage was measured as a simple count of the balls that dropped through the blast plate from the target plate.

There is some evidence that the game Pachinko, which uses a maze of pins on a board to control the rolling patterns of balls passing through it, influenced Paxson. It is believed that he did understand that he could account for windage during bomb falling by adjusting the "pins" in his mental Pachinko image.

It is also known that Paxson wanted to control the bomb behavior during fall in three dimensions.[25] The mechanical machine could not fulfill such expectations, but fortunately the digital computer came along to do such simulations.

Ed Paxson's bomb machine—while apparently not extensively exploited—is properly included in the history of RAND's utilization of analytic machines for policy studies.

The Air-Combat Room

Air combat was also a topic of high interest. To explore aerial duels and maneuvers between single aircraft as well as large groups of aircraft, a special room was built at the first RAND headquarters at 4th and Broadway in Santa Monica. Its surfaces were covered with inscribed grids so that, by stretching strings across the room from point to point, ranges and bearing angles of flight paths could be measured as they vary with time. Fire-control errors from ground weapons could also be computed. Both high- and low-altitude behavior could be simulated.

These examples are two of many in which RAND built a specialized device or computing process for its own need. Others include the random-number generator machine, specialized circular slide rules, punched-card numerical procedures, analog-computer processes, and, of course, numerous instances of computer software.

System Research Laboratory

In the early days, the RAND staff included a wide variety of academic disciplines.[26] In particular, a group of psychologists (among them, John L. Kennedy, Robert Chapman, William C. Biel, Boguslaw Boghosian, and Milton G. Weiner) became interested in cognitive learning, especially the training and associated task learning of organized groups. As a research vehicle, the group chose an Air Force Air Defense Center (ADC). Its mission and set of organizational tasks were well understood (e.g., track aircraft, receive tracks from and pass tracks to adjacent centers, vector-interceptor aircraft to targets, plot data from the associated radar, receive messages from and send messages to higher echelons of command). A large number of such centers existed throughout CONUS and

---

[25] Conversation between Ed DeLand and Willis Ware.

[26] For further information regarding the SRL, see Kennedy and Chapman (1955), Chapman and Weiner (1955), and Chapman (1955).

The air-combat room used point-to-point strings to simulate aircraft trajectories.

could provide a basis against which to measure research results; the work would be of interest to RAND's major client.

To test the thesis that an organization can improve its performance faster and to a higher level when trained as a total entity, as opposed to skill training of individuals, a laboratory facility would be required.

In a warehouse at 4th and Broadway, RAND constructed a replica of an ADC using the electronic and mechanical shop facilities of the numerical-analysis department (see photo on next page). As a pseudoradar display, the paper-handling mechanism of an IBM 407 printer was used. Successive sheets of fan-fold paper were fed through the 407 handler to emulate the radar scan; each sheet of paper remained in place (and in view) for the duration of the 360-degree radar scan. X marks on the paper represented the posi-

RAND constructed a laboratory replica of an air defense center to study the design, training, and operation of complex human-machine systems.

tion of air traffic. Thus, all targets in the radar's volume of coverage were displayed at one time, unlike a real radar display, which is painted on the terminal CRT as the radar sweeps around. Participants adapted quickly to the difference. Moreover, this approach was inexpensive, used the available computing technology of the time, and avoided an R&D effort to develop more-realistic terminals and displays.

A large, plastic tote board was used to plot tracks of traffic and other identifying data. Other plastic backlit boards posted, for example, air-fighter readiness, maintenance status, scheduled air traffic through the sector, weapon availability. Finally, audio links were provided to surrounding air-defense sectors and to FAA air-traffic–control centers. A balcony provided space for observers, the experiment team, and the individuals who staffed the other end of the audio links (e.g., higher command echelons, adjacent defense centers, FAA centers).

The scenario for a run was prepared on NAD's 701: the long reams of pin-fed fan-fold paper to run through the simulated terminals, the scripts for all players, the calculations that positioned Xs depicting air objects properly on the output paper.

The initial trial runs were done with UCLA students as participants. The results were so successful that USAF teams were brought to the facility for many following runs, the most exciting of which were the days on which higher command sent a message that war had been declared.

The USAF became so enthusiastic about the results that it was decided to field the work throughout the USAF ADC. RAND formed the system-development division with Melvin O. (Mel) Kappler in charge. Willis Ware of NAD was assigned to him for engineering and computing matters. The following contractor team was assembled:

- IBM, to design, develop, and fabricate a high-resolution CRT output-display device for the 701
- Mitchell Camera Company, to design and build a high-resolution 35-mm camera with precision positioning of the film in the film gate. It was also to provide shutter-open and shutter-closed signals for synchronizing the camera with the 701
- Eastman Kodak, to provide an appropriate lens with high linearity across a field of view that would cover the face of the CRT display
- RCA in West Los Angeles, to design and produce a device to transport 35-mm film, read the spots thereon, and electronically couple the output in synchronism with the actual CRT terminals of an actual radar site.

Computer fan-fold paper became actual radar terminals; long lengths of successive sheets of paper became film. X marks on the paper became dots on film. When the camera signaled that the shutter was open, the 701 painted a radar scan's worth (360 degrees) of air-object–position dots on the output CRT display. When the camera signaled that the shutter was closed, the 701 calculated that next scan's worth of position data (i.e., a full 360 degrees) and paused until the camera again signaled that it was ready.

Kappler and Ware would periodically visit all contractors to monitor progress and resolve problems. The latter spent many weekends at the IBM plant in Poughkeepsie in the company of B. O. Evans, the IBM engineer in charge and an ongoing friend of RAND's computer department.[27] They would connect the display to one of the 701s in final test on the production floor and spend endless hours displaying dot patterns and peering through a microscope measuring dot positions on the CRT face—all in the name of ensuring adequate end-to-end linearity so that tracks would be smooth and not jump around erratically on the radar displays.[28]

With delivery of the system components, RAND's part of the story ended. The system-development division of RAND was spun off to become the System Development Corporation with Kappler as the founding president. He took with him several

---

[27] For many years, Evans arranged annual, several-day visits for RAND's computer managers to IBM's research projects.

[28] The digital-analog converters in the display devices were high-precision, specially designed analog operational amplifiers built by Reeves Analog Computing of Long Branch, New Jersey.

senior RAND programmers; among them were Wes Melahn, John Matousek, Mort Bernstein, and Pat Haverty.

The remainder and future of the SDC story have been written elsewhere.[29]

The RAND Tablet, Videographics, and Related Projects

Motivated by J. C. R. Licklider's well-known 1960 paper "Man-Machine Symbiosis"[30] and later (1962 onward) by his influence as director of ARPA's Information Processing Technology Office, members of the department commenced work on the human-machine interface in the very early 1960s. The work focused initially on an input device for free-hand input to a computer.

Over a period of a few years, the effort produced a device commonly known as the RAND tablet, which became the user interface to a series of projects that exploited a user's ability to input free-hand actions to a computer. It also became the input device (along with a keyboard) for the RAND videographic system.

The RAND Tablet

The initial effort was a reverse-flatbed plotter; that is, instead of driving the print head from a computer, the user manually moved the head, whose positioning mechanisms reported its position to the machine. Even after stripping the print head of all unnecessary plotting mechanisms, the head was hard to move smoothly and precisely. A user's ability to move the head fluidly and to position it accurately was simply not good enough for the purpose.

The next step was to use a woven grid of Formex® wires, which provided a resolution of 0.1 inches.[31] Each wire of the grid was driven by a digital signal indicating its position in the matrix. A free-hand stylus moving over the surface then picked up a signal unique to its position. While significantly better than the reverse plotter, its resolution of one part in 10 was not adequate for the anticipated user desires.

Fortunately, printed-circuit technology had matured to the point at which a grid of copper strips on a biaxially oriented polyethylene terephthalate (boPET) surface (such as Mylar®) could provide a resolution of 0.01 inches. This approach led to the final product design. The boPET surface was covered with a plastic wear layer and the whole thing mounted in a metal frame that afforded a central 10-inch by 10-inch work area. The peripheral area of the frame covered the digital encoders that drove each copper strip with a unique signal indicating its position.

---

[29] Baum (1981). See especially Chapter Two for background on the System Development Division.

[30] See Licklider (1990).

[31] Formex wire is a special copper wire insulated with a thin flexible coating and is normally used in the field windings of electric motors. RAND convinced a local weaving vendor to make the special wire-based grid.

The user instrument was a penlike object with a tiny click-switch in the end that the user would depress to send signals to the machine.

Sometimes, one or more wires on the copper-boPET mat would be broken, and, rather than discard it, Nelson Lucas (the department drafter at the time), working under a magnifying arrangement, laboriously repaired the break.

Ultimately, ARPA funded RAND to construct roughly a dozen tablets for additional internal projects and for use by other researchers in the ARPA family, e.g., Herb Teager at MIT. Handmade in an R&D facility, the unit cost of a tablet was $18,000.[32]

Interestingly, one early concern had to do with a person's ability to write on one surface (the tablet, which was horizontal) but look at a different surface (the display, which was vertical). Normally, in handwriting, a person is looking at the surface on which the writing instrument makes markings. This proved not to be a problem: Users quickly adapted to the geometry.

The device did not catch on commercially, perhaps because of inertia in user habits and familiarity with a keyboard; perhaps, as is true for many R&D successes, the world was not ready for this very different way of communicating with a computer; or perhaps commercial interests did not perceive applications that would require and exploit the tablet capabilities. It was not until the personal computer with its mouse brought computing to the masses did tablet-based machines begin to appear commercially in the latter part of the 20th century.

Mal Davis and Tom Ellis characterized the tablet in this way:

> a low-cost, two-dimensional graphic input tablet and stylus developed to conduct research on man-machine graphical communications. The tablet is a printed-circuit screen complete with printed-circuit capacitive-coupled encoders with 40 external connections. The writing surface is a 10" x 10" area with a resolution of 100 lines per inch in both x and y. The system does not require a computer-controlled scanning system to locate and track the stylus.[33]

This last statement is of some importance: Unlike many screen-pointing arrangements, the tablet reported where the stylus was located; the machine did not have to repeatedly scan the work area, in effect asking, "Stylus, where are you?"

Handwriting Recognition

One of the projects that stemmed from the presence of the tablet in the department's research environment was the recognition of user handwriting. Groner described the work as follows:

---

[32] Complete tablets, relevant documents, and the printed boPET sheet have been deposited with the Smithsonian Institution in Washington, D.C., and with the Computer Museum in Santa Clara, California.

[33] Excerpted from Davis and Ellis (1964, p. v).

A program, written in IBM 360 Assembler Language, that allows the user of an on-line computer to print data and directives on the RAND Tablet with a special pen and have them recognized and displayed immediately. The scheme recognizes 53 letters, numbers, and symbols in a wide variety of printing styles, requiring only the usual conventions followed on coding forms. High-resolution point-by-point pen location data are gathered, displayed on the cathode ray tube screen, and analyzed while the character is being written or drawn. An average 100 data points per stroke (one each 4 msec) are collected, filtered, and thinned. A stroke is identified by such clues as sequence of directions, corners, and end-point location, and also by contextual clues when necessary. Multiple stroke symbols are recognized by the identification and relative location of the constituent strokes, regardless of the order in which they are written. The pen track is displayed until the character is recognized, and is then replaced by a standard hardware-generated version of the character. Previously written material remains on the display until removed. Changes, insertions, and deletions are easier than with pencil and paper. Experiments with groups of programmers, engineers, and secretaries indicate that a half-hour training period is sufficient, with 90 percent immediate recognition by the system. The scheme is in daily use in an experimental problem solving system at RAND.[34]

Chinese-Character Lookup

A companion project was the lookup of Chinese characters. The important point here is that the sequence in which the several strokes in the character are drawn is an important aid in finding a dictionary entry. Groner, Heafner, and Robinson described the procedure:

A method for using sequential positional information to recognize hand-printed Chinese characters, and a computer program that uses this method to provide a translation aid. The desired character is drawn on the RAND graphical input tablet and is reproduced on the CRT display page, which includes the asked-for character together with its pronunciation and its identification number in the standard Chinese-English dictionary. The program can be used for any forms that are drawn in a particular sequence of strokes. Both recognition routines (Chinese and Roman characters) analyze the point-by-point locations as each stroke is being drawn, and identify it within milliseconds after completion. The program could be used in preparing a hardcopy dictionary index or teaching aids by use of a graphical output printer.[35]

Map Annotation

Another project was map annotation, that is, the addition of markings, words, and symbols to maps for any of a variety of purposes. Historically, this had commonly been done by manual writing methods on a transparent overlay of the map. Bob Anderson and Norm Shapiro described the project as follows:

---

[34] RAND (2007d).

[35] RAND (2008b).

The RAND tablet and the videographic system could be used to look up handwritten ideographs in an electronic Chinese dictionary.
SOURCE: Groner, Heafner, and Robinson (1967, p. 10).

A discussion of the key features of an interactive map display system that affects both the usefulness of the system and the design and architecture of its hardware and software. Recent developments in computer graphics offer the possibility of creating interactive map display systems having many of the advantages of traditional paper maps, but significant additional advantages as well. This report presents observations and guidelines for developers of interactive map systems. The techniques and design principles discussed are applicable to command and control systems ranging from support of a field commander through systems tailored to the needs of the National Command Authority.[36]

---

[36] RAND (2007a).

Prior to this work, a pilot project had addressed the military problem of map annotation, a task that military analysts commonly performed for many purposes.[37] It proved straightforward, convenient, and easy to position boxes, lines, arrows, text, and other annotations over the displayed map. The net effect was to make annotation significantly quicker and more efficient. It is believed that the contact point was the DoD/Defense Intelligence Agency (DIA) acting through the USAF R&D facility at Rome Air Development Center, which provided the digitally scanned maps for display on the CRT on which the user actions and activities were also displayed. It is possible that the RAND group produced the digital maps in house. It is also possible that it was a demonstration effort intended to interest the USAF or the intelligence community in the technique.

Bob Anderson and Norm Shapiro summarized the map work as follows:

> Maps play a fundamental role in planning and decisionmaking activities related to command and control. The abstractions used and the cartographic decisions that result in traditional paper maps have evolved over thousands of years and provide a compact and highly useful representation of geographic information.
>
> The essence of a map is abstraction: Maps generally present a highly abstract representation of reality. They are abstract in that information is omitted (for example, minor roads may not be shown), they are stylized (a city may be represented by a single dot), and they are encoded (the population of a city may be denoted by the size and shape of the dot).
>
> Traditional paper maps must contain all the information that a user is likely to need; hence there is a continual need for cartographers to balance the amount of clutter with a user's need for information.
>
> Although paper maps have many advantages—for example, they are inexpensive and highly portable—they have many disadvantages as well: They cannot represent rapidly changing information; they omit needed information; they do not incorporate useful computational aids such as minimum-path algorithms or time-of-flight calculations.
>
> Recent developments in computer graphics and the continuing decline in the cost of electronics offer the possibility of creating interactive map display systems (IMDSs) having many of the advantages of traditional maps, but significant additional advantages as well.
>
> These systems are not merely maps but are aids to geographic planning and problem-solving in the broadest sense. Experimentation on such systems conducted by the authors during the past year has produced the following observations and guidelines for developers of IMDSs:

---

[37] No documentation of this work has been found. Perhaps it was a low-level effort or simply done as a trial application or demonstration.

- Due to their fundamental differences, the design of electronic maps should not mimic that of paper maps. Each cartographic decision or design feature must be reconsidered based on its underlying purpose.
- In a system with reasonable computational agents, continuous display controls such as knobs or joysticks are in many situations considerably inferior to discrete controls such as function buttons.
- Users have preconceptions that are quite uniform about the direction in which continuous controls should be moved to shift the display. In some cases, the expected direction changes when the size of the object being viewed exceeds the size of the display window.
- Aircraft-type controls are inappropriate for almost all geographic display applications.
- Aircraft-type controls can be learned in a few minutes by most subjects.
- Given control over clutter, users act responsibly and limit clutter effectively.
- Given a choice, users often prefer to receive voice-output data rather than CRT-presented data.
- Disorientation can be caused by abrupt changes in view, lack of visible features, and interruption of the user.
- Disorientation can be reduced by specific training of users and occurs less frequently among trained pilots than among other subjects.
- A variety of simple techniques can be used to retain user orientation in map displays; disorientation is therefore not a significant problem.
- Discrete zoom or translation increments greater than certain limited values cause disorientation and should be avoided.
- Continuously displayed legends giving names of entities (and displayed text giving other properties of geographic entities) seem less valuable in interactive maps than in paper maps.
- Electronic map index programs can greatly increase a user's ability to locate information. They depend, however, on a system design in which the computer does not act just as a camera but understands the names and attributes of the data being displayed.
- Users can tolerate and effectively use variable abstractions, provided they can control the abstraction process.
- Users' abilities to tolerate variable abstractions increase with experience.
- Interactive maps are effective problem-solving devices, even when supplied with rudimentary computational and information retrieval facilities.[38]

Videographic System

One of the early requirements for graphical input was the capability to merge information provided by user actions—or generated by computers—with information coming from other sources, such as maps. Initially, high-resolution TV technology was used to scan and display "other information." Eventually, it was realized that an all-digital system would provide superior quality and performance. RAND entered into a partnership with an IBM facility at Los Gatos, California, to design and produce such a system.

---

[38] Anderson and Shapiro (1979, pp. v–vi).

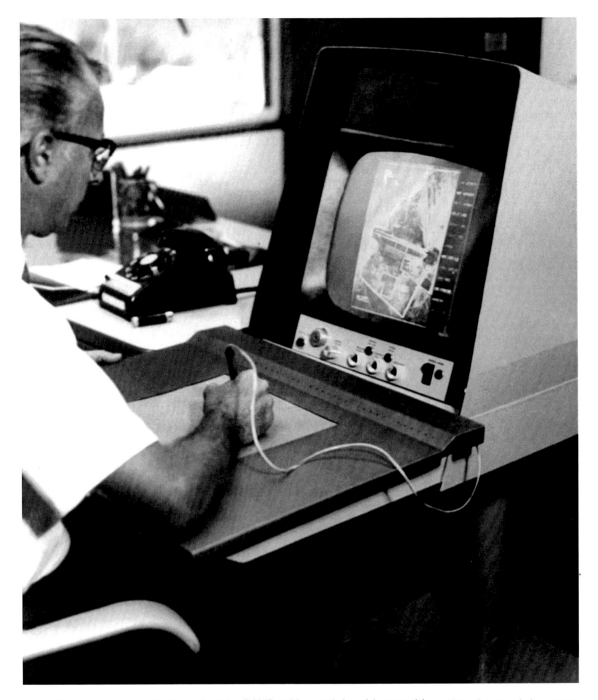

Tom Ellis, an engineer, shown using the RAND tablet and the videographic system to annotate maps

Not only was the system to be all digital but it would also have many consoles for multiple users.

Uncapher summarized the effort as follows:

> Cathode-ray-tube graphic displays offer one of the most powerful and useful man-machine communication paths. The RAND Video Graphic System offers one implementation. It serves 32 consoles; each has a full range of interaction and full

graphics, and accommodates up to 8 different input devices. Each console serves as the general graphic terminal for all the user's computer-based needs. The user can access several computers from any terminal. The system is based on the use of an 873-line TV monitor in each terminal. Scan conversion and buffered storage are centralized to improve performance and reduce cost. An all-digital approach to the video system is now being designed at RAND.[39]

A videographic console included a tablet, keyboard, CRT display, microphone, and a speaker. The computing heart included an IBM 1800 computer, a scan converter, and a huge (approximately 36 inches in diameter) magnetic disk to store scanned images and to maintain synchrony among parts of a displayed composite image.

The system proved to be tricky, particularly to maintain synchronism between scan-source material and terminal-source material. Moreover, commercial developments were overtaking its technology. For various reasons, development of the effort was terminated before the audio part was undertaken.

GRAIL

Another project stemming from the presence of videographics was the development of a flowchart language that could be used to construct models and simulations or to describe complex information-flow situations.

Ellis, Heafner, and Sibley described GRAIL as follows:

> The important organizational concepts of the flowchart language are the sequential flow of control, the hierarchy of subroutines, and the language (flow diagrams) that pictorially relates their interdependence. A fundamental facility of the man-machine interface is the automatic recognition of appropriate symbols, which allows the man to print or draw appropriate symbols freehand. GRAIL's text-editing features include placement, replacement, and deletion of characters, character-string insertion or deletion, and line deletion. Control functions include displaying text page-by-page, requesting specified display frames, moving symbols, and test line editing. The flowchart processes may be compiled and executed at CPU speeds or the man may control interpretative execution by direct stylus actions. He may use overlay displays or split screen displays to debug.[40]

GRAIL, in turn, spawned related projects, such as BIOMOD and CLINFO, described next.

BIOMOD

Building on GRAIL, the BIOMOD project was devoted to modeling of biological and related systems. Groner, Clark, Berman, and DeLand described it as follows:

---

[39] RAND (2007c).

[40] RAND (2007b). See also Ellis, Heafner, and Sibley (1969b, 1969c).

The videographic system used a rotating magnetic-disk storage unit to combine digital and analog information.

BIOMOD [is] an operational system designed to enable unsophisticated computer users to study models of dynamic systems. . . . BIOMOD employs a graphics console comprising a television screen, a data tablet, and a keyboard. A user constructs a model by drawing block diagrams and hand-printing or typing text while receiving immediate feedback about the interpretation of his actions. Each component of a model block diagram may be defined either by another block diagram, or by one of the other user-oriented languages: analog-computer-like elements; algebraic, differential, or chemical equations; or FORTRAN statements. During model simulation, displayed curves are continually and automatically updated; the user may stop the simulation and plot different variables, change scales and/or parameter values, and then continue the simulation.[41]

CLINFO

CLINFO was implemented on a Data General Nova machine.[42] While not closely related to other graphics projects, it borrowed from their techniques. For its time, it was a unique project in that it involved individuals external to RAND as part of the team. Groner, Baker, et al. described it as follows:

The CLINFO Project is an effort to identify the information processing activities and needs critical to clinical investigation (medical research involving human subjects which is aimed at improving diagnostic and therapeutic techniques) and to recommend how to satisfy these needs.

To date the project (1) has determined that the most critical needs [that] can be met effectively using state-of-the-art computer technology lie in the areas of managing and analyzing clinical-research data collected by individual investigators, (2) has developed prototype minicomputer-based systems designed to satisfy these needs in the General Clinical Research Center (GCRC) setting, and (3) has installed, and is successfully operating, two prototype systems in GCRCs where they are being evaluated.

The project is being conducted by computer scientists, clinical investigators, and National Institutes of Health (NIH) staff members. It has involved several phases of activity, beginning with a determination of user requirements by means of informal and formal discussions and interviews.

The present phases address the incremental and iterative design and development of a prototype, and the collection of detailed information about its utilization by diverse users at more than one site. If justified by user acceptance and estimated costs and benefits, the project will next specify a system appropriate for a large number of clinical researchers.

---

[41] Groner, Clark, et al. (1971, p. v). See also Clark, Groner, and Berman (1971) and Clark and Groner (1971).

[42] The choice of a minicomputer narrowed down to DEC versus Data General. Data General was selected because its operating system and Beginner's All-Purpose Symbolic Instruction Code (BASIC) programming language provided capabilities closer to project needs and were more flexible than were DEC's equivalents. Also, Data General seemed to provide better customer support. The language C and UNIX were not appropriate for this application.

The CLINFO project was initiated in 1972 to answer two fundamental questions, namely, (1) what are the information processing activities and needs of clinical researchers who investigate physiology and diagnostic and therapeutic techniques in GCRCs and (2) what, if any, computer technology can meet the major needs of a variety of investigators at scattered geographic locations while being fiscally and otherwise acceptable to their institutions?

To answer these questions in depth, the National Institutes of Health established a consortium comprising clinical investigators (T. G. Christopher, a nephrologist at the University of Washington, A. W. Nunnery, a pediatrician at the University of Oklahoma, and H. K. Thompson, a cardiologist at the Baylor College of Medicine), computer scientists (primarily G. F. Groner, N. A. Palley and N. Z. Shapiro at The RAND Corporation), and NIH staff members (W. R. Baker, Jr., and W. F. Raub at the Biotechnology Resources Branch, and W. R. DeCesare and his assistants at the GCRC Branch).

Although each of the participating clinical investigators had prior experience with computer technology and the computer scientists had prior experience with biomedical research, none of us had previously worked with the consortium members from other institutions.

Although the consortium had some initial difficulties, the interdisciplinary approach has been instrumental to the success of the project because (1) expertise in medical research and in computer science and technology, in addition to NIH viewpoints, have been required and utilized throughout the project, (2) the viewpoints of the developers of any eventual computer system, as well as those of potential users, have been represented at all stages of the project to ensure that any computer system or systems recommended would be useful, acceptable and feasible, and (3) the medical and institutional diversity of the participating clinical investigators has helped to ensure the wide applicability of any recommendations.

Finally, because of both the composition of the consortium and the investigative interests of its individual members, our approach has been to examine real-world problems in detail and then attempt to find or devise solutions rather than to start with existing solutions and try to mold problems to fit them.[43]

As a historical note, an early version of BIOMOD was used to schedule chemotherapy treatments for a cancer patient.[44]

---

[43] Groner, Baker, et al. (1976, pp. 2–3).

[44] Lincoln, Groner, Williams, and Lukes (1976).

Time-Shared Computing: JOSS

JOSS was the creation of Cliff Shaw. The functional structure of the user interface; the subtle details of system behavior; the elegance of its arithmetic processes;[45] clever user options, such as attaching conditional statements to commands—it all came from Cliff Shaw. Every last line of implementing code—including the supporting utility programs—came as well from him; he steadfastly declined help from anyone.

The motivation for building JOSS was Shaw's perception of the need for a ready and efficient system in which users could frame and execute small algebraic problems. JOSS was not a programming language per se; it was a complete, operational, user-friendly environment.

The original JOSS (later called JOSS-1) was implemented on JOHNNIAC, which had been patterned after the von Neumann machine at IAS, but many elements were unique to JOSS and JOHNNIAC and not a part of the Princeton model: These included the JOSS user console (centered on an IBM electric typewriter), the swapping magnetic drum added to the machine, and the communication arrangements for connecting terminals to the machine.

Cliff Shaw, trained as a mathematician, worked as an insurance actuary and became a superb programmer.

JOSS-1 serviced a few USAF users via dial-in telephone connections. It also accommodated a limited number of internal staff users. Because of users' vigorous acceptance, RAND launched a follow-on JOSS-2 version that, in effect, was a production-engineered version hosted on a dedicated DEC PDP-6 machine. It too supported both internal and external users.

It is hard to appreciate the elegance and sophistication of JOSS without having used it, experienced it first hand, and studied the user language. As Cliff once said: "The success of a system depends on thousands of decisions, every one made right." He made all of the decisions undergirding JOSS exactly right.

The following excerpts from two papers give additional facts about the two JOSS versions.

---

[45] For example, the square of the square root of 2 is 2, not 1.99999.

JOSS-1[46]

Abstract: JOSS (JOHNNIAC Open-Shop System) is an experimental on-line, time-shared computing service. It is in daily use by staff members of The RAND Corporation for the solution of small numerical problems. The users compose stored programs and interact with JOSS through remote typewriter consoles by using a single, high-level language. The system is described with emphasis on those features [that] have led users to accept it as a convenient new tool. JOSS provides use of familiar typewriters, exact input/output, decimal arithmetic, high-level algebraic language with English punctuation rules, easy modification and repair of programs, and report-quality formatted output.

Introduction

The JOHNNIAC Open-Shop System (JOSS) is an experimental, on-line, time-shared computing system [that] has been in daily use by staff members of The RAND Corporation since January 1964. It was designed to give the individual scientist or engineer an easy, direct way of solving his small numerical problems without a large investment in learning to use an operating system, a compiler, and debugging tools, or in explaining his problems to a professional computer programmer and in checking the latter's results. The ease and directness of JOSS is attributable to an interpretive routine in the JOHNNIAC computer [that] responds quickly to instructions expressed in a simple language and transmitted over telephone lines from convenient remote electric-typewriter consoles. An evaluation of the system has shown that in spite of severe constraints on speed and size of programs, and the use of an aging machine of the vacuum-tube era, JOSS provides a valuable service for computational needs [that] cannot be satisfied by conventional, closed-shop practice.

This paper concentrates on the numerous, small, hardware and software design decisions [that] have influenced the acceptance of the system by its intended users. Several figures, produced on-line, are included, providing readable examples of features of the JOSS language. An austere version of the system saw limited use during most of 1963.

Background

From the earliest days of construction of the JOHNNIAC computer, a Princeton-class machine built at The RAND Corporation in 1950–53, it has been the author's dream to have an economical, personal, remote communication station for on-line control and programming of a computer. With so much to be learned about programming and operating large general-purpose computers, it isn't surprising that the additional investment in communications equipment, remote stations, and corresponding software was postponed.

---

[46] Excerpted from Shaw (1964, pp. 2–7). Shaw wrote, "This paper was prepared for presentation at the 1964 Fall Joint Computer Conference, sponsored by the American Federation of Information Processing Societies, October 27–29, 1964, at San Francisco, California."

In its early days, JOHNNIAC served well as a production machine. Then, because it has only a 4096-word core memory, a slow 12,288-word drum, slow copy-logic for card I/O and printing, no tapes, and a very austere order code, production computing was gradually shifted to more modern IBM equipment. Yet, the very accessibility to this unsaturated second machine made JOHNNIAC attractive as the basis for simplified programming systems for small, open-shop problems and for experimental work in heuristic programming, new software systems, and hardware for better interaction with a computer. In November 1960, after years of discussion of personal remote consoles with T. O. Ellis, I proposed to the management of RAND's Computer Sciences Department that JOHNNIAC be committed full time to providing a modest computing service to the open-shop via remote typewriters.

The purpose of the JOSS experiment was not to make JOHNNIAC machine language available, but rather to provide a service through a new, machine-independent language [that] had to be designed specifically for the purpose. It was to be an experiment with the goal of demonstrating the value of on-line access to a computer via an appropriate language, and was intended to contribute to a project with the long-range goal of a sophisticated information processor. T. O. Ellis, I. Nehama, A. Newell, and K. W. Uncapher were the other participants in that project.

In 1961–62, Ellis and M. R. Davis designed and directed the construction of the required multiple typewriter communication system adjunct to JOHNNIAC. The hardware was ready well in advance of the first version of the system program, and only a few select users were subjected to this very limited system. Their feedback, including encouraging remarks on the usefulness of JOSS, helped shape the full version.

Comparison

Other on-line, time-shared computing systems have become operational in recent years. All are pioneering efforts. By comparison, JOSS is special-purpose, even though it encompasses a wider class of problems than one might guess at first reading. Most of the others provide the user with access to machine language. F. J. Corbato has aptly described them as open systems and JOSS as a closed system. In the open systems, an executive routine is prepared to help the user at the machine-language level or to pass control to one of several subsystems providing adaptations of pre-existing programming systems. JOSS, however, was designed with on-line interaction in mind, and resources were devoted to making it smooth and easy to use. The future lies with the open systems, but it remains to be seen whether the open-system executive will absorb JOSS-like systems simply as additional subsystems, or whether JOSS-like systems will absorb the executive function and thus serve as the user's computing aide and single contact with the computer.

We wanted to do a controlled evaluation of the system at the time of the introduction of the full version of JOSS, but the new users taught others so quickly that we had to resort to after-the-fact questionnaires!

Hardware Components of JOSS

Physically, JOSS consists of the JOHNNIAC computer, ten remote consoles, and a multiple typewriter communication system to mediate between JOHNNIAC and the consoles. Because JOHNNIAC was ill-equipped to handle the message traffic required in JOSS service, a special-purpose buffering system was built to process characters within messages and to monitor the remote stations. The alternative of modifying the main frame to handle the message traffic directly would have required a major rework of the JOHNNIAC control and would still have yielded degraded performance in JOSS service. Thus, JOHNNIAC remains a very primitive machine with no indexing, no indirect addressing, no floating point, no error checking, no memory protect, no interrupts, no channels, no compare, no zero test, a miserable format of two single-address instructions per word, and a 50-ms add time.

Chuck Baker at work on a JOSS-2 terminal

The JOSS system program runs about 6000 words, the low-frequency portions residing on drum and overlaying each other in core when called in for execution. A large part of the JOSS system program resides permanently in core. It was a considerable challenge to compress it sufficiently to leave room for the processing of a user's block in core.

More than once I regretted the lack of an adequate subroutine linkage operation; it would have saved much space in this deeply hierarchical program.

The 12,288-word JOHNNIAC drum is divided into three sections, accessed by moving heads at a rate not quite so fast as a modern disk unit unless the heads are luckily in the correct position. Average swap time (i.e., the time to write one user's block of information out onto drum and read a second user's block into core for processing) is, therefore, quite slow at about half a second.

Communication System

The multiple typewriter communication system provides sixteen line-buffers, controls the states of all ten remote consoles, and registers signals from them. The limit is 81 consoles—well beyond our needs and our budget. The JOSS system program in JOHNNIAC commands block transfers between core and the line buffers. It also commands the communication system to enable or disable a console, request or relinquish control of a console, clear a line buffer, assign a line buffer to a console, or transmit a line buffer to a console. It also commands the communication system to report any signals from consoles indicating a carriage return, a page ejection, or the depression of one of the console control keys.

JOSS-2[47]

Though JOSS is implemented on a high-speed, general-purpose, time-sharing computer, it is a special-purpose system designed to provide the user with a personal service through remote computation. The only component of the system that the user is aware of is his own console—a mobile unit that is plugged into his office outlet and that supplies computational power. The console itself consists of a standard IBM Selectric typewriter with a slightly modified character set. The conventional characters take up 73 of the standard 88 keyboard positions, leaving 15 positions available for special graphics, which, since the JOSS system is restricted to numeric computations, have been chosen from the usual set of mathematical symbols.

An auxiliary control box, equipped with indicator lights, activates the console. The JOSS console has been designed so that control of the typewriter is proprietary: Either JOSS has control for output purposes, or the user has control for typing in to JOSS. Which of these situations is actually the case is indicated by visual, tactile, and audible signals. The user's input of instructions and data is typed in green, and JOSS responds with output in black.

---

[47] Excerpted from Baker (1966, pp. v–vi).

JOSS commands are limited to one line; take the form of an imperative English sentence, and in fact may be read out loud; begin with a verb; and obey the conventional rules of English for spacing, capitalization, punctuation, and spelling. The ability to append a conditional clause to any JOSS command is an extremely powerful feature of the language. Three brief examples are presented that touch on almost every feature of the JOSS system: the readability of the language, including the identity of the "speaker," its computational ability, its logical ability, and JOSS's response to errors.

In addition to computing directly with numbers, JOSS can assign values to letters, to help in working with numbers that are repeated many times, or initially have unknown values. Further examples demonstrate that JOSS operates with numbers that are (1) always in decimal, (2) limited to 9 significant digits, (3) are exact on input and output, (4) are expressed in scientific notation where appropriate, and (5) may be denoted by single letters. Any legitimate algebraic expression involving letters, numbers, and functions may replace any number, anywhere in the language, without reservation, and JOSS will interpret the result appropriately. JOSS arithmetic also provides us with the true result, rounded if necessary, to 9 decimal digits, for the operations of add, subtract, multiply, divide, square root, and selected cases of exponentiation.

Supplementing the basic operations of arithmetic, the JOSS functions fall into three groups: elementary transcendental (log, exp, sin, cos, arg), number dissection (sgn, ip, fp, dp, xp), and iterative (sum, prod, max, min, first).

Several "real" problems are next presented to illustrate how the user can add to JOSS's power to work with him in specific problem-solving situations. We see how JOSS can store values, expressions, functions, and forms, as well as sequences of commands, called steps, for subsequent interpretation.

The ability of JOSS to produce, easily and quickly, report quality output, in a standard format of 8-1/2 by 11 in., contributes a great deal to the power of the system. The value of the JOSS language itself lies not in the user's ability to continually expand and refine the language in many small ways, but in his ability to combine a few highly refined basic features in a variety of ways without restriction. The language is highly readable, and the JOSS user will soon come to actually "think" in the JOSS language—or, at least, to express his problem using JOSS's vocabulary.

JOSS influenced the design of many other systems. A list of them—in Shaw's handwriting and compiled by him in 1967—was pinned on his office door (Fig. 6.1). Ed Bryan later added the bottom three entries, identified as weak influence.[48]

---

[48] Ed Bryan provided the list in electronic form; Irv Greenwald has the original list.

Figure 6.1 Early Systems Influenced by JOSS

jcs 3-8-67

JOSS influenced systems

	Organization	System name	Status	Computer	number
1.	RAND	JOSS	Retired	Johnniac	
2.	RAND	JOSS	Running	PDP-6	
3.	BBN	TELCOMP	Running	PDP-1	(2)
4.	BBN & MGH	TELCOMP	Running	PDP-1D	
5.	U.C. Irvine	~~JOSS I~~ ISIS	Running	IBM-1410	
6.	U.C. Berkeley	CAL	Running	SDS-940	(3?)
7.	U. of Pittsburgh	PIL/L	Running	IBM-360/50	
8.	NASA Huntsville	AMTRAN	Running	IBM-1620	
9.	NASA Huntsville	AMTRAN	?	B-5500	
10.	Burroughs	INTERP	?	B-5500	
11.	Applied Data Research	ESI	Running	PDP 5, 8, 85	(~)
12.	Cal Tech	CITRAN	Running	IBM-360/50	
13.	Oak Ridge		?	CDC-1604	
14.	EAI	HYTRAN	Running	EAI-8400, 8800	(?)
15.	AECC		?	B-5500	
16.	NRL		?	NAREC	
17.	NEL		?	M-460	
18.	Applied Data Research	JOSS	Running	PDP-6	
19.	Medinet	File Comp	"	GE 465 ?	
20.	Mitre				

Weak influence

	Organization	System name	Status	Computer	number
1.	ABC	RUSH	Running	IBM-360/50	
2.	SDC	TINT	Running	IBM-Q-32	
3.	Dartmouth	BASIC	Running	GE-265	(~)

Networked Computing: Packet Switching and Distributed Communications

The concept of breaking a digitally expressed message into chunks for transmission along possibly different routings through a redundantly connected digital network has been discussed under the terms *message blocks*, *packets*, and *distributed communications*. The surviving name, as is well known everywhere, is *packet*; the original name was *distributed communications*.

Paul Baran originated the seminal concept in the early 1960s, and the story of it was told in his address at the Franklin Institute in Philadelphia, Pennsylvania, on the occasion of his receiving the 2001 Bower Award and Prize for Achievement in Science. The following excerpts are from that paper, which was also published in the *IEEE Communications Magazine*.[49]

[49] Baran (2002). The reprinting here has been lightly edited, and a few new footnotes have been added. Baran acknowledged his RAND colleagues: "I am particularly indebted to Frank Collbohm, John D. Williams, Frank Eldridge,

The Beginnings of Packet Switching: Some Underlying Concepts

Cold War Background

When I joined RAND in 1959, a glaring weak spot in our strategic forces command and control communications was a dependence on shortwave radio and the national telephone system, AT&T, both highly vulnerable to attack. H-bomb testing in the Pacific revealed that long distance short-wave (high-frequency) sky-wave transmission would be disrupted for several hours by a high-altitude nuclear blast. Computer simulations showed that weapons targeted at U.S. retaliatory forces would render long distance telephone communications service inoperative by collateral damage alone. While most of the telephone facilities would survive, the paucity of switching centers formed a dangerous Achilles' heel.

To cool tensions at this stage of the cold war, a retaliatory force capability was needed that could withstand a surprise attack, and survive sufficiently to return the favor in kind in a controlled manner. A survivable command and control communication infrastructure would be mandatory to get away from the guns loaded, hair trigger doctrine of the time.

Paul Baran invented a networked topology called distributed communications that was later used in the Internet.

RAND computer simulations [had] showed that the telephone system would fail, while most telephone facilities survived. I believed that the problem was obviously in the topology of our communications networks, and there might be a solution. (I had worked on the subject of survivable networks while at Hughes Aircraft before coming to RAND, so I was not new to the subject.)

Introduction[50]

This activity was undertaken in 1960 at the RAND Corporation [which had been] established by the U.S. Air Force to preserve the operations research capability created by the Air Force in World War II, and to work on issues of national security. The freedom of the staff to choose projects, try novel approaches, and disagree with the bureaucracy along the way is difficult to imagine in the present environment. Today, proposals must be written, projects excessively monitored, and reports pre-

---

Albert J. Wohlstetter, Paul Armer, Willis Ware, and Keith Uncapher among others at RAND for continuing strong support while undertaking my highly controversial activity."

[50] The work on distributed communications is described in a series of research memoranda (Baran, 1964a, 1964b, 1964c, 1964d; Baran and Boehm, 1964; Smith, 1964).

pared whether or not there is anything worthwhile to report. It was a different era then, and I enjoyed a remarkable degree of freedom that encouraged far out, and sometimes wild, thinking that would be hard to duplicate today.

Why Networks Are Vulnerable

[The essential argument is that a singly connected network (i.e., one in which there is a single thread of connectivity between any two subscribers) is vulnerable to a break in the thread anywhere along the thread even though many other network facilities survive.] Shortly after I arrived at RAND I began to study the behavior of distributed networks with different levels of redundant connections. When we reached redundancy levels on the order of 3 an interesting phenomenon occurred: the network became extremely robust. If a node survived physical damage, it would likely be connected to all other surviving nodes in the largest single group of surviving nodes. This meant that it would be theoretically possible to build extremely reliable communication networks out of unreliable links. In other words, if a redundantly connected node survived the physical attack, there is a high probability that this node, at least on paper, was somehow connected to all the other surviving nodes. Somehow was the issue, and was the motivation for packet switching.

State of the Art, 1960–1964

In those days (around 1960) we didn't know how to build communication switches where signals could traverse many serially connected nodes and operate reliably in the face of damage. The AT&T telephone system had a limit of five switched tandem links before a phone call was unacceptable. A new way was needed to get usable signals through a large number of nodes, traveling via highly circuitous paths that could not be determined in advance. The new network would have to relay signals along without errors. I considered several analog transmission approaches, but kept hitting a brick wall. The only way I could think of around this restriction was to transmit all signals digitally to avoid the distortion build-up, and the routing information would have to go along with the data itself.

The Broadcast Station Distributed Network

My first RAND distributed network proposal in 1960 was for a survivable teletypewriter network to carry what was then called "minimum essential communications." Carrying briefing charts and slides around to the Pentagon and various military command centers, I found [that] the term was unrealistic. Far, far more capacity was needed than was previously realized. So I went back to the drawing board and took on the challenge to come up with a scalable communications switching structure capable of dynamically routing high-bit-rate traffic among a large set of potential users, and where user requirements could not be predicted in advance.

Meanwhile, the broadcast teletypewriter concept crept slowly through the Air Force process and was eventually assigned to the Rome Air Development Center in upper New York State for implementation. An experimental network was built to cover the northeast section of the US. Its only stress test was the massive Northeast power blackout in 1965 when it was said to have worked well.[51]

Network Synchronization

My interest was now focused on creating a new, very high-data-rate (in 1960s terms) network. For example, since the data flow in the network had to traverse many tandem nodes, I felt it would be impossible to synchronize all individual links in tandem to operate at the exact same data rate. Instead, I proposed small computer-based switching nodes, to provide a small amount of buffering to eliminate the need for overall network timing, letting each link operate at its own natural data rate.

This choice meant that there would be no physical real-time connection between the transmitting and receiving ends. But I felt that would be okay; if the transmission data rate was high enough, the user would be fooled by the illusion that a real-time connection existed.

Mix and Match

This breaking of the lock step nature of the circuit switch link meant that it should theoretically be feasible to build the network from a collection of different types of links, each operating at a different data rate if desired. From the earlier study of the effects of redundancy, high link reliability would not be needed in a distributed network anticipating heavy damage. This is unlike the case of circuit switching, where a single failed tandem element prevented end-to-end communications. This fundamental difference may seem obvious and even trivial today, but its statement tended to generate an undue number of livid words from otherwise competent communications transmission engineers. Those not versed in digital computer art tended to excessively strong objections. And most of those whose day-to-day occupation was caring for telephone lines thought that I must be crazy, a complete fraud who didn't understand how a telephone worked, or both. With some notable exceptions, the proposed ideas were not universally received with great joy.[52]

---

[51] Selover (1965), Costa (1966).

[52] The author sat in on some of the discussions with high-level AT&T officials. It was clear that they "were not buying into this new fangled digital world." This is understandable in view of the sunken cost of in-place network facilities; the expense of converting from analog to digital technology; and the mind-set of the top-level management, who had grown up in an analog communications world. History has, however, demonstrated otherwise, as the present-day AT&T can testify.

In the words of Paul Baran,

"AT&T and I had a long running battle about packet switching that went on for many years starting in about 1961. In brief, their position was that the notion of packet switching was idiotic, totally impractical and couldn't possibly work. Further, it wasn't needed as the Bell System was not vulnerable as RAND simulation suggested.

"I recall once presenting the concept to their top brass at 195 Broadway in New York, their headquarters at the time. In the middle of my presentation I was interrupted by their transmission engineer, who asked, 'Son, did I hear you to say that you opened up a switch in the middle of a telephone conversation?' I said, 'Yes, and . . .' And his eyeballs rolled looking at the ceiling while he tossed his hands up in the air and then proceeded to tell me how a carbon button telephone worked."

Choice of Switching Data Rate

The next design choice was the approximate data rates for the switching node processing. At the time, there was some interesting early work under-way at Bell Labs by John Mayo and others, on what would become the T-1 multiplexing system. By replacing telephone loading coils, nominally at 1-mile spacing, with limiting amplifiers, 24 separate 64 kb/s digital voice channels could be multiplexed on existing copper telephone pairs at 1.54 Mb/s. The system was limited to a maximum range of about 150 mi before the jitter built up to make the link unworkable. But that was okay in my mind because I contemplated that the switching nodes would be retiming the digital signals anyway. So 1.54 Mb/s seemed like a good design data rate.

Getting Through the Damaged Maze

The scheme I settled on to quickly find paths through a network of changing topology while it was being attacked was to route data through the network based on adaptive learning of past traffic. Intuitively it seemed that it should work. But, of course, I couldn't really be sure until after a computer simulation. My RAND colleague Sharla [Perrine] Boehm ran many simulations under different conditions confirming the network's behavior. The simple switching protocol exhibited remarkable intelligence, routing traffic efficiently, yet responding quickly to changes caused by damage. For example, under simulation we found that upon half the network being instantly destroyed, the remainder of the network reorganized itself and was routing traffic effectively within less than one second of simulated real world time.

The routing protocol was simple. Each message block, these days called a packet, had a TO and FROM address field together with a handover counter field that was incremented every time the packet was sent from node to node. The value of the handover number was an estimator of the length of the path taken by each packet. Each switching node regarded recent handover numbers as better estimators than older measurements. The network not only learned; it also had to forget, and thus be able to respond to changes in link and node availability.

The Post-Office Analogy

John Bowers, a RAND colleague, suggested that it was easier for him to visualize the concept by imagining an observant postman at each node (or post office). The postman could infer from the lowest received cancellation date (handover number) of the letters (packets) coming FROM any direction (link) the best direction to send traffic TO in the future to that address. By observing traffic passing through the node and by recording the handover numbers of the FROM station, together with the link number, the imaginary postman could determine the best TO link, the second best TO address, the third, and so on. When the shortest path link is busy or out of action, the next best path will be taken. Since the postman explanation was so easy to understand, I have used this explanation to this day.

Hot-Potato Routing

To dramatize the need for speed in the switching nodes, I described the switching process by saying that each message block should be regarded as a hot potato, tossed from person to person, without gloves. You want to get rid of the hot potato as quickly as you can. If your first choice recipient is busy, toss it to your second choice recipient, and so on. If you have no better choice you are allowed to throw the hot potato back to the previous thrower. Everything had to be essentially instantaneous, if voice was to be transmitted, because voice is intolerant of delay. This early routing scheme is called the hot potato routing algorithm, and has been reinvented the usual number of times, and now is most often called deflection routing.

Sequence Number

Since sequential packets can travel by different paths, they often arrive out of sequence. A short serial number in the header indicates the sequence of packets sent. The receiving unit notes the short modulo serial number and sorts the received packets into their correct sequence buffers, so packet after packet comes out in correct sequence even if some packets travel through a longer path than others.

Cyclical Redundancy Check

Part of the housekeeping field in each packet is dedicated to error detection. The original RAND plan used a cyclical redundancy check (CRC), which is still the preferred error detection approach today. The CRC provides an efficient but not foolproof error detection test. If the error detection test fails, no acknowledgment is sent and the packet is retransmitted. Generally, an acknowledgment of the properly received packet is required before the responsibility for further relaying action is transferred.

An end-to-end error control measure . . . ensures that the few distorted packets that get through the process will be caught and replacement packets requested. As a result, the system can be made arbitrarily error-free, even when using links with high error rates.

Suppression of Silence

In most circuit-switched communication applications, silence is the usual message since no information is transmitted most of the time (remote computer terminals, voice, two-way video, etc.). There is an economy to be gained by not sending long strings of 0s or 1s that contain no information, necessary in conventional circuit-switched networks. The magnitude of this economy can be large, because the common facilities are so effectively shared. In packet switching, we avoid sending packets unless there is information to be sent. If there is no change in the data stream relative to the content of the last packet, why bother sending a packet?

Reliability

There are two components of reliability: the probability that a path exists between two users, and the probability of no errors when using that virtual circuit. The factors that combine to provide super-reliability possibly include:

- The redundancy of the routes allowed;
- The policy of keeping a carbon copy of the transmitted packet until each node is certain that the packet sent has been correctly received by the next recipient;
- End-to-end control to replace any lost packets. If in doubt, the packet is retransmitted and the sequence number used to clean up the duplicates.

Where Did the Name *Packet Switching* Originate?

I used the term message block in the early 1960s. In 1965, Donald W. Davies of the British National Physical Laboratory, unaware of my earlier work, independently came up with the same basic concept and chose the same data rate, 1.54 Mb/s, and the same packet length, 1024 bits. Davies called his system "packet switching," a far better choice of words, and it has become the name that stuck. Davies said he specifically chose the term packet switching to distinguish it from message switching, an earlier technology dating from the telegraph and later the teletypewriter era. Davies wrote a paper shortly before he died in June 2000[53] describing his contribution to the field, followed by a "careful, thoughtful, and scholarly" analysis[54] of a 1962 doctoral thesis recently cited by another highly regarded early worker in the field, who recently began claiming priority for the invention of packet switching. It is Davies' position, on detailed examination, that the cited reference dealt not at all with packet switching, but solely on the older message switching art.[55]

Disclaimer

From time to time, I have been assigned credit for all sorts of things that I haven't done. For example, I am not responsible for the ARPANET [ARPA network]. Its initiator was Robert Taylor, and it was a project managed by Larry Roberts who provided the high-level conceptual specifications with the design detailed and implementation by Bolt, Beranek, and Newman, Inc. [BBN]. My role was very minor, as described by Abbate [1999, pp. 36–37]:

> [Paul Baran, too, became directly involved in the early stages of planning the ARPANET. Roger Scantlebury had referred Lawrence Roberts to Baran's earlier work. Soon after returning to Washington from Gatlinburg, Roberts had read Baran's 'On Distributed Communications.' Later he would describe this as a kind of revelation: "Suddenly I learned how to route packets" [Norberg, O'Neill, and Freedman, 1996, p. 166].

> Some of the ARPANET contractors, including Howard Frank and Leonard Kleinrock, were also aware of Baran's work and had used it in their research. In 1967, Roberts recruited Baran to advise the ARPANET planning group on distributed communication and packet switching. Through these vari-

---

[53] Davies (2001).

[54] Ware (2001).

[55] Hafner (2001).

ous encounters, Roberts and other members of the ARPANET group were exposed to the ideas of Baran and Davies. And they became convinced that packet switching and distributed networks would be both feasible and desirable for the ARPANET.

The ARPANET grew and flourished through the effort of many, including graduate students around the country who turned the basic BBN-designed packet switching network into a computer communication network by the work of many others in the research community. It is appropriate to give credit to those who had a major role in that early activity. That list would include, among others, Vint Cerf, Danny Cohen, Steve Crocker, Howard Frank, Frank Hart, Bob Kahn, Len Kleinrock, John Melvin, Severo Ornstein, John Postel, Larry Roberts, Elmer Shapiro, and Bob Taylor.]

Text Editors (NED and e)

The early RAND text editors actually began at the Washington-based Institute for Defense Analysis (IDA), which had an outpost in Princeton, New Jersey, called the Communications Research Division.[56] IDA maintained a close interaction with departments of the university, and among other aspects of its mission was the development of advanced computer-science tools, especially those of the human-machine interface.

R. Stockton (Stock) Gaines, who was at the IDA facility at the time, recalled how development of a text editor began there:[57]

> The starting point was a two-dimensional editor created at IDA in Princeton, of which the principal authors were Ned Irons and Franz Djorup. A paper describing this editor was published in CACM [*Communications of the ACM*] in the 1970–72 time frame. It is where many of the basic features of today's editors first appeared. For example, "copy" and "paste" first appeared here (called "pick" and "put" at the time). Others are given credit for this pair, but the CACM publication clearly predates any other mention I have seen.

> The hallmark of the editor was the concept of an infinite quarter plane, in which one could insert text, characters, or (later) objects anywhere below the start of the page and to the right of the left hand [border], without filling in characters to get there. This is in contrast to the infinite string model [that] (unfortunately, in my opinion) has come to dominate.

> When Ned Irons left us to go to Yale, my understanding is that creating that and certain other software we had at IDA (we had, among other things, done our own operating system) were among the things he undertook right away. Others

---

[56] Information from this section relies in part on Bilofsky (1977; for PDP-11 with an Ann Arbor terminal) and Kelly (1977).

[57] This and the subsequent quotations in this section are excerpted from email exchanges with Willis Ware.

can describe when Walt Bilofski got involved (I think he was at BBN around that time). He had worked at IDA when the editor was being developed there, but my recollection is that he was working on other things then.

Peter Weiner was responsible for bringing Walt to RAND in late 1974 or 1975 to implement the RAND version, named NED to honor Ned Irons. So the 3rd incarnation of the editor was the first version to run on Unix.

Later the Apple Pie editor was developed for the early Apple computers (pre-Mac) and a version was done for DOS on the PC. Also, David [Dave] Yost did a lot of work on the RAND version.

Peter Elliot Weiner, also at IDA at the time, picked up the story:

I was personally involved in both the first version at IDA, and then with the RAND version and Walt, and can answer some further questions. Later history (after 1980) is past my involvement.

I was a user of the editor at IDA, and was aware of its advancements. When Ned [Irons] and I started the Yale Computer Science department, we didn't have such a tool. After a fight with the Yale Computer Center, the university administration *asked* if we would take $275,000 to buy a PDP-10 to prove the concepts we had been talking up. I went to DEC and negotiated for a PDP-10, as we didn't have as much money as we needed. DEC had line-oriented editors and wasn't interested in our concepts at all.

After the PDP-10 came in, we found a supplier of the right kind of CRT. I think Ned wrote the code for an early version of the Yale Editor, using a language of his creation. I then hired Walt on a consulting basis to write it over in assembly language—and improve it with additional features. I also worked on the code.

After coming to RAND [from Yale], and getting funding to come up with the money for a small minicomputer (and after confrontations with the RAND Computer Center who believed in [WYLBUR]) I hired Walt [Bilofski] to come to RAND and write the first UNIX version. I do think we made an impact with this work, particularly because we got ARPA to drop ANTS and ELF in favor of UNIX and the RAND Editor.

Weiner then left RAND to found Interactive Systems. He continued:

At Interactive Systems, once again Walt improved the editor—together with code that cut down the bandwidth between the central UNIX system and otherwise dumb CRTs, allowing many more terminals to work at once. Here it was called the Interactive Editor.

Later Ned did a system called 10+ [that] tried to simplify the system to ten buttons.

I agree with Stock [Gaines] that many features of the CRT editors in this family are missed in current commercial products.

Meanwhile development of the editor continued at RAND. David (Dave) Crocker, one of several who worked on the editor, wrote:

To mention a truly awesome subroutine package that Bruce Borden built, which I then incorporated into the editor. It served as a replacement for the standard Unix buffered input/output routines, except that it cached [the] buffers. I believe the size of the buffer was compile-time configurable, but it might have been run time.

For something like editing, caching of the local "working set" of buffers has a spectacular performance impact, particularly when modifications are done with a change-list or file index list, rather than just jamming the new text in, thereby requiring a full write-down of the rest of the file.

The two major changes I did were to add this package, for file access, and to buffer screen output—that doesn't sound like much work, but Walt's code was a challenge to modify. The effect was startling. At the time Walt left, the PDP 11/70 used by our department could painfully support 2–3 editor sessions. After caching file buffers and buffering screen output, I think it could comfortably handle 20 or 25!

This was a very basic computer science exercise, but it certainly demonstrated the importance of taking an optimization pass over an initial system.

I inherited the code when Walt left RAND for the startup of Interactive Systems. I maintained it for a year, or so, until I left RAND in August 1978 for grad school. As I recall, Dave Yost took it over from me.[58]

Eventually, through a continuing evolution of e at RAND, it reached version 19, which is still in use as of this writing. Crocker continued:

Dave Yost mentioned his own, commercial effort. I think he said he built it from scratch. . . . [T]he RAND editor was a re-implementation of a display editor built at the Institute for Defense Analysis, while Peter was there. When he came to RAND, he commissioned Walt to write one for Unix, as I heard the story.[59]

Rick Kiessig at RAND picked up the story:

There were a few other features of the editor that I believe were unique at the time:

[58] Crocker (2006).

[59] Crocker (2006).

Replayability. If the editor (or the OS) crashed, the files being edited at the time could be recovered back to a point within a few keystrokes before the failure. This feature was crucial for user acceptance.

The Line Access Package, which I started and Dave later improved, was one of the earliest reusable libraries of text editing functions (including replayability).

I believe that the editor was one of the first Unix-based text editors to support multiple windows. Especially cool, the same file could be opened multiple times, so you could refer to one part of it while changing another part.

The ability to quickly switch from one open file to another in the same window with minimum screen updates led to a feature we called "video diff," that allowed you to visualize the differences between one version of a file and another. By maintaining context, it was much more useful for software version management and integration than the standard Unix diff utility.

Automatic "as-you-type" word-wrap was not added until pretty late in the game. Early versions of the editor displayed long lines with a marker (">," I think) on the right edge of the screen. You had to scroll the whole page to the right to see the rest of those long lines.

I used the editor so much that even after maybe 10 yrs of being away from it, when I ran it again one day, I could still quickly and easily remember the keystrokes and commands.

Remember the Ann Arbor terminals at RAND, with the fancy color-coded keys for various editor functions?

Crocker continued:

My understanding of the earlier history is that Peter brought the design from a display editor that had been done in the 60's at Institute for Defense Analysis. That is, my understanding is that he replicated onto Unix a display editor's function that had been originally developed on a very different platform. I do not know any details about the IDA system.

I had not heard that he brought code. My impression was that all the code was written by Walt.

It was originally called RAND Editor but the ARPA funding program manager mandated that we remove the RAND name from the name of the editor, so we moved it to NED.

The version I inherited was a complete, basic, WYSIWYG [what you see is what you get] 2-D [two-dimensional] display text editor. As Dave explained, an extremely noteworthy human factors characteristic was the end of the text on a line was not the end of the line. In other words, the model really was a (very) long sheet of paper, rather than a series of text strings ending in CR-LF [carriage return, line feed]. Hence, hitting the down [arrow] moved the cursor directly down, whether there was text on that far out on the line or not.

This might not seem a big deal, but the usability impact was significant, since it substantially simplified the user's cognitive model; they did not have to "learn to use an editor." They just typed. This dramatically reduced the learning curve, especially for new, non-technical users.[60]

Rick Kiessig continued:

Having used most of the older versions, I can confirm that there have been at least 19 of them. Dave Yost was responsible for most of them after the early work done by Walt and Dave Crocker. He did the majority of the ongoing maintenance and improvement starting in early 1979, first as a contractor to RAND (with some help from me), then later for the Davis, Polk and Wardwell law firm and also on his own. I believe that most, if not all, of the versions since 1979 were built by Dave Yost. [Dave Yost's] commercial product, the Grand Editor (for which he published a great hard-copy full-length book/manual), was derived directly from the RAND Editor. It was not written from scratch. There was a version branch at one point for GE, but I don't remember exactly when.

Word Processing

By the mid-1970s, the previously unified Computer Sciences Department—one part to conduct research and the other to provide computer services to the corporation—had split.[61] Keith Uncapher and his group had left RAND to form the Information Sciences Institute at the University of Southern California (USC). The remnants of the research activity in the Computer Sciences Department were not organized into a specific group, although Bruce Borden had organized a few of them into an ISL to support the computer-science research. Later, Michael Wahrman, James Guyton, and James Gillogly successively became the heads of the ISL. The programming people and the machine-service people became the Computer Services Department (still CSD).

As a result of an in-house secretarial training program, a committee had been formed to study the needs of the secretarial and administrative staff; this led to an interest in computer-based text processing. Commercially available CRT terminals had become

---

[60] Crocker (2006).

[61] This section is based on an email conversation that included Sue Payne, Lynn Anderson, Christine Taylor, Rosalind Chambers, and Terry West. These people variously conducted training, served as a help desk for user questions, wrote instructional documentation, and created software. Email excerpts from various people have been blended with original writing to create a readable flow.

available, and prototype software was available in the research community, particularly for the DEC minicomputers. The time was right to convert RAND's secretarial and administrative staff from typewriters to computer terminals.

The ISL group was generally pro–UNIX-based systems; the CSD, pro–IBM-based systems. In part, the different positions reflected the fact that "programmers didn't understand that the rest of the Corporation needed a word processor because they wrote documents [with intricate formatting, tables, font choices, and such] . . . whereas the programmers were only interested in a [simple environment that would support] programming" and do so from a remote terminal. The difference in viewpoints is reflected in the decisions that were made for the first corporatewide text- (word-) processing environment.

ISL had been testing word processing in 1976. The initial text-processor machine was a single DEC PDP-11/45. A limited number of users could be supported, a dedicated telephone line connecting each one from his or her office to the machine. When a user wanted to use the text system, an active line might not be available. One had to call the computing center because there were not enough computer ports for the number of users, so they would move the active incoming lines around as needed. Innovative users soon discovered that wedging the point of a pencil into the keyboard beside the request key improved the odds of capturing the first available computer slot. People also would run to different offices and keep pressing keys to keep a login active.

As the demand grew, users were grouped and assigned to particular machines—tp [text processor] 1, tp2, and so on through tp5. The single PDP-11/45 became two DEC PDP-11/70s by 1981, then a VAX 780, and, finally a VAX 11/785.

The first terminal was just called an Ann Arbor terminal (users typed "aa" to set terminal type when logging in). A later model of the terminal had colored keys around the edges (orange or red for special keys, such as Ctrl or Esc). Then came the Ambassador terminals (users typed "aaa" when logging in).

The full-screen editor NED had become available as early as 1976.[62] By 1981, it had been improved and renamed to "e" or the "RAND editor." The UNIX command nroff was used as a formatter in 1977 until Terry West, in a pro-bono effort, wrote a new formatter for e called eR in 1980. A handful of people used the command nroff to do text processing for several years. The creation of eR perturbed the CSD organization, which preferred the IBM-based WYLBUR[63] package. The research staff demanded the

---

[62] See the preceding section on NED and e.

[63] According to Bob Patrick,

[ORVIL] and [WYLBUR] were developed at Stanford in the late 1960s by a team led by Rod Fredrickson [who later joined RAND to head the computing-service organization]. Orvil was a component of Wylbur. Wylbur was an extension to [IBM's] OS/360 for a computer literate environment [that] was geographically dispersed and had customers writing small jobs. The competitors to Wylbur were MIT's Timesharing, and IBM's Timesharing Option (TSO). Wylbur was most efficient and, in some ways, the best, but it did not have the publicity that the others had. Wylbur was originally written for the IBM model 67 (a Model 360/65 with [memory] relocation). At Stanford, remote terminals were connected to the center by private dedicated wires. They terminated in a communications control unit. Wylbur ran in a high priority [mainframe] partition and handled the terminal traffic. A user could create a new job, amend an existing job, and submit a job to OS/360 for execution. Output could be viewed from a terminal or printed centrally and picked up.

e/eR environment, and, in the end, it won out as the initial text-processing system at RAND.[64]

The combination of the editor NED, email, and text-processing utilities available on UNIX (along with the relative ease-of-use utilities that UNIX offered) made it the platform of choice from the users' standpoint.

Although "nroff/troff was incredibly slow," a small number of users in the publication department and a few of the secretarial staff used troff as a formatter.[65]

A RAND economist[66] ported e into a DOS-based version that he called esp and also created a formatter for it called end. This provided users a word-processing capability on their individual desktop machines. No longer did one have to wait in line for an available connection to a central machine. Terry West also recompiled his UNIX-based formatter—eR—to run under DOS, and, as a result, end never became popular within RAND.

By the end of the 1980s, commercial machines and Microsoft office products had become widely available. Thus, RAND opted to move its user base from the in-house environment that had evolved onto a Macintosh and PC commercial one.[67]

The Mail Handler

In his mail-handler (MH) manual, Jerry Peek recounted how the mail-handling system came to be developed:

> Early in 1977, R. Stockton Gaines and Norman Z. Shapiro of the RAND Corporation laid out the MH principles in a way that's been followed amazingly well since. At that time RAND had an electronic mail system called MS [Mail System]. MS worked the way most mail software still does today: it was a monolithic system [that] didn't take advantage of the UNIX file and directory structure. Among the ideas laid out in the MH memo were: storing messages in a directory as normal text files, which could then be read by other UNIX programs as well as MH; deleting a message by changing its name (moving it to another directory); and having a "user environment" file that keeps track of what the user did last. The

---

[64] This statement suggests that WYLBUR and the e and eR systems were in competition, and, in a way, they were. The computer center had long been an IBM-only shop, and it was natural for it to favor IBM-oriented software. On the other hand, the ISL was familiar with and favored the newly evolving text-handling systems generally funded by ARPA in the research community.

WYLBUR had been designed primarily to support programmers at remote terminals who were preparing programs to be run under OS/360. While WYLBUR had some simple word-processing commands, it did not have the flexibility and functional completeness to satisfy the quite different needs of the research staff.

[65] Both nroff and troff formatters were included in the UNIX software distribution from Bell Laboratories.

[66] William Rogers had a small, private software company—Software Resources.

[67] The status of the RAND text-processing system is described in the following documents distributed to users in a large, indexed, orange binder, which also contained several other items, such as cost, letter preparation, classified computing, and printing guide: Lynn Anderson et al. (1986); Lynn Anderson and Batten (1986); Phil Klahr, Payne, and Anderson (1987); Westbury (1981, 1982); and Payne (1985).

MH commands were a lot like MS commands except that they became individual programs, one for each task, executed with a UNIX shell.

By 1979, Bruce S. Borden had developed MH; it has remained conceptually the same ever since. Of course, some changes and a fair number of additions have been made to MH since it was created. Since 1982, Marshall T. Rose, aided by John L. Romine, with some help from Einar Stefferud, Jerry Sweet, and others at the University of California, Irvine (UCI), have extended and maintained MH. (Marshall Rose has since left UCI.) Performance enhancements were also made at the University of California, Berkeley, and MH has been included with later versions of Berkeley UNIX (4BSD). Versions of MH also come with Digital's ULTRIX, IBM's AIX, and others. People at UCI, along with help from contributors, updated MH until the late 1990s.

In 1997, Richard Coleman started work on nmh, the "new MH." As MH development at UCI ended, the nmh developers—first Richard Coleman, then a team spread across the Internet—have revised some MH programs, added new features, and tried to fix its code to be simpler and more portable. At this writing, in mid-2003, nmh development has slowed but not stopped.[68]

The Original MH-Proposal Memorandum

Stock Gaines and Norm Shapiro lay out the design ideas underlying MH in an undated memo:

```
To:      Bob Anderson
From:    Stock Gaines, Norm Shapiro
Subject:       THE NEXT MESSAGE SYSTEM
Copies: Dave Crocker, Dave Farber, Carl Sunshine, Steve Tepper, Steve
Zucker


While the creators of MS[69] are to be congratulated in having produced
a substantial advance over SND and MSG, the current system, in a cou-
ple of ways, falls short of the software for dealing with messages
that we should have in UNIX. MS as it stands is in two fundamental
and important ways at odds with the UNIX philosophy and approach. We
think that another iteration on message software should take place
which will provide us with software dealing with messages that is
again an advance over MS and will fit in naturally with UNIX in a way
that MS does not, from which a number of practical advantages will
follow. The two ways in which MS is basically incompatible with the
UNIX approach are first that it is a monolithic system rather than
being a set of functions which are callable from wherever is appro-
priate, and second that the storage of messages is not done by making
appropriate use of the file and directory structure (an exceedingly
elegant, simple and powerful one) already existing in UNIX.
```

---

[68] Peek, Wohler, and Welch (1996).

[69] David Crocker and others at RAND in 1976.

Let us discuss the UNIX way of storing messages first. As an alternative to the clumsy method of using a text file and a structure file, we suggest that instead a mailbox be simply a directory. Each message would then be a separate file in that directory. If it is necessary to keep additional information about the files in the directory, that can be done by entering in the message directory a file containing information about the messages in the directory. Notice how many of the things we are trying to do with the structure file get handled automatically if this occurs. For instance, each time a message is written or read, the file system already automatically updates this information. Therefore, a clear indication that we have a new message in a mail folder is that the instant of writing and reading is the same. If they are different then we can test the time last written to see if the message was received recently or not. Dave Crocker has in the past pointed out that the rm command has the disadvantage that it throws a file away. It would be quite appropriate to add a shell command called, say, dis (for discard) which moves a message from the directory it is in to a subdirectory of that directory which we may think of as the discarded messages directory.

These messages can be cleaned out by some sort of a cleanup command or by software that carries out this task at appropriate times. The point is that IF the garbage retrieval function is desirable for messages, then it is so for files. Of course, in the directory structure we have no information concerning the contents of messages. However, there is some reason to believe that the current design which retains pointers to each of the components of a message is of no advantage and may be more costly in execution time than if no such information were available. In any event, it is merely an effort towards efficiency and one [that] appears to have little value.

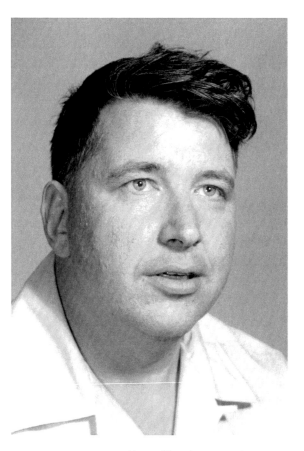

Norm Shapiro, a senior mathematical programmer, codeveloped MH, RAND's early electronic mail system.

The additional value [that] would accrue if messages were files is substantial. They then become accessible to other software in the system in a natural, convenient and highly useful way. The lack of such accessibility of messages is currently one of the major deficiencies of MS. As Steve Tepper has suggested, the draft message might itself be a directory to expedite its processing, although it is not clear that the advantages of this outweigh the advantages of leaving the whole draft as a single file.

The second major difference we are suggesting between the current MS and the approach we believe is appropriate for UNIX is that the functions for dealing with messages should be embodied in individual command level routines which can be executed by themselves rather than only being available through a subsystem. The subsystem approach is appropriate for special situations such as NED, but inappropriate where there is not some overriding consideration such as the consistency [that] must be maintained between the different functions in a special environment. It is, of course, desirable to maintain a certain amount of consistency between the functions. Right now, for instance, it is nice (but not critical) that MS remembers which message a user last referred to, and will show the next message without his having to remember what number to type next. However, there is a natural and useful way of achieving that effect without a subsystem; have a "user environment" file available which the message software (in contrast to a message system) knows about, updates and understands. In such a user environment there could reasonably be a description of which message was last examined (and in which directory).

This approach has the advantage that such information is not lost, as it currently is when one exits from MS. It is quite evident how to implement most of the current MS functions as individual subroutines. For instance, the scan routine must examine a mailbox [that] is now a directory and summarize the messages in it. This is nothing but an extension of ls [the UNIX command to list a directory's contents], which reads some information from the header of each message in addition to reading the directory itself, and would be very straightforward to implement. Reply clearly initializes the draft message in a very straightforward way. The "Show" command is nothing but a variety of ls. "Next" and "Previous" work in a straightforward manner if the user message environment file is maintained.

There are other advantages to this approach. Users who learn UNIX would not have to become familiar with a whole new language but only with three or four new functions. As message handling software evolves much of it will be applicable to other text handling functions. For example, a program to display all messages, in a given directory or set of directories from, to or about a given UNIX user, would also be useable to display all files in a "source" directory of C programs which use a given function. Dually, as general UNIX software evolves, it will tend to be more applicable to message handling. MS has made important contributions to our ideas concerning messages and how to handle them. It is not the subsystem itself, but the basic ideas about messages underlying it, which represents the important contribution of its creators. It seems likely that breaking the functions of MS out of a subsystem into a set of separately executable subroutines would not be a terribly difficult task, would give us an opportunity to redo some of those in ways that correct some of the existing flaws, and would integrate message handling into UNIX in a much more natural and useful way. We suggest that this approach should be followed in contrast to investing very much more effort into upgrading MS.

We would be delighted to discuss these ideas more fully.

Implementation

Bruce Borden implemented the ideas outlined in the Gaines and Shapiro memo. He described the process in an email to Willis Ware:

> I joined the RAND Corporation in 1978. My first assignment was to "improve" the MS [3A] mail system, which had been developed over the previous two years by Dave Crocker and others at RAND. MS was synthesized from the various mail packages the authors had used and researched on other systems, most notably, [DEC's] TENEX [and TOPS-20]. It was the ultimate in monolithic mail packages, attempting to provide every feature provided by all other packages. It was terrible. It was so unlike common UNIX programs that I found it totally unusable. It was also huge and slow. (We were running on a PDP-11/70!) I was supposed to speed it up and make it more robust. After about a month, I gave up. I went to my management and recommended that MS be discarded, and a much simpler package built from the ground up. MS was developed on government contract, and RAND was committed to delivering a product.
>
> At that point, I started talking with Stockton Gaines and Norm Shapiro about a memo they had written, in which they had proposed that standard UNIX files and directories be used for mail messages, along with standard UNIX commands like ls and cat [concatenate] to list and display messages. They also proposed that UNIX environments be used to hold things like current message number. Finally, they suggested that the user chdir [change directory] into a working folder to operate on it. They had proposed these ideas at the start of the MS project, but they were not able to convince anyone that such a system would be fast enough to be usable. I proposed a very short project to prove the basic concepts, and my management agreed. Looking back, I realize that I had been very lucky with my first design. Without nearly enough design work, I built a working environment and some header files with key structures and wrote the first few MH commands: inc, show/next/prev, and comp. Show/next/prev were one command—it looked at its name to determine which flavor to be. With these three, I was able to convince people that the structure was viable. This took about three weeks.
>
> About this time, I also came up with the name MH—Mail Handler; I needed a name, and I couldn't think of anything better. I've never liked the name! Over the next six months, I completed the basic MH commands: inc, show, next, prev, comp, repl, forw, (Steve Tepper wrote dist), rmm, rmf, folder(s), scan, refile, and pick. I then wrote mhmail, anno, ali, and prompter (because I was tired of using [the editor] vi to do simple composes).
>
> There were so many "small" decisions made during this process, it is amazing how consistent MH turned out to be. For example, I needed a way to name a folder as an argument to the MH commands, and I didn't want the user to have to type -folder foo. Even with abbreviations (a very non-UNIX design decision), this was too cumbersome. So, I introduced the +folder syntax. This also simplified the syntax when two folders could be specified (refile, for example).

Because everything was modularized, I was able to add message names, like first and last without changing anything but a library routine. Many initial users wanted shorter names for commands—even the mostly four-letter lengths were too long for most users. Rather than rename the basic commands, I designed MH for use with shell aliases. Most users preferred n and p for next and prev, for example. Another common request was to combine rmm and next, which was commonly aliased as rn, or, for me, as , (that's right, a comma).

There are a few other design decisions which have been very successful. Default switches and global settings in the .mh_profile file worked very well. Pulling files out of the user's mail drop into an MH folder with inc provided a clean interface between the external mail delivery environment and MH.

Some early decisions have been changed by later developers of MH. For example, I felt that the backquote conventions of the [UNIX] shell were too clumsy for most users, so I didn't provide an mhl program, and pick had scan and file switches to make it useful. I also kept most changeable information in the .mh_profile file in an attempt to speed up MH operations. Most of these variables have been moved into other context files within the MH tree. I think MH worked and has survived for many reasons. First, it is very UNIX-like. There isn't much to learn to use it. Second, it keeps its own context, which is almost completely independent from anything else the user is doing. A user can run inc or comp anywhere and any time without affecting his current context. Mail isn't something you stop to do—mail processing is interwoven into the fabric of a user's daily activities. You're running a program and discover a bug, you send a quick mail message, perhaps piping the output of the program into mail. No other package that I know of makes this type of interwoven mail handling so easy and intuitive.

Finally, the structure of the source tree and the implementation of a comprehensive support library have made MH command development and support very easy. Any good UNIX programmer can modify an MH command, fix a bug, or add a new command with a few hours of source tree review.

I have a few regrets with MH. After using MH for a few years, I decided that some fundamental functionality of e-mail communication was missing. For example, I'd send a message to someone asking some simple question, and when I finally got a "yes" message back, I had no idea what the original question was, and no easy way to find it with MH. The bigger requirement here is for conversation support. Embedding replied-to messages in the body of a reply message is insanity. E-mail packages should provide automatic retrieval of the replied-to message. The In-reply-to: component is sufficient for this. Imagine being able to walk down a multi-branching tree of messages [that represents] a long-running conversation on some topic and its related topics. This is still missing from MH and other mail packages.

For many years, MH was limited to 999 messages in a folder. I made this decision consciously—anyone with that many messages in one folder needed to divide it up into subfolders. I'm not sure I should have imposed my own views this way. It was many years from the time MH was completed until it was put in the public domain. I developed MH on RAND's own money (the MS development contract had been completed), and RAND worried about legal ramifications of releasing MH to the world. I'm very glad that MH has become public domain and that it is so widely used. Although I've done many exciting things in my career, I get the most satisfaction from MH, knowing how widely it is used and how well it has aged. I am also thankful to all the people who have worked on MH and enhanced it over the years. MH still has the same flavor, and when I look at the source tree, it is still familiar after 14 years!

Another Perspective

Stock Gaines provided another perspective with his recollections in an email to Willis Ware:

It is now 15 years since the beginning of MH, and inevitably there are some differences in what we all remember about those days. Herewith, I include some of my own recollections. The memo from Norm and me speaks for itself. After the memo, there was a meeting to discuss it, at which almost everyone present (who shall remain nameless) opposed it. Arguments were given about inefficiencies, etc. Bruce arrived at RAND a month or so after this. When he discovered our memo in the late spring of 1977, he came to talk to me and told me that he thought it would be pretty straightforward to create a mail system such as Norm and I had described. At that time, I headed a project funded by the Air Force, and I thought that this work would be appropriate, so I provided the support for Bruce.

My recollection is that six days after our conversation, Bruce showed us an initial version with about six commands working! I was extremely impressed with what Bruce was able to do, and naturally pleased that the ideas from the memo were validated. Bruce suggests that there was an initial working version in about three weeks, so probably what he demonstrated earlier wasn't complete enough to use.

The next several months were quite exciting. It is a prime example of experimental computer science, and it is impossible to imagine that MH would have evolved to what it became with more formal software engineering practices. To have begun with a full requirements specification and a top-level design would have been to rob the whole project of its creative energy.

During the initial period of development, all of the work and most of the ideas came from Bruce. However, others did contribute, including Norm and me, and also Bob Anderson. Bruce made one significant invention that I found particularly impressive. The various commands for handling messages (for example, forw) needed to be able to work on subsets of the messages in a directory. Specifying a range was easy, but specifying by date or other contents of a message or header was not. We appeared to be in danger of ending up with an extremely complex command format for MH.

Bruce's elegant solution was to define a separate function, pick, to do the selection. The initial implementation simply linked all selected messages into a subfolder, from which the desired activities could be carried out (also an elegant idea). Subsequently, other ways of using the results of the pick command have been devised, but the insight of making pick a separate function was profound and has contributed greatly to the success of MH.

A User's Perspective

Funded by RAND's contract with the USAF, MH had a varied history: From a hallway conversation about a memorandum in 1977 through a small, few-command demonstration of the central ideas over a long weekend of six or so days through full-scale development within a year or so through a long series of improvements, refinements, and documentation to its most recent version 6.8.3, it—and its descendants—have achieved widespread distribution to an estimated tens of thousands of sites.

Nonetheless, there was only limited interest in the commercial world. The product was known in academic and research circles, but there was little effort to promote it commercially. While RAND did indeed license IBM to use it in its own products, MH never caught on as a commercial product, probably due in part to the concurrent rise of the desktop microcomputer, its specialty software, and its attraction to an entirely different user community. RAND did make extensions to MH in 1984 that aimed it toward becoming a component of a corporatewide office information system. At the request of the University of California, Irvine, which had taken over MH maintenance in 1982, eventually RAND put the MH software into the public domain. For many years, on request and for a modest fee, RAND distributed a magnetic tape containing MH and (usually) a companion RAND editor (e).

Marshall Rose and colleagues at UCI picked up MH and maintained it with bug fixes, documentation, and small revisions in its coding. Eventually, the effort drifted from UCI completely into the open-software community and was renamed New MH [nmh].

There is an important distinction between users who send and receive mail and those who send and receive but also process mail—that is, deal not only with individual messages one at a time in correspondence fashion but also with single messages or with groups or collections of messages for various other purposes. The latter addition—processing—is in the context of an office information system as opposed to an office mail system. Undeniably, contemporary personal-terminal mail systems have features that are important in the information-processing–system sense, e.g., the ability to handle attachments to email messages, the automatic handling of attachments or text in other languages or other formats, such as images or graphics. At the same time, some processing that can efficiently be done in MH is awkward in them, e.g., selecting a subset of unsorted messages on the basis of some criteria, such as sender, subject, date, or content, and dealing with the group as a single unified entity.

In the case of MH, imaginative innovations that occurred more than 25 years ago have often influenced or become incorporated into contemporary email systems. Among them were the following:

- First and foremost, MH is fully integrated with the OS under which it runs—generally, UNIX or one of its variations. This, in turn, implies that MH commands are executed in the UNIX shell and thus can be freely used in UNIX scripts to process email messages. Thus, processes—or combinations of actions—unique to a given user can readily be implemented, e.g., find all messages from a given sender and refile them into another folder or folders, maintain a log of all such actions, forward one or more messages to a prescribed group of addressees.
- Secondly, each MH message is a UNIX file which means that it is available via an editor to make, for example, annotations; content corrections, such as spelling errors; add references; combine messages; or extract sections from a message for other uses (for example, to incorporate into a document). Moreover, each message is accessible to any UNIX command.
- MH can efficiently put a message into any number of additional email folders with a single command and the names of the folders. If the same set of other folders is repeatedly used, a UNIX alias or script can implement the whole process. Compare that to the multiple mouse actions and clicks of graphically based mail systems for desktops that move a copy to other folders, one at a time.
- Moreover, filing a message into many folders uses the UNIX file-linking feature. There is only one copy of a message; all others link to it. Thus, storage space is conserved whereas, in desktop systems, there is usually a separate copy of the message for each destination electronic folder. This ensures that all copies of a message are synchronized with respect to content.
- MH has a pick function that allows identified groups of messages to be scanned for specified entries or words or Boolean combinations thereof. Moreover, the resulting set of messages (identified by number and by folder name) can be processed (e.g., refiled to a different folder, forwarded as an email, deleted, scanned).

Thus, processing large amounts of email in MH and maintaining the collection in an orderly library or archival structure can be done efficiently and even in an automatic or scheduled fashion.

There was an independent effort by James Guyton to provide MH with a more efficient 2-D graphical user interface—in particular, one that made scanning, reading, and deleting mail more convenient. Known as hm, it was in limited use within RAND and provided a split-screen display, with a list of inbound messages in the top half and the content of a selected message in the bottom half.

Unfortunately for MH, it suffered from a lack of funding commitment to add features that would have made it more competitive with current desktop mail systems. However, the principles and features laid out for MH in 1977–1978 are as valid today as then, provide much extensibility to accommodate the desires and needs of individual users, and can help point the way for future office information systems.

The Developers' Present Views

The innovators of MH expressed their current views in these brief snippets.
Norm Shapiro provided these observations in May 2006:

> There are three important things about MH.
> 1. Each msg is a UNIX file; hence, the full power of UNIX is available to process (manipulate) messages.
> 2. MH commands are UNIX shell commands; it is fully integrated with the OS [UNIX]; it has full access to the OS command structure.
> 3. MH has a .context file to keep track of itself and also user activities.

> The netnews way of storing and distributing news postings is due to mh.

> Nearly 30 years after it was conceived, mh and its progeny continue to be used by thousands—probably tens of thousands—of people. Few computer systems can claim that. By any reasonable measure mh is a rousing success. If I [were] to be asked what was my life's most important intellectual accomplishment, I will say it was the role that I played in mh.

> Because of its architecture, every year mh grows more powerful and useful. Every time somebody invents a more versatile shell, mh grows more versatile. Every time somebody invents a more efficient file system, mh becomes more efficient.[70]

Bruce Borden offered this recollection by email in April 2006:

> I remember [the demo version] taking about 4–5 days, one weekend plus 2–3 days to demo the first commands: inc, show (and its variants next [and] prev), comp [and] send [and] rmm, file, repl and others followed over the next couple of weeks. A complete, usable environment took less than 2 months. Then we ran into the 1000 message limit I coded in, and when I upped that to 10,000, we bumped into that a few months later, which led to a lot of work to handle arbitrary size folders. Then we started working on mime messages, and other things that kept people busy for years.[71]

Dave Crocker provided this commentary in April 2006:

> A Personal view of the impact from email work done at The RAND Corporation in the mid-1970's: MH took MS user functionality and implemented it in a style far better suited to the Unix operating and file system, as well as the Unix quick-commands user model. That is, each function was a Unix command, with inter-command context being stored externally. The evolution of MH affected an entire generation of network R&D engineers, since it was the email client of choice around the Arpanet and Internet for perhaps 15 years.[72]

---

[70] Norm Shapiro (2006).

[71] Borden (2006).

[72] Crocker (2006).

Artificial-Intelligence Research

The Beginnings of Artificial Intelligence

The RAND Corporation played a major role in the early development of AI.[73] Of the 20 chapters in the first published book on AI,[74] six had been previously published as RAND research reports. Much of this early work in AI was the result of the collaboration of two RAND employees, Allen Newell and Cliff Shaw, and a RAND consultant, Herb Simon of the Carnegie Institute of Technology (later to become Carnegie Mellon University).

Newell, Shaw, and Simon: The Development of List-Processing Languages

Beginning in the mid-1950s, Newell, Shaw, and Simon's (NSS's) research on the LT machine, their chess-playing program,[75] and the GPS defined much of the AI-related research during the first decade of AI. Their work encompassed research areas that are still prominent subfields of AI: symbolic processing, heuristic search, problem solving, planning, learning, theorem proving, knowledge representation, and cognitive modeling. At RAND, they left a legacy of publications that gave AI many of its building blocks and much of its momentum.

It is important to note that this surge of AI activity at RAND did not take place in isolation. It occurred at a time and place at which a host of fundamental notions about computer science and technology was being generated. In the 1950s, RAND was involved in designing and building one of the first stored-program digital computers, the JOHNNIAC (named after John von Neumann, a RAND consultant in the late 1940s and early 1950s). It was in operation from 1953 to 1966, and NSS used it extensively in their work on information-processing theory.

George B. Dantzig and his associates were inventing linear programming, Lester R. Ford and Raymond Fulkerson were developing techniques for network-flow analysis,[76] Richard Bellman was developing his ideas on dynamic programming,[77] Herman Kahn was advancing techniques for Monte Carlo simulation,[78] and Lloyd S. Shapley was revolutionizing game theory.[79] Stephen Kleene was advancing understanding of finite

---

[73] Bob Anderson excerpted this discussion from Klahr and Waterman (1986a). The original paper has an extensive bibliography of 123 entries; it gives a sweeping overview of the RAND research on AI and related topics and introduces a comprehensive book. Willis Ware edited and added some footnotes and other material.

[74] Feigenbaum and Feldman (1963).

[75] Cliff Shaw is reported to have said that one of the most difficult decisions in the chess-playing work was the methodology for representing the chess board and the position of the players' pieces within the software.

[76] Ford and Fulkerson (1962). Also published by Princeton University Press, 1962. Also see their reports in the series *Notes on Linear Programming* (Dantzig, 1953, 1954a, 1954b, 1954c, 1954d, 1955, 1956, 1958; Dantzig, Ford, and Fulkerson, 1956; Dantzig and Fulkerson, 1954; Dantzig, Orchard-Hays, and Waters, 1954; Dantzig and Orden, 1953; Dantzig, Orden, and Wolfe, 1954; Ford and Fulkerson, 1954, 1955, 1956a, 1956b, 1957; Fulkerson, 1958).

[77] See, for example, Bellman and Kalaba (1959).

[78] Kahn (1955).

[79] See, for example, Shapley (1951a).

Herb Simon, Cliff Shaw, and Allen Newell, the famous NSS team of early artificial-intelligence research

automata,[80] Alfred Tarski was helping to define a theory of computation,[81] and James T. Culbertson[82] and Alton S. Householder[83] were investigating the relationship between neural nets, learning, and automata.

Within this milieu, Newell, Shaw, and Simon were developing methods and directions for AI research. Perhaps equally important was their development of appropriate computational tools for AI programming. Using the notion of linked-list structures to represent symbolic information, Newell and his associates developed the first symbol-manipulating and list-processing languages, a series of information-processing languages

---

[80] Kleene (1951).

[81] Tarski (1951).

[82] Culbertson (1952).

[83] Householder (1951a, 1951b).

(IPLs) that culminated in IPL-V.[84] In their 1963 paper, Daniel Bobrow and Bert Raphael (both of MIT at the time, but also RAND consultants) included IPL-V as one of the earliest and most highly developed list-processing languages.[85] Because of RAND's unique computing environment and its close ties to the Carnegie Institute of Technology, several Carnegie graduate students were attracted to RAND, and several Ph.D. dissertations emerged, including those of Fred Tonge[86] and Ed Feigenbaum.[87] During the early 1960s, Feigenbaum, in collaboration with Simon, continued to publish RAND reports describing his experiments with his verbal-learning program, elementary perceiving and memorizing (EPAM).[88] Even after completing his work at Carnegie, Feigenbaum remained a RAND consultant and was highly influential in RAND's research on expert systems and expert-system languages that emerged in the early 1970s.

Newell and Simon also were RAND consultants during the 1960s and 1970s. One of their associates, Donald A. (Don) Waterman, joined RAND in the mid-1970s and brought much of their influence on the use of production systems to RAND's first work on expert systems. But AI also had its share of controversy, at RAND as elsewhere. Given its quick rise to popularity and its ambitious claims, AI soon had its critics.[89] One of the most prominent, Hubert Dreyfus, published his famous critique of AI while consulting at RAND.[90]

Expert Systems

In the early 1970s, Bob Anderson and his associates began directing their attention toward providing aids for inexperienced computer users. The objective was to enable these users to exploit the power of computers, and even to program them, without having to become computer sophisticates. At the same time, RAND researchers were becoming increasingly interested in intelligent terminals and the possibility that such terminals might eventually be developed into powerful, individualized, computer workstations.

One of the initial goals of this group was to develop a simple, English-like language for computer users who were not programmers. Such a language, combined with intelligent terminals, could bring computers to a wide range of potential users by providing an easy-to-use, interactive environment in which to work.

The consulting work of Feigenbaum and his associates at Stanford in the early 1970s, particularly in their use of rule-based models in a system that became known as MYCIN,

---

[84] Newell (1963), Newell and Tonge (1960).

[85] Bobrow and Raphael (1963).

[86] Tonge (1959, 1960).

[87] Feigenbaum (1959, 1961). He is the Kumagai Professor of Computer Science Emeritus at Stanford University. Prior to coming to RAND, he was a graduate student at Carnegie Institute and studied under Simon.

[88] Feigenbaum (1964), Feigenbaum and Simon (1961a, 1961b, 1961c, 1962), Simon and Feigenbaum (1964).

[89] Simon and Newell (1958).

[90] Dreyfus (1965).

influenced the RAND effort.[91] Anderson and his associates were particularly impressed with MYCIN's explanation facilities and its very readable, English-like output. MYCIN's input, however, lacked this English-like quality, because it had to be programmed in Lisp, a high-level programming language that was much too sophisticated for novice computer users. Therefore, RAND set out to build a language that allowed simple, English-like input as well as output.

That effort resulted in RITA (RAND intelligent terminal agent), a language for developing intelligent interfaces to computer systems.[92] Nonprogrammers could read RITA's unique, English-like syntax fairly easily, and its control mechanism gave RITA programs easy access to the local OS. The language was used for developing not only interface programs but also simple, exploratory expert systems. Problems that arose from attempts to develop expert systems in RITA (e.g., slow execution speed and the limited expressiveness of the syntax) led eventually to the development of the rule-oriented system for implementing expertise (ROSIE).

When Philip Klahr and Stanley J. Rosenschein joined RAND's AI staff in 1978, rule-based systems became a major focus of research. Six RAND researchers specializing in rule-based systems gathered for an intensive, two-day workshop to design the next-generation rule-based language. The result was the initial design of ROSIE.[93]

ROSIE was used in the development of several expert systems in a variety of application domains. In one application, RAND researchers developed the legal-decisionmaking system (LDS), a prototype expert system to assist attorneys and claim adjusters in settling product-liability cases. This system enabled researchers to explore the feasibility of applying knowledge-engineering techniques to the legal area. The work on legal reasoning, which initially focused on product liability in general, was later narrowed to the analysis and settlement of asbestos cases.

A second noteworthy application of ROSIE was in the area of military planning. A prototype expert system called the tactical air-target recommender (TATR) was developed to help targeters select and prioritize airfields and target elements on those airfields.[94] The resulting program contained approximately 400 ROSIE rules.

Another military application of ROSIE was also under way at RAND during the early 1980s. The RAND strategy-assessment center (RSAC) was designed to provide military strategists with a war-gaming facility.[95] It combined a set of automated programs, or agents, with human teams to model superpower decisionmaking in conflict situations. RSAC used ROSIE to develop and implement the rule-based scenario agent,

---

[91] The name derives from the pharmaceutical world in which many antibiotics include the suffix letter-group -mycin (Shortliffe, 1976; Buchanan and Shortliffe, 1984).

[92] Robert Anderson et al. (1977), Anderson and Gillogly (1976).

[93] Waterman et al. (1979).

[94] Callero, Waterman, and Kipps (1984).

[95] Paul Davis and Winnefeld (1983).

a policy-level model of nonsuperpower behavior. ROSIE also influenced RSAC's development of RAND-ABEL™,[96] a C preprocessor that facilitates the encoding of rules and decision tables in a C-based environment.[97]

As expert-system research grew at RAND and in the AI community, Frederick (Rick) Hayes-Roth, Don Waterman, and Douglas B. Lenat (of Stanford University at the time, but also a RAND consultant) organized a workshop in 1980 on rule-based systems and their application to the development of knowledge-based expert systems. This workshop produced the first comprehensive book on building expert systems, which included a detailed comparison of expert-system–building languages. Expert systems quickly became a prominent subfield of AI research and provided a new set of tools for application in government and industry.[98]

Knowledge-Based Simulation

Simulations are most often costly to build, poorly organized, inadequately understood by users, difficult to modify, and poor in performance. Since the early 1960s, RAND has explored and developed techniques to make simulations more useful, understandable, modifiable, credible, and efficient.

Much of RAND's research in simulation methodology in the 1960s revolved around the development of the SIMSCRIPT language and its successor, SIMSCRIPT-II.[99] A research group headed by Philip Klahr focused on applying AI and expert-system technology to simulation. The goal was to develop a research environment that would help users build and refine simulations with which to analyze and evaluate various outcomes. ROSS, an English-like, object-oriented simulation language, was the primary result of this work.[100] ROSS provided a programming environment in which users could conveniently design, test, and modify large, knowledge-based simulations of complex mechanisms.

Simulations written in ROSS were expert systems: They embodied a human expert's knowledge of the objects that comprise the simulation domain. To build a ROSS simulation, it is necessary to specify the domain objects, their attributes, and their behavioral rules. ROSS was used to design and build several military simulation systems, including a strategic air-battle simulation called SWIRL and a tactical ground-based combat simulation called TWIRL.[101]

The TWIRL system simulated a ground-combat engagement between two opposing military forces. It included troop deployment, artillery firing, air interdiction, and

---

[96] "The name RAND-ABEL stands for nothing in particular" (Hall et al., 1985, p. 1, fn. 1).

[97] C is a computer programming language.

[98] Philip Klahr and Waterman (1986b).

[99] Kiviat, Villanueva, and Markowitz (1968).

[100] McArthur, Klahr, and Narain (1984, 1985).

[101] Philip Klahr et al. (1984).

electronic communication and jamming. TWIRL was developed to experiment further with the ROSS language and to provide a prototype simulation that could be used to explore issues in electronic combat.

RAND's work in the general AI field also included exemplary programming, which generates computer programs from examples;[102] machine-aided knowledge acquisition;[103] knowledge-based systems;[104] and distributed AI.[105]

Computational Linguistics[106]

In the same period as the major impetus on AI, the early promise of automatic machine translation of text from one language to another (the emphasis at RAND was on translation from Russian to English) produced only modest systems, and the goal of fully automated machine translation was abandoned [at RAND] in the early 1960s. The research in machine translation did, however, serve to elucidate the difficult problems of automated language understanding and translation. As a result, work in this area turned more toward fundamental and generic issues of linguistic theory, and RAND engaged in over a decade of activity in computational linguistics.

By 1967, RAND researchers had produced a wealth of literature (over 140 articles) on linguistic theory and research methods, computational techniques, the English and Russian languages, automatic content analysis, information retrieval, and psycholinguistics.[107] In addition, David G. Hays produced one of the earliest textbooks on computational linguistics.[108]

During the 1960s, RAND provided a center in which natural-language researchers from all over the world could meet, communicate, and collaborate. Special seminar programs and summer symposia provided ample opportunities for researchers to exchange ideas and test theories.[109] Work at RAND during this period included a number of developments: Martin Kay and his associates were working on the MIND system which focused on research in morphology [Kay and Martins, 1970], semantic networks [Kay and Su, 1970; Shapiro, 1971; Shapley, 1951a, 1951b, 1952a, 1952b], and parsing [Robert Kaplan, 1970, 1971; Kay, 1967]. Jane Robinson [Robinson and Marks, 1965a, 1965b] was developing a new syntactic

---

[102] Faught et al. (1980).

[103] Hayes-Roth, Klahr, and Mostow (1980).

[104] Lenat, Hayes-Roth, and Klahr (1979).

[105] Waterman and Peterson (1980); Thorndyke, McArthur, and Cammarata (1981).

[106] The following discussion is excerpted from Philip Klahr and Waterman (1986a), with slight editing and carrying over of references by Willis Ware.

[107] Hays, Henisz-Dostert, and Rapp (1967).

[108] Hays (1967).

[109] Kochen et al. (1964).

analyzer; Roger Levien and Melvin "Bill" Maron were developing the Relational Data File for information retrieval and question answering [Levien, 1969; Levien and Maron, 1965, 1966]; Larry Kuhns [1967, 1970] was developing a sophisticated query language for database inference; and, in a somewhat different area, work was beginning on a new theory of "fuzzy sets."[110]

The Perfect Buddy

This story is best told in a memorandum written by Willis Ware in January 1983.[111] The material that follows is an excerpted and slightly edited version. It illustrates another but somewhat different interaction between RAND and its clients, in this case the USAF and the Defense Advanced Research Projects Agency (DARPA, formerly ARPA).

There is a future vision of how an aircrew will relate to, interact with, and control the air vehicle, its sensors, and its weapons. What is this vision? Can it ever happen? Whether it ever takes place exactly as characterized below is in a sense immaterial; but it can provide a way to judge whether other advanced avionics programs are on an appropriate path.

Imagine a bubble in the sky that contains an aircraft, together with its weapons and sensors and crew. The design task is to organize the whole thing from a system-level point of view. In that bubble, the pilot—or larger aircrew—is faced with a workload that basically is a collection of cognitive tasks. What happens is that the relative priorities of all such tasks are constantly shifting as the pilot proceeds through his mission plan, or as external events of the world intrude. At one moment the top priority will be to miss an obstacle; at another moment, to search for threats. At yet another, the top priority will be to search for a target; but at yet another, the first importance will be splitting for home. The design job is to partition the total workload of handling the aircraft—together with its weapons and sensors all set in a combat environment of an unpredictable world—between the crew and the automated systems that support it.

There are several points to be made. First, the partitioning is undoubtedly dynamic and dependent on the mission phase. Second, on some parts of the mission the crew might well be able to adequately handle most of the workload that is present. Obviously, on other parts of the mission, though, the crew will be hard pressed to

---

[110] Bellman, Kalaba, and Zader [sic: Zadeh] (1964).

[111] This material was originally presented to an Air Force Studies Board (AFSB) meeting in November 1981 at Wright-Patterson Air Force Base; present were members of the board, the commander (Gen. Robert T. Marsh) and chief scientist (Bernard Kulp) of the Air Force Systems Command, and various participants from the Aeronautical Systems Division and Air Force Wright Aeronautical Laboratory (AFWAL). AFSB is an advisory group to the Air Forces Systems Command. It functions under the National Research Council or the National Academy of Engineering. The written document was provided on March 16, 1982. This present version is slightly edited and excludes the discussion of a USAF program on advanced avionics architectures. The term *buddy* was chosen with great care because of the connotation normally associated with the word in common usage—e.g., a friend ready to help, who does not intrude, who is supportive but not competitive.

handle the few cognitive tasks at the top of the then prioritized list. From this point of view, the automated information infrastructure of the aircraft must be astute enough to:
• "Know" where the dynamically changing partition is,
• Fill in underneath the partition on those tasks that the crew cannot do at the moment—if they need doing; and conversely,
• Relinquish tasks to the crew as it chooses to take them back or has time to.

Such a characterization would be called, in the computer science world, a perfect intelligent agent. In an operational world of aircrews, it would probably be called the "perfect buddy"—in the same spirit as a "perfect wingman." There is a whole host of questions as to just what capabilities and characteristics the buddy should have, how it would sense the partition, how it could support the pilot or aircrew, what information it needs and/or can supply.

How does one communicate with such a buddy? It is quite clear that pushing buttons and flipping switches will not be wholly satisfactory. Possibly single- or few-word spoken instructions would do for some circumstances; but on other occasions, especially in high stress periods, it would be necessary to give the buddy statements of intent probably, and, in addition, statements of purpose. Under certain circumstances, it would be satisfactory to use exemplars by means of which the aircrew would illustrate or demonstrate to the buddy what is needed and the automated system would provide it.

For that part of the task load that it is handling, the aircrew will need:
• An efficient information environment in which to work,
• An efficient means to communicate statements, and
• An expectation that the automated buddy will somehow know the context in which such statements are to be interpreted.

Thus, the unambiguous single-word command (e.g., right, left) is not likely to be satisfactory and must be replaced by simple sentences of intent or purpose (e.g., avoid the ground). Hence, the research issue in such a futuristic vision revolves in part around a language processing issue and not a simple voice recognition matter.

To illustrate, a helmet-mounted sight gives only a statement of intent; its wearer is looking in a particular direction, but he might be doing so for a variety of purposes. He intends to do something in a particular direction. For example, he might wish to:
• Train the radar,
• Train a laser designator, or
• Sight a navigational checkpoint.

Of itself, sighting in a given direction does not give a statement of purpose unless there is but one purpose in looking. Therefore, it would appear important to keep statements of intent and statements of purpose conceptually separated while we seek to understand the novel environment being outlined herein.

In this regard it is noted that voice control as now envisioned by research programs is intended as a more efficient and faster means to push buttons, select switches, and possibly shove levers. While obviously this is an important step, it is only the beginning of what spoken statements can be advantageous for.

Both statements of purpose and statements of intent will undoubtedly be voice communicated. Immediately there arises the question of what language will be permitted in the dialogue between a pilot (or aircrew) and the automated buddy. What words will be allowable? In what simple sentence structures may such words be combined for statements of intent, or statements of a purpose, or explicit commands, or exemplars? How do we exploit language processing and voice communication to provide an efficient work station for the aircrew?

Much of the research program now under way at such places as the Air Force Avionics Laboratory is clearly pertinent to the vision, but there seems to be a missing part. There is much effort on sensors; there is much effort on local processing of data; there is effort on bus systems to connect things together; but the "cerebral cortex" appears to be missing. There is no research program focused on the top-level issue of providing the automated information infrastructure that can support an aircrew as an automated buddy of some reasonable IQ. Getting there from here will almost certainly require very sophisticated computer science including heuristic programming, knowledge engineering, and exemplary programming. Classical control theory will not get us there.

The rest of the story comes from a letter of May 1984 to another USAF adviser, Charles R. Vick of Auburn University.

I want to make sure that you know about the enclosed presentation that I made to the AFSB on February 5, 1982 and of subsequent events.

I had been trying to get an AI project incorporated into the [USAF research] effort which was otherwise largely an engineering development. I decided that one way to promote the cause was to discuss it before the AFSB meeting which included both General Marsh and Dr. Kulp. I subsequently wrote the whole thing down but later extracted just the AI portion which I had called "The Perfect Buddy"—a research [effort to provide] an AI system [that] has a dynamic interface to its user.

In December 1982, Drs. [Robert S.] Cooper and [Robert E.] Kahn of DARPA visited RAND to discuss ideas for a new program. I mentioned Perfect Buddy to Bob Kahn, and in January 1983 I sent it to him as an idea for consideration. I do not have direct evidence that my paper was directly responsible for the "Pilot's Assistant" (also called the "Pilot's Associate") in DARPA's present program, but I would assume that it had some influence.

When I learned of the DARPA project, I wrote (August 1983) to Dr. Kulp and suggested that he interact with DARPA to make sure that the Air Force had a major piece of the effort. His reply of September 1983 indicated that the conversations were taking place and, to my amusement, acknowledged that [the program] "in 1982 your briefing went a little unnoticed. . . ."

I give you this background so that you will know what the AFSC has already been told via the AFSB, and where it stands in thinking about AI. Incidentally, it is still an uphill battle. It might come to pass if the Air Force and DARPA get coordinated, in which case AFWAL will probably become the "executive agent" in behalf of DARPA for the AI-in-the-cockpit work.

By way of epilogue, there is no oral or documentary evidence that the "perfect buddy" paper lead to the "pilot's associate" program, but the calendar timing suggests that it might have. In any event, the USAF and DARPA did get together.

Department of Defense Computer Institute

In the beginning of the computing phenomena, there were two kinds of movers and shakers.[112] The categories were roughly academic and industrial. The academics had time to meet and think and an incentive to document. The industrials were so engrossed in their activities that sometimes little record of events was set down.

The military had pressing problems and embraced computing before laying a proper skill foundation for such activities. They were led into expensive and frequently unsuccessful developments by teams of enthusiastic sales people and marketeers (both in-house and out) who would accept any set of requirements if the reward were high enough. The world had many cost-plus military contracts, and some contractors may have bid low feeling that there was nothing to lose or without an adequate skill and experience base. There was no clearinghouse of contract progress and completion information, with the result that companies with massive overruns and late deliveries were not penalized in bidding for new work.

The distant early warning (DEW) line of northern radars led the way; the military needed radar defense against a Soviet threat coming over the polar regions. RAND was following these developments quite closely and became interested in team training as opposed to individual skill training. Eventually, this led to a RAND spinoff of the SDC to do the analysis and programming for the new air defense system—SAGE.

Bob Patrick and Willis Ware lived in different worlds but met frequently to discuss trends and the computing outlook in general. Bob worked in industry and was a RAND consultant one day per week. Willis traveled extensively in high USAF circles and got to see military decisionmaking. With colleagues Keith Uncapher and Pat Haverty, they formed a critical mass of computing opinion. Together, they concluded that the USAF needed to make better computer-procurement decisions.

---

[112] The following discussion mixes excerpts from email conversations with Bob Patrick and Pat Haverty, quoted sections from a summary discussion of the Department of Defense Computer Institute (DODCI) written by Patrick, and original parts by the author. Additional wording has been inserted into the quoted sections to improve the flow of readability.

At that time—the turn of the 1960s—the Strategic Air Command (SAC) had decided to implement a wholly new, computer-based command-control system nicknamed 465L. Concurrently, an SAC colonel stationed at RAND (Col. William M. Jones, who joined RAND after his retirement) was involved in a project to create a computer-based flight planner.[113] Thus, RAND had an established relationship with SAC and from visits were able to observe first hand the 465L effort—and its problems. RAND was seeing the USAF (among others) sign on to decisions for the "big-L" systems without understanding the technology, the pitfalls, their management and implementation (e.g., problems, software management, tightly controlled status reviews, realistic and stable functional system requirements and specifications). RAND sensed that it was important to educate the general officers who were the decisionmakers and could ask the right questions of other officers and of their contractors.

The RAND computer people had often discussed the skill-training issue in the government at large, and particularly in the USAF. Everybody was having trouble managing large computer-system procurements; failures outnumbered successes significantly.

At SAC, Gen. K. K. Compton was in charge of the 465L program, but he reported that he had a problem communicating with the commander in chief (CINC) of SAC—Gen. William H. (Butch) Blanchard at the time. The unfamiliar language and subtle technical issues of computer systems were not in the background of USAF officers then. It is not clear who made the proposal—it was probably the RAND people—but it was decided to put on a several-day informational series of presentations for the SAC command structure.

Haverty, Patrick, and Ware planned the "curriculum"[114] and subsequently entertained the SAC officers, including General Blanchard, for 2.5 days of lectures on the basics of computers, how they worked, the concepts of software, their special terminology, and the like. The event concluded with a "graduation dinner" at the Fox and Hounds restaurant in Santa Monica (since closed).

The success of the SAC affair led the RAND team to consider running a similar series of events in the Washington area for high-ranking officials who had to deal with this strange new thing called a computer. The proposal was made—with SAC's support—and eventually all details were worked out. General LeMay had meanwhile moved from SAC into the Pentagon; he would have been familiar with the matter.

General LeMay had become chair of the DoD Joint Chiefs of Staff. In the spring of 1964, General LeMay established the DODCI under DoD regulation 5160.49 and assigned the Navy as host agency.[115] A press release announcing the DODCI was dated March 16, 1964.

---

[113] Jones, Shapiro, and Shapiro (1959). According to RAND lore, the abbreviation was initially FLOP; General LeMay, head of the SAC until July 1957, refused to hear the work briefed until the abbreviation was changed to remove the suggestion that anything in SAC "flopped."

[114] The curriculum planning was done in a rented room at a motel that once stood on Sunset Boulevard in Los Angeles just west of its intersection with the I-405 freeway.

[115] DoD (1976).

The Navy had several large computer developments under way, all managed out of the Washington Navy Yard in southeast Washington. Since there was space at the Navy Yard and since all of the initial DODCI students were to be from the Washington military establishment, the chosen initial site was the Navy Yard. Navy CAPT Horace Stan Foote would be the host.

The students were generals and admirals—you had to have stars to come. The sessions lasted about a week, and Patrick served as acting director, as well as lecturing on computer applications.

While the official bureaucracy ground on, several major defense and other military organizations provided a group of about a dozen civilian lecturers: Bellcomm; director, defense research and engineering (DDR&E); DIA; IBM; MITRE Corporation; Planning Research Corporation (PRC); RAND; SDC; secretary of defense; U.S. Navy; and UNIVAC. Many of us knew one another, all had encountered decisionmakers who were uneducated about computing, and each of us convinced management that it was a worthy cause and that they should stand the time and costs. The initial set of instructors reran the course several times.

The transition to the permanent cadre was unremarkable. There was no coaching or transition; the permanent director answered to Captain Foote. The DODCI cycled for about two years from the Washington Navy Yard and later became a part of the curriculum at the National Defense University. The RAND team saw a problem, solved it, a temporary solution grew into a permanent one, and the services were better able to handle their assigned duties.

Officer Career Paths

In a related development, Willis Ware and Bob Patrick got the USAF to properly identify officers with computer skills and assign them correctly.[116] When Patrick was in the USAF, each officer's personnel records contained a military occupational specialty code (MOS). The MOS reflected the experience, education, and skill set of each individual. When computing burst on the scene, there was no MOS to reflect that skill set. Officers with essential and scarce computer skills were routinely assigned to noncomputing jobs. Willis Ware and Bob Patrick discussed this problem and decided that it needed correcting.

RAND was closely tied to the USAF and had unusual access to the top officers. RAND also had a procedure that guaranteed that such access would not be abused. With coaching from Willis, over a period of months, Bob made a case for an MOS in computing.[117] The arguments were written up, vetted thoroughly within RAND, and finally

---

[116] This section is based on material provided by Bob Patrick in April 2006.

[117] The MOS was renamed to AFSC.

published as a formal RAND recommendation to the air staff: "Identifying and Training Computer Personnel to Meet USAF Needs," in the fall of 1965.[118]

Nelson Lucas, the department drafter, made a pyramid out of Styrofoam® showing how individuals with various base computer specialties could grow (with proper career paths) into the senior decisionmakers that USAF needed. The team made several trips carrying this pyramid in its special fitted case to brief various groups (within the USAF and out).

With the AFSC skills properly identified, together with a career progression through the ranks defined, senior USAF officers would eventually have proper experience and seasoning. Thus, the DODCI solved an immediate education problem, and the official computer-specialty codes provided a permanent solution.[119]

The importance of this action lay in providing the USAF with a mechanism for attracting and retaining officers—especially younger ones—with a broad background in computer and information matters. Previously, younger officers with a computer background would find themselves assigned to some minor computer task (e.g., running an IBM 1401 machine at some remote location) or to a completely non–computer-related activity (e.g., running an administrative support function). They quickly discovered that the way to a computer career was to leave the USAF for a civilian position. Prior to the 51xx codes, there had been no way for an officer to have a career in the USAF and specialize in the computer field, which, at that time, was in vigorous growth everywhere.

Given the freedom that RAND had to interact with the USAF at all organizational levels and given the research staff's freedom to engage in collateral activities that were not formal studies, RAND did two things that made an enormous difference to the USAF and the world: DODCI and the AFSC-51xx career path for USAF officers. Both are examples of things that helped make RAND well known in the computer field.

Software

Any profession has its unique and specialized tools. In the case of software, the people who communicate the desires of a user with a problem to an analytic machine of some sort play such a role. For punched-card equipment, the intermediary people are called procedure writers; for high-speed digital machines, programmers. In either situation, the

---

[118] The formal recommendation process was very exacting and thoroughly controlled within RAND; the bar for producing one was very high. The output—a formal RAND recommendation—was addressed to the USAF chief of staff, and the USAF was obligated to provide RAND a reply stating how it would—or would not—respond together with supporting arguments and actions. Needless to say, there were only a few formal recommendations ever issued.

[119] The set of codes became known as the "51xx series," so named because the four-digit computer-related AFSCs all began with 51. The AFSC codes in computing for USAF officers set the stage for similar USAF enlisted-personnel specialties. It also provided a pattern for similar specialties in the other services. At one point, prior to the establishment of the 51xx codes, the officer-assignments desk at Brooks AFB would discuss a pending assignment action with the RAND people to make sure that officers with a computer background would be placed into appropriate job positions.

person with the problem had to describe it in enough detail that the numerical procedures to solve it could be formulated and put into the machine.

In the early days of using analytic machines, the details for using them were so complex and extensive that specialists qualified in their use emerged. This was the time of closed-shop programming. Inevitably, users who sought solutions to problems would train themselves in machine details—or come to RAND already having the knowledge—and do their own programming. This became known as open-shop programming. Most computing organizations have a mix of the two kinds.

Sometimes a programmer would have had other training and, in effect, become a peer of the research team, as opposed to being support to it. To single out a few from among many across the spectrum of peer-to-support:

- Nancy Brooks was trained as a mechanical engineer and became a superior programmer. She worked closely with the RAND physics department and contributed new insights to certain nuclear weapon–effect physics.
- Phil Wolfe, trained as a mathematician, worked closely with Dick Bellman to formulate the mathematical and software foundation for dynamic programming problems.
- Bill Orchard-Hays, trained as a mathematician, worked closely with George Dantzig and others in the development of the simplex method of linear programming.[120]
- Herbert Shukiar was long involved with military logistics studies and later personnel studies.
- Bernard Hausner and Richard Villanueva developed the SIMSCRIPT-I and -II languages, which were later commercialized and led to the founding of the California Analysis Center by Harry Markowitz.
- Thomas Sawtelle and Stephen Glaseman worked with DoD and USAF command-and-control networks.
- Many others worked so long with a particular category of problem that they accumulated enough knowledge about it to become subject-matter experts and rise to peer relationship.

Indeed, of the RAND application-programming staff, most of them were at the peer end of the spectrum. Other programmers designed and implemented utility and support software for both the JOHNNIAC (e.g., Mort Bernstein, Leola Cutler, Shirley Marks) and for commercial machines.

Leola Cutler was a senior programmer.

---

[120] Dantzig (1963). See also Dantzig (1953, 1954a, 1954b, 1954c, 1954d, 1955, 1956, 1958); Dantzig, Ford, and Fulkerson (1956); Dantzig and Fulkerson (1954); Dantzig, Orchard-Hays, and Waters (1954); Dantzig and Orden (1953); Dantzig, Orden, and Wolfe (1954); Ford and Fulkerson (1954, 1955, 1956a, 1956b, 1957); Fulkerson (1958).

Remember that JOHNNIAC needed a software suite from scratch and that early IBM machines were delivered with barebones software support.

Yet others became peer members of the several computer-science research projects—e.g., the IPL work of the NSS triumvirate, CLINFO and the various other efforts of videographics, JOSS.

As RAND moved into a completely networked computing posture entirely dependent on commercial products, the system software (i.e., the infrastructure software that makes the whole system work together properly) demanded system-level programmers as unique specialists.

Finally, in this modern environment, closed-shop application programming has attrited significantly, while open-shop, user-level programming has flourished. The dividing line between user with a problem and programmer has nearly disappeared. Moreover, a new kind of programming group has appeared—they who form a dedicated team to support and customize commercial software that is used for corporate administrative purpose (e.g., payroll and time-keeping, personnel records, library functions).

Security and Privacy

Security

In the 1950s and 1960s, the prominent conference gathering places for practitioners and users of computer technology were the twice-yearly Joint Computer Conferences (JCCs)—initially called the Eastern and Western JCCs but later renamed the Spring and Fall JCCs (SJCC and FJCC, respectively) and, even later, the annual National American Federation of Information Processing Societies (AFIPS) Computer Conference.[121] From this milieu, the topic of computer security—later to be called information-system security and currently also referred to as protection of the national information infrastructure—moved from the world of classified defense interests into public view for the first time.

A few people—Bob Patrick, Pat Haverty, and Willis Ware among others[122]—all then at the RAND Corporation (as its name was then known) had, in the late 1950s and early 1960s, been talking about the growing dependence of the country and its institutions on computer technology. It concerned them that the installed systems might not be able to protect themselves and their data against intrusive and destructive attacks. While there had been a few papers at the conferences on social effects of burgeoning computer technology, they decided that it was time to more directly bring the security aspect of computer systems to the attention of the technology and user communities.

---

[121] The first few paragraphs of this discussion are slightly edited and elaborated ones excerpted from a foreword written by Willis Ware for Pfleeger and Pfleeger (2006).

[122] Others would have included Paul Armer, Keith Uncapher, and Jim Tupac.

A fortuitous enabling event was the development within the National Security Agency (NSA) of a remote-access time-sharing system with a full set of security-access controls, running on a UNIVAC 494 machine, and serving terminals and users not only within the headquarters building at Fort George G. Meade, Maryland, but also worldwide. Willis Ware knew of the existence and details of the system.

It proved possible to have a paper about the NSA system presented in a public forum, and, with two others from RAND to help—Harold Petersen and Rein Turn—plus Bernard Peters of NSA, a group of papers was organized and offered to the SJCC conference management as a ready-made additional paper session to be chaired by Ware. The conference accepted the offer, and the session was presented at the Atlantic City (N.J.) Convention Hall in 1967.[123]

On an independent thread of the story, speaking in a light vein, Ware observed that, "in a city far, far away on the banks of the Mississippi River—St. Louis to be precise—there was installed a mighty and expensive 'big-iron' computer, naturally painted blue."[124]

In an effort to accommodate the costliness of its installation, the defense contractor had asked permission to commingle classified work for a fighter aircraft with unclassified work in a single computer functioning in a remote-access mode. The idea was to attract local businesses to use the system via remote job-entry terminals.

Driven by this request, DoD, acting through ARPA and later the Defense Science Board (DSB), organized a committee and requested that RAND provide the leadership. Chaired by Willis Ware, it was to study the issue of security controls for computer systems. The intent was to produce a document that could be the basis for formulating a DoD policy position on the matter.

The report of the committee was initially published as a classified document and was formally presented to the sponsor, DSB, in January 1970. It was later declassified and republished by RAND in October 1979 (Ware, 1979). It was widely circulated and became nicknamed "the Ware report."

The USAF followed up with two study committees that formulated an R&D plan, and the NSA sponsored a many-year series of workshops leading to the orange book and related documents and standards. But that part of the security evolution is external to RAND and its activities.[125]

Approximately concurrently, RAND was asked to conduct penetration testing of the target installation, which it did with the full knowledge of the target. Access was achieved, and, as the story goes, the RAND team offered the sponsor, ARPA, three options:

---

[123] Ware (1967b), Petersen and Turn (1967).

[124] "Big Blue" is a nickname for IBM.

[125] See, for example, James Anderson (1972), Computer Security Center (1983), Ware (1995). Most of these documents are in the bibliography of Pfleeger and Pfleeger (2006). Also, for electronic images of these historical papers, see Bishop (undated).

1. Put an appropriate message on all terminals.
2. Crash the system.
3. Inform the installation of the success.

The sponsor chose the third action.[126]

Subsequently, the RAND involvement with computer security was an occasional paper, talk, or discussion with officials or interested parties.[127] The RAND work had planted a vigorously growing seed; it was for others to nourish the effort.

It is clear that, if a data organization is to be subject to internal or external rules or law governing usage of its data (e.g., rules of use regarding privacy), then security policy and safeguards must be in place (1) to protect the installation and its data, and (2) to control access to and dissemination of the data.

Privacy

Meanwhile, in the early 1970s, Secretary of Health, Education, and Welfare Elliot Richardson had become concerned about the vast amount of personal data that the government held about its citizens. In particular, he was very sensitive to the growing use of social-security numbers (SSNs) as personal identifiers. He impaneled the Secretary's Advisory Committee on Automated Personal Data Systems to examine the issue and solicited the participation of Willis Ware (who had just completed his tenure with the DSB security activity) as an individual knowledgeable about system security. Through a series of events, Ware became chair of the committee that he described to a colleague as "the most politically balanced group I've worked with. We had young v. mature people, ethnicities of all kinds, lawyers v. non-lawyers, experts v. lay persons, male v. female, politically active individuals v. politically passive ones."

Eventually, in 1972, the committee report was delivered to HEW secretary Caspar Weinberger.[128]

The report achieved several significant goals:

- It conceived and defined the Code of Fair Information Practices, which has become the foundation for personal-information privacy law and privacy doctrine in the United States and worldwide (e.g., the European Union position).
- The Code set the relationship—one might call it the rules of engagement—between (1) the organizations collecting personal information and the data systems that held it and (2) the individual citizen about whom the personal data had been assembled.
- It provided the intellectual basis for the Privacy Act of 1974,[129] which, in turn, set the framework for other law.
- It created the Privacy Protection Study Commission (PPSC).

---

[126] James Anderson et al. (1971).

[127] Turn and Ware (1976).

[128] HEW (1973).

[129] P.L. 93-579.

Not surprisingly, President Gerald R. Ford chose Ware to be a member of the seven-person commission, and Ware served as its vice chair. The final report and five appendixes were delivered to President James Earl Carter in July 1977.[130] At the time, the PPSC report was the most complete and extensive analysis and documentation of personal-data practices in the private sector.

While the government was seen as "the privacy problem" in the 1970s, the private sector has gradually become an equal—if not dominant—part of the issue. After a flurry of privacy laws in the late 1970s and early 1980s, the social cause of personal-information privacy remained largely quiescent until the turn of the century; since then, there has been some legislation and occasional court cases. Now, data practices in both the U.S. government and in private industry drive the personal-privacy issue.[131]

Fair Information Practices

At a 1993 talk for a U.S. Department of Health and Human Services conference on health records, Willis Ware reviewed the origin of the name "Code of Fair Information Practices." He wrote as follows:

The Origin of the Phrase 'Code of Fair Information Practices'

The following reconstruction of history is based on my recollections of the time, an interchange of electronic-mail messages with John Fanning [presently with the U.S. Public Health Service, Commissioned Corps, or USPHS], and correspondence with David B. H. Martin, Executive Director of the [HEW] Secretary's Advisory Committee on Automated Personal Data Systems [SACAPDS]. The associate executive director of SACAPDS was Carole Watts Parsons, now Mrs. William Bailey.

The so-called "HEW committee," assembled and tasked by [then HEW] Secretary Elliot Richardson, had often met in Bethesda, Maryland and held meetings at the local Holiday Inn. Occasionally we would also use the NIH facilities at Bethesda for a meeting. The agenda would normally call for a 3-day meeting and on at least two occasions, a Saturday was included.

On a particular occasion, we had met on a Saturday in one of the NIH buildings. It was out-of-hours for the building and the security guard required us to sign in individually and also to give our SSNs. There was a lot of joking among committee members about this because we had been discussing the SSN in committee and regarded this activity by NIH as completely inappropriate. It was in winter because everyone had street coats.

---

[130] PPSC (1977). The appendixes were "Privacy Law in the States," "The Citizen as Taxpayer," "Employment Records," "The Privacy Act of 1974: An Assessment," and "Technology and Privacy."

[131] For a comprehensive collection of current and archived materials on privacy and its many related issues, see EPIC (undated). See especially EPIC (2002).

There had been a discussion on Friday night between me and David Martin in which he outlined the concept of adopting a set of rules that would be the basis for the relationship between a data subject and a record keeper. On Saturday morning, I made a presentation about the concept of a list of standard practices as a way of dealing with privacy issues and I also presented arguments supporting it as a reasonable and sensible approach. In discussing it, the committee undertook to construct a list of what features might be on such a list.

As we thought of them, Professor Layman Allen from the University of Michigan Law School and member of the committee wrote them on a board at the end of the meeting room. I remember that initially, there were only a few entries on the list. Computer-oriented people in the group of course thought of all manner of rules to [ensure] accuracy, correction of errors, etc.

One such proposal was to require the record keeper to notify all who had received personal information from it of the correction. We quickly estimated that it would be a back breaking task for the record keeper, and that it would be a superb source of income for the U.S. Postal Service.

David Martin and I departed the meeting for some outside obligation. We left Layman Allen in charge and when we came back an hour or so later, the group had expanded the list to [I think] about a dozen items. By that time, it was mid-afternoon and we adjourned the meeting and went home. David and I exchanged some private comments as we left that the list of rules had become very complex; we were both a little dismayed at what had happened.

The committee report . . . lists the dates of the meetings but not the places. Comparing them to calendars for 1972 and 1973, and given that the time of year was winterish, the meeting in question could have been December 16, 1972 [Saturday] or March 3, 1973 [Saturday].

The December date is more likely to have been "winterish" and had only one speaker scheduled whereas the March date seems too late, given that the agenda for it is shown as "discussion of the final report." Keep in mind that the final report printed by the U.S. Government Printing Office was presented to [then] Secretary Caspar Weinberger in June, 1973. Thus, December 16, 1972 appears to be the day on which the committee framed the essence of a Fair Code, but did not name it.

The dates of March 1–3, 1973 are shown to be the 7th and final meeting of the committee, and we would certainly have had the details of the "list of rules" and its name settled by then. While there were no formal committee meetings between December 1972 and March 1973, there were additional drafting meetings, and draft review meetings among David Martin, Carole Parsons and myself.

In the December–March interval not only did a full draft of the report get created but the lengthy list of features from December got boiled down to its present size.

I believe that this was primarily the work of David Martin and Carole Parsons, probably in discussion with me either by phone or in a review meeting in Washington. I do recall that David and I often had very lengthy phone conversations. We also worked out an arrangement for exchanging draft materials and comments between Washington and Santa Monica on an overnight basis. The December–March period was an intensive one of writing and re-writing.

After such a drafting/review meeting, David, Carole, and I were sitting around a table in the north building of the old HEW complex, probably on the 5th floor which was where the offices of the committee were. It would have been around dinner time and other people, mostly friends of David, drifted in and out. We were winding down after the day and chatting about various details of the report.

Someone came into the room, was introduced to me, and [I believe] was also characterized as having worked with or was presently with the Department of Labor. The 3 of us had been talking about our list of protective mechanisms and I suspect toying with names for it.

The individual who had drifted in mused out loud to the effect: "What we're talking about is just like the Code of Fair Labor Practices." That was a pivotal comment and promptly, David Martin first voiced the phrase "Code of Fair Information Practices." I believe we might have bandied about variations on the phrase—such as where to put the word "fair"—but one struck us as best and has survived.

The identity of the individual who commented about the similarity to the Fair Labor Practices is uncertain. There is a possibility that it was John Fanning, presently with USPHS. He believes it was not he, so for the moment, the person's identity is unknown.

It is clear however that David Martin did coin the phrase "Code of Fair Information Practices" and that it occurred in the period between December, 1972 and March 1973. Since the December event was only a week before Christmas, and drafting really got started in January, it is likely that the actual date is in February or the first part of March, 1973.

Slightly ahead of the [HEW] committee was the work of the Younger [Committee on Privacy] in the UK. There were also study groups in several other countries; there are brief summaries of reports and activities in the report about Sweden, France, Germany, Canada, and the UK.

With respect to the Younger committee specifically, pp 173–174 of the report [summarize] its work and [list] ten "safeguards" [that] bear some resemblance to a Fair Code, but are much less specific and not as crisply stated as the provisions of the Fair Code. The British Computer Society had also adopted a Code of Ethics for its people and the Younger report supported and adopted it also. There is no mention of the term "Fair Code" or even of a "Code" in the summary of the Younger report. In fact, we used its own phrase "safeguards." Had the Younger group used the phrase "Fair Code" or even "Code," I feel certain that we certainly would have acknowledged it and also used it in what we wrote.

Thus, "Code of Fair Information Practices" appears to be uniquely American and to have been originated by David B. H. Martin.[132]

---

[132] Ware (1993).

CHAPTER SEVEN

Lore, Snippets, and Snapshots

The Great Machine Fire

Since there are inevitably heat-producing components in electronic equipment, there is always the risk of fire. IBM, as would any vendor, used nonflammable components to the maximum extent feasible, and, especially, it used wire whose insulation was fire resistant. In addition, it conducted flammability tests by deliberately overheating components and areas of a completed cabinet. Nonetheless, on an otherwise routine day, there suddenly was a shout of "Fire!" in the machine room.

Fortunately, plentiful CO_2 fire extinguishers had been provided throughout the machine room, and the fire was quickly out. The unit in question—the mainframe, as the CPU was called—was, however, damaged.

On investigation, it turned out that a resistor dissipating its rated heat load had ignited nearby wiring. IBM had tested specifically for this circumstance, but, as luck would have it, the test had been conducted with the resistor and wiring in a horizontal position. The actual machine as it was built had both wiring and resistor in a vertical position, with the result that the chimney effect of the rising heat was sufficient to ignite the insulation.

The Gavel Caper

Frank Stanton, then president of the Columbia Broadcasting System (CBS), was chair of the RAND Board of Trustees from 1961 to 1967.[1] At some meeting of the board, Goldy Goldstein, RAND's executive vice president at the time, imagined a special gift for the chair and approached the computer-science department for implementation of his idea. In the words of Mal Davis,

> [Goldy] came to Ray Clewett with a [chime device] and a gavel; and told Ray that they were having a Board meeting and he wondered [whether] Ray could fix it so that when the gavel was struck it would [chime]. Ray talked to me and we came up with the idea to put a radio transmitter inside the gavel. Ray sketched out a

---

[1] There is no known documentation on this event. The facts, as related, are based solely on memories—particularly those of Mal Davis, who worked on this project.

weight [and] spring switch device that would trigger the radio transmitter to send out a pulse. I built a radio transmitter and super regenerative receiver, and tested them to be sure they would trigger the chime. George [Dietrich, member of the mechanical-shop staff] did the work on the gavel all the while consulting with Ray. Of course, the transmitter had to be rebuilt after we knew exactly what space and configuration we had to work with [in the interior of the hollowed out gavel head]. The available batteries were a big part of the space limitation.

The ingenious part of the thing was the spring [and] weight switch mechanism that George and Ray built. Mechanical damping was such that it was ready for another whack of the gavel before the [chime] was finished. There was no clue that anything was there other than a gavel. I don't remember [whether] Ray bought another [larger] gavel, but I don't think so. Anyway the gavel was pretty much normal size.

The transmitter and receiver [were] similar to what was being used for radio controlled model aircraft at the time. The gavel [electronics] package was so well done that normal handling did not reveal any movement inside.[2] If you shook the gavel hard the shaker could barely detect the insides moving around, but it didn't trigger a radio pulse. The Board meeting was [to be] held in the main conference room. The [chime] mechanism and receiver were located off stage.[3] There was no way we could monitor the show, but we were lucky. Jim Beavers[4] was in the projection room to run their slides, and he gave us a full account of what went on.

At the opening meeting, the gavel was presented to Stanton with appropriate ceremony and remarks. He, of course, wielded the gavel to call the meeting to order, and, as he banged it on the table, the gavel played forth the famous three-chime broadcast signature gong of NBC (CBS's main rival).

I believe that, after the stun of the first rap of the gavel, Stanton rapped it a number of times, even on the blackboard. There was a lot of amazement and laughing before the meeting got started, and I believe even after the meeting was over. [Goldy] later thanked Ray and told him that everything worked out just as he had hoped. The gavel was given to [the chair,] and that was the last we saw of it.

Presumably, Stanton took the gavel back to New York with him, but its whereabouts, if it even still exists, is not known.

---

[2]   Tom Ellis and Mal Davis of the department's engineering staff did this part of the project, supported by the electronics shop. Since the integrated circuit as an electronic component was yet to appear, the electronics would almost certainly have used discrete-component transistors.

[3]   Presumably, the chiming mechanism was connected to the conference room's sound system.

[4]   James (Jim) Beavers had been a member of the RAND security-guard detail but then became RAND's official photographer and audiovisual person.

Department-Head–Office Decor

At one point, probably inspired by Goldy Goldstein, who tended to be gadget-prone, some of the upper management's offices were upgraded with such features as a remotely operated automatic door closer, special accent lighting, sound-recording arrangements, and special furniture. Reluctantly, John Williams (then head of the mathematics department), also accepted a modest upgrade.

Directly across the hallway from Williams was the office of the Computer Sciences Department head—Paul Armer at the time. In his absence, a trio of pranksters,[5] in the spirit of what had happened to other offices, decided to "upgrade" his also. The automated door closer was a series of pulleys and ropes activated by a tug on a handle borrowed from a Sloan lavatory flush valve; it actually did work. The accent lighting was a rusty old kerosene lantern hung from a hook in the ceiling. The time-keeping device was a plastic child's clock—which did not function.

Upon his return, Armer was overwhelmed by the changes wrought to his office. He and John Williams shared a laughing good time about it.

After upgrading, Paul Armer's office decor included an old kerosene lantern.

---

[5]   Robert Reinstedt (the CSD administrative assistant at the time), Mort Bernstein, and Fred Gruenberger.

Oliver Alfred Gross and JOSS-1

Ed Bryan remembers this practical joke that Cliff Shaw played on a colleague intent on debugging JOSS:

> It was 1964 or so and JOSS had just become operational. Lots of RAND research-ers and [people] from around the nation were connecting to this new time-shared computing service to solve problems in the algebraic language, which was also called JOSS. My job was to help folks learn how to use the system, to write some user manuals, and to find problems with the system. Cliff Shaw, author of JOSS, did all the fixes. Oliver Gross from the math department got very interested in the system, and was a "national resource" in system debugging for [two] reasons: (1) the model in his head of how the system worked was unrelated to how the system actu-ally worked, but it was quite accurate in predicting what it did, and it suggested

Oliver Gross, mathematician, at the JOHNNIAC console

many things to try that seemed bizarre to us; and (2) Oliver always prepared an elegant presentation of the error, which he would bring in, saying, "How do you suppose that this happened?" He kept us going day after day as he found obscure problems with JOSS that needed fixing.

Cliff decided to play a trick on Oliver and modified JOSS just for Oliver. He fixed [it] so that if Oliver (and no one else) caused the same programmatic error (i.e., divide by zero, syntax error) within 5 minutes, it would send out a special message, "Dammit, Oliver, can't you get anything right?" Then it would disable itself so that the message would not reappear, at least for that day, but would appear again the next day. This foiled Oliver in trying to provide an elegant demonstration of the strange problem that he had found.

We could see his frustration as he tried to reproduce the problem, wandering the halls and scratching his head. We were having fun watching.

After a few days, he came to one of us and showed us the message, saying that he couldn't reliably reproduce it. We would just say, "That's amazing, Oliver. How did you do it?" We kept him going for several days before telling him about the trick. Happily, he forgave [us] and kept on finding and displaying real problems in JOSS.

The Soviet "Threat"

As RAND military studies became visible in the world at large, the Soviet media took to labeling the organization as "the Academy of Death and Destruction."[6] Internally, there was casual hallway talk about the possibility that it would become a target of Soviet spying or, worse, that its staff might be subverted or harmed, especially those people with high visibility.

For some reason, not known, there arose a concern in management's view that the incidence of illness in the staff seemed to be higher than might be normally expected. There was indeed concern that the staff had become a target. A study (whose details are unknown) compared the medical status of the staff with that of the general population. It is not known who did this comparison, how it was done, what data were used, or the methodology, but, in the 1950s, RAND had a full-time nurse, Lucy J. Nowicki, who probably participated at least as a source of data about the staff. The whole thing was kept very quiet.

The outcome of the study showed no significant differences between the medical problems of the staff and those of a general population. The conclusions were persuasive enough to offset any fears of deliberate Soviet intervention into RAND's personnel. However, concerns about spying continued in some minds for several decades.

---

[6] The general threat is real, and details are believed accurate, but there is no known documentation on this incident and only a minimum of memories.

Social Events

RAND sponsored annual dinner-dance events for many years. In addition, the computer people had department-level gatherings for retirements, departures, and other purposes. On one occasion—probably RAND's 25th anniversary—the affair was at the Ambassador Hotel's Cocoanut Grove in Los Angeles:

> Carol Channing entertained that night and she coaxed Frank (Collbohm) up onto the stage for a lot of banter. She called him "Mr. Cold Bomb" several times. I think she also got [Goldy] Goldstein up too, but no one recalls how she referred to him.[7]

In other years, the corporation parties were held at the several beach clubs in Santa Monica—the Jonathan Club, the Deauville Club (which burned and became a parking lot), and the Casa del Mar Club (which Synanon took over before it eventually became the Casa del Mar Hotel).

Department affairs in and around Santa Monica are reflected in the following quotations. The Surfrider was a motel at 1910 Ocean Avenue that the Loews Santa Monica Beach Hotel replaced. The other references are to restaurants in the Santa Monica area except for the Castaways, which is in Glendale.

> I certainly remember the Surfrider. We attended the lounge regularly after work. And often dropped by when waiting for [a] batch program debugging run from the computers. It was an interesting cycle: put in your job, go to the Surfrider while waiting for the job to be scheduled and run, back to RAND for the results, problem fix and re submittal, back to the Surfrider to wait. Sometimes far into the night.[8]

> At the Castaways party, the speaker was particularly funny with his dialogue. I think his name was Stan but I'm not certain. His dialogue seemed so out of character for him from my experience running his jobs in the computer room. Jim Tupac was our department head at the time. Anyway, the comment that has stuck with me in my warehouse of useless facts was his closing remark "Just remember that Tupac spelled backwards is Caput!"[9]

> I remember the Surfrider Hotel, but I don't remember retirement parties. . . . RAND had access to their shower room for noontime jogging, volleyball, etc. . . . We also had a CSD party at the Castaways, which overlooked the San Fernando Valley and had a Hawaiian theme. . . .

> One other memory: we had a CSD party at a country club . . . sometime in 1965. Shirley Marks asked me to be part of the entertainment (she was tagged to put the

---

[7] Excerpted from Ware (2006).

[8] Bryan (2006).

[9] Allen (2006).

Bill Gunning, shown standing beside the seated Willis Ware, was the chief engineer of the JOHNNIAC project.

secret entertainment together, with original songs that a few of us performed). Also in this company was Ed DeLand, who insisted on wearing a tux to the event. It was during the weeks of rehearsing for this event that I took to calling Ed "Uncle Ed," and this was a good thing for Ed because whenever he saw me he called me "nephew" rather than having to remember my name.

Among many other functions, Herman Kahn's going away party to head the Hudson Institute was held at the Surfrider.[10]

Also, should not be forgotten is the Bellevue on Ocean Avenue, [several] blocks [at the corner of Santa Monica Boulevard] from RAND. Several noon events were held there.[11]

The One-Way Wire

Punched-card machines (e.g., the IBM 407 Printing Calculator) had the capability to implement Boolean operators (e.g., AND, OR) by using the contacts of built-in relays. Electrical signals could be combined to make choices (i.e., logical decisions) about the processing flow of a problem. However, the complexity of the calculations that RAND undertook taxed the vendor-supplied capacity.

To extend the logical capability available via the plug boards on these machines, the "one-way wire" was innovated. It consisted of a small, solid-state diode (which had become available during World War II) spliced into a normal plug-board wire. Thus, electrical signals could pass one way through a wire but not the other. Two such wires could implement an AND or OR operator.

This technique was the precursor of the "diode logic" construct that became popular in the design approach to later electronic computers.

Soviet Cybernetics

In the late 1950s, exchange visits of technical delegations between the Soviet Union and the United States were occasionally arranged through diplomatic channels. One such was in computer technology. As the reigning representative of the field in the United States, the National Joint Computer Committee (NJCC)[12] organized a two-week visit to the USSR for a group of eight individuals—and a few spouses—in 1959.

---

[10] Reinstedt (2006).

[11] Rumford (2006).

[12] This group consisted of four members each from the IRE, the American Institute of Electrical Engineers, and the ACM. Its original purpose was to sponsor the twice-annual JCCs. Some years later, AFIPS, whose name was inspired by the International Federation for Information Processing (IFIP), replaced the NJCC.

At the time, Paul Armer was an ACM member of the NJCC and Willis Ware, an IRE member. Thus, two of RAND's staff were in the delegation. Upon its return, RAND volunteered to assemble the group's report. Subsequently, an oral presentation of it was given at a Boston NJCC conference, and RAND published the well-known *Soviet Computer Technology*.[13] It gave a very definitive checkpoint on the status of computer technology in the USSR.

Given such a head start on USSR computing technology, RAND was funded to translate much relevant Soviet literature and, for several years, published the *Soviet Cybernetics: Recent News Items* and the *Soviet Cybernetics Review*.[14]

Inter/Exhume

In the early days of mainframe computing, machine cycles and memory space were limited and "precious commodities." Accordingly, programmers learned to play tricks to exact the most performance from their machine. One such was nicknamed inter/exhume.[15]

In those olden days when memory was scarce and limited, programmers wanted the most possible of it, and vendors (notably IBM) would put a primitive OS into unprotected memory, and a programmer would "inter" the OS onto a tape and take all of the machine's memory for his or her problem. At the conclusion of the run, the program would then "exhume" the OS back from tape to memory, and no one need be concerned.

The procedure is not quite like the "push/pop" construct, but it is similar.

Ed Bryan provided more details:

> On unprotected machines of the day, once the application program was given control, it simply wrote out the lower part of memory, containing the OS, to a tape, and then used the memory for itself—in the case of IPL V,[16] it used it for a memory linked list. When the program finished (IPL was interpreting the [user's] instructions) it restored the OS from tape—the OS was none the wiser. Of course the program had to be such that it didn't need to call on the OS for any services—easy for IPL.

> There were also schemes for the FORTRAN OS (or IBM systems including FOR-TRAN). Lee Scantlin, at RAND, ran big calculations that needed the memory (even though the FORTRAN OS was tiny). He needed the FORTRAN format-ted I/O for the results, so, after "INTERing" the OS, he wrote that data and

---

[13] Ware (1960).

[14] For example, the first issue of *Soviet Cybernetics Review* is available (Holland, 1971). To locate other issues as well as related documents on cybernetics (about 80 total), search the RAND online publication catalog using either search parameter: "Holland, Wade" (author search) or "cybernetics" (title search).

[15] The origin of the name is uncertain, and there may also be other names for the same procedure.

[16] IPL-V is the one of the list IPLs that Newell, Shaw, and Simon innovated.

the required format statements to tape, and in a subsequent pass, with the OS restored—"EXHUMEd"—them and wrote out the formatted results.

And Ivan Finkle contributed:

> Lee Scantlin and I wrote a paper . . . that described how we got rid of the operating system to get us more usable memory.[17]

From that paper:

> A description of an operating system called NOSY (for non-system), designed to provide more core storage for the programmer than is available when using the IBM system IBSYS. This is achieved by sacrificing efficiency of input and output and, in the RAND system, at the expense of decoupling two machines and using only one. It should therefore be used only for programs that cannot run under IBSYS because of core storage requirements.

The RAND Computer Symposia

Once a year for (probably) five years in the early 1960s, RAND CSD sponsored an annual symposium to which leaders in the emerging computer industry were invited—top-level managers, research individuals, and gadflies. The origin of this event is not documented, but it probably arose from private discussions between Paul Armer and Fred Gruenberger.[18] Both shared a common interest in how the industry was advancing and in it maturation problems. Gruenberger carried the burden of putting on the affair, but he enlisted the aid of Bob Patrick, longtime consultant to the department.

Patrick wrote as follows:

> I was most impressed with his "RAND Symposium" series on computing. Each year he got official support, invited movers and shakers, prepared the agenda, ran the meeting, and produced an edited transcript. He really performed a useful service to a fledgling industry. When manufacturers were cutting each other's throats he bridged the gaps so we could educate ourselves and each other. I think he held five of them. I was invited as a participant in 1961 and 1962 and got those proceedings abstracted and published in *Datamation* [magazine].[19]

---

[17] Finkle and Scantlin (1965, p. iii).

[18] In regard to Gruenberger per se, Patrick wrote:
"At RAND his interests involved computers but he was into academic usage, not hardware or software. He did prime numbers . . . , obtained an IBM 1620, installed it (in a RAND facility) and pursued solutions to academic problems. He made a few movies and was delighted with video tape as an audio/visual medium. He attempted to "sell" video tape technology within RAND and found little interest, but that technology is now standard."
Gruenberger also ran classes for the Santa Monica Middle School—students and faculty alike. He is remembered not only for the effort itself but for his emphasis on teaching "computing," not teaching "computers."

[19] For three RAND contributions to *Datamation*, see Armer (1967), Boehm (1972), and Reinstedt and Berger (1973).

My list of *Datamation* pieces shows:
1961 RAND Symposium, Part I (Participant), 9/61
1961 RAND Symposium, Part II (Participant), 10/61
1961 RAND Symposium, Part III (Participant), 11/61
1962 RAND Symposium, Part I (Participant), 10/62
1962 RAND Symposium, Part II (Participant), 11/62

Among the participants—some of whom attended in successive years—these symposia were highly regarded as a forum in which prominent individuals in the field could have a place—a "summit meeting"—in which to exchange private views about the industry and its problems and behavior.

In an oral history taken by the Computer Museum in Santa Clara, California, Patrick continued:

TCM: And back to RAND, I'd like to ask about Fred Gruenberger and the RAND Corporation symposium series that he was responsible for.

Patrick: Gruenberger recognized a need for technical information interchange. And he organized the RAND symposiums to bring leading edge technical people together. And did that very well. I was invited to several of those, and being a member of the Datamation staff, I managed to get RAND symposiums into print. Fred taped them and transcribed them, and they ended up being inch-thick books. Datamation abstracted sections and published them.

I seem to recollect some two-part articles on consecutive months in Datamation, to try and get that same kind of information to a broad population because at that time the only education that was taking place in the field was manufacturer specific, and it was [specifically] to sell hardware. There weren't any computer sciences courses in colleges at that time, and there weren't any Ph.D.s in computer sciences. All of us had training in some other discipline.

TCM: And are you aware of any occasions where you would say that the ideas and the discussions at these meetings had any particular effect in the broader world where ideas that surfaced during a meeting were acted upon or had an impact?

Patrick: Well, the RAND tablet was discussed there. It wasn't a commercial success—RAND had one, but the mouse came out of the Xerox Parc people. It was a graphical input technique, which was the predecessor of the mouse that we all know as a way to move a pointer around on a screen. And that was an outstanding development that comes to mind immediately. I'm sure there were several more.

Professional Societies

Concurrent with the evolution of a commercial industry and the parallel development of the department came related professional societies. In the late 1940s and the early 1950s, the dominant electronically oriented ones were primarily devoted to communications and electrical power. However, small groups of practitioners aggregated around the forming computer technology and so were born the IRE Professional Group on Electronic Computers—PGEC-16 (later to become the Professional Technical Group on Computers and eventually the Computer Society of the IEEE)—the ACM, the Computer Committee of the American Institute of Electrical Engineers, and the JCC, with representatives from each of these groups.

The JCC's sole function was to sponsor and manage the twice-annual computer conferences known as the Eastern JCC and the Western JCC; later, they became the SJCC and FJCC, and, finally, the JCC was to become AFIPS, which took over the sponsorship of the conferences.

Department members were very active in these organizations, both locally in the Los Angeles region and nationally in the parent societies. At various times, department members were chairs, vice chairs, treasurers, members, or chairs of program and other conference committees or had other roles in the conferences; they were also chairs (or presidents) or vice chairs of the national organizations. The department provided the first and founding president (Willis Ware) for AFIPS.

So much activity and significant contributions by department members led to high visibility for them, so much so that many became as well known outside RAND as well as inside. The collective impact of their presence was to leave many vectors of influence within the computing community.

From the department's and corporation's point of view, the payoff was visibility in the marketplace for recruiting and for a reputation of professionalism. RAND's clients at the time were the USAF and the AEC, neither of which wanted exposure. The computer people, working primarily on unclassified, basic computer science and exploitation of computer power, provided a window to peek inside the company and give it public exposure.

The department also supported vendor user groups, whose purpose was to provide a forum for vendor and users to meet and discuss issues of mutual interest. The principal such group for RAND was IBM's SHARE, whose annual meetings were attended by several department people. As one wit put it: "It's the place to beat up on IBM." RAND provided the SHARE president for one term, James Babcock.

Microvignettes

The Marchant March
The early mechanical desktop calculators did not have a divide function; accordingly, the operator had to laboriously work through the process of long division, step by step, each time the work flow demanded a division. Therefore, processes or procedures that did not require division were much to be desired.

The later models did include a divide function, and someone quickly discovered that, by putting the right operands into the machine and calling for the divide function, it would rhythmically churn through all 20 steps of the division, making the same sound at each step. Thus, one had, in effect, 20 identical noises of wheels, gears, and levers working.

The sequence quickly became known as the Marchant march (Marchant being one of the major manufacturers of calculators).

Getting Out the Documents

The department editor, Wade Holland, had the usual trouble with authors—namely, each so liked his own words that resistance to editorial change was strong. A marked-up hard copy from the editor would often trigger a confrontation with the author. Finally, Holland hit on the solution: return a retyped copy to the author so that changes were largely hidden. Voila! Things went smoothly thereafter.

Hero of the Week

Before physical threats against computing facilities became a reality, the drapes along the north wall of the computer room were open, giving a view out over the north parking lot. One day, Jim Brown of the machine room staff glanced out and noticed an interloper attempting to steal a motorcycle parked in the north lot. A big man, he did not hesitate but went scurrying outside and foiled the attempt. Memories do not recall whether he apprehended the culprit or chased him away, but the bike was saved.

Department management immediately commissioned Ray Clewett (head of the mechanical shop) to make a multipointed, star-shaped medal several inches in diameter and to engrave on it "Hero of the Week." Hanging from a length of brass chain, it was publicly presented to Brown in the machine room within an hour after the event.

The Chiquita® Banana War

Two senior staff members mischievously started a bit of horseplay by affixing Chiquita stickers (the small ones used to identify that brand's bananas in the market) to various places in one another's offices. The byplay became known as "the great banana war."

The Mengel Joint

When Mengel returned to RAND from Harvard, one of his first assignments was to help with the assembly and installation of the newly arrived REAC. This, of course, involved much soldering, but, regrettably, Mengel's technique was not up to par. Many of his joints proved to be "cold"—i.e., the joint had not been heated enough for the solder to flow and alloy with the wire but simply stuck to them mechanically. Therefore, the joint was unreliable and the source of electrical noise.

To commemorate these events, Keith Uncapher commissioned the shop to manufacture an appropriate memento. The memento consisted of a wooden annulus approximately 4 inches square and 0.5 inch or so thick. From the midpoint of each side, a stain-

Arnold Mengel holding his replica of a Mengel joint

less steel wire ran across the open interior space to the opposite side. Where they crossed in the middle, they touched, and a glob of solder was affixed. Needless to say, the solder would not alloy with the stainless-steel wire, and so it made itself a glob, much in the image of a cold solder joint.

It is not known whether the item had a nameplate or note, but, if it did, it would be called the Arnold Mengel joint.

John Williams' Jaguar

Ray Clewett recalled,

> John D. Williams's Jaguar [roadster] to which the shop helped to add a turbo-charger. To make room under the hood for the turbocharger, a large part of the inner wall of the right front fender had to be cut away. Hence, the assistance from the shop.

John and Evie [his wife] used to do [acceleration] trials out on the Pacific Coast Highway at night. Evie held some sort of pendulum device that John had rigged up to measure acceleration.

One of the shop guys (George Dietrich) was driving the Jag on Ocean Ave. one day during the day when the accelerator stuck nearly wide open. He and John recovered the situation safely but I don't know how they did it.

Programmer Sweepstakes

As the new discipline of computer programming emerged in the 1950s, there was ongoing interest at the management level in the question: What training, what personal characteristics, what experience makes a good programmer? Since there were no academic programs training this new type of individual, the hope was that a screening test could be developed to identify persons—no matter what their experience or formal training might have been—who had promise to become a qualified programmer.

From time to time, RAND—and other organizations—would individually and sometimes collectively run a "programmer sweepstakes." A group of trained programmers would be selected and each given the same problem to work and build a running program. There is no known documentation on these trials, so it is not known the length of time allowed to complete the assigned task or how the quality of the individual programs was judged. However, since the era in question was one of limited computer-memory size and limited computing power, presumably memory demand and run time on the machine figured in the ranking of the outcome.

There is an insightful quote from Paul Armer[20] that is recalled: "Every time it's the same outcome; no matter what the training or experience of the individual, the one going in that is considered to be a good programmer proves to be the winner coming out."

Later on, psychologists and behavioral scientists were involved in trying to develop screening tests for programmer candidates. When the SDC needed a huge number of programmers for its work with the USAF air-defense systems, extensive tests were developed for measuring an individual's latent programming capability and promise.

---

[20] As head of the NAD at the time, he was instrumental in organizing the sweepstakes effort.

CHAPTER EIGHT

Epilogue

Well, that's it—the story of the RAND department that was born as part of the mathematics division, became independent and flourished until all departments were abolished, and left its mark on the world with many notable achievements.

This is not an exhaustively complete recounting. I hope that this telling includes most, perhaps even all, of the highlights of the computer-science efforts and gives at least a taste of what the department's application-programming side was all about. There is much more to the latter, but its chronicling is for others to do. Similarly, there is a story of the computer folks' interaction and close cooperation with the mathematics department and its own roster of achievements.

To be sure, the several decades of work by the department progressively named NAD, Computer Sciences, and Information Sciences did not achieve the goal suggested by Figure 8.1. But those decades did establish a broad foundation from which such an ultimate goal may be achieved.

To say again what was said in Chapter Two, primarily with USAF funding, encouragement, and concurrence, but also with support from the AEC and ARPA, Project RAND, and the RAND Corporation, the department

- helped lay the foundation for modern-day computing and the professional societies that support the field
- designed and built an outstanding (for the time) computer
- innovated much of the support software to facilitate programming and make computer usage efficient and convenient for all users
- pioneered the application of computer- and mathematically-based approaches to analytic studies
- was the first to exploit many mathematical techniques for real-world USAF (and others') problems
- evolved a close-knit mathematical and computer-science in-house staff to jointly handle increasingly complex problems (e.g., war games, simulations, battle models)
- conducted a computer-science R&D effort focused on the needs of computer users and the real problems of the USAF and other clients
- developed the first online, interactive, terminal-based computer system to which a number of USAF users had remote access via telephone connections
- handed off these achievements to USAF centers as they materialized and developed

- helped USAF to move facilely into the emerging field of analytic studies based on extensive computing hardware and software, as well as into a computer infrastructure for the operational and support forces
- handed off to the emerging discipline of computer science and to the computer users of the world much knowledge and intellectual advances to computer-based problem solving—largely in the form of innovative and operational software packages, usually complete with relevant end-user documentation
- supported a wide range of RAND policy studies with computer-supported know-how
- made significant contributions to important national policy issues, sometimes in a direct manner (e.g., information security, personal privacy), sometimes in a supporting role.

Figure 8.1. Some Goals Were Not Achieved[1]

_____

[1]   The author originally used this cartoon in a RAND Paper (Ware, 1967a). It is an adaptation by a RAND artist (possibly George Margadonna) of a somewhat different version that Bo Brown drew for the *Pennsylvania Gazette* (published by the University of Pennsylvania) and was used by permission. The author also used it in slide form as part of a popular "gee whiz" lecture that he widely presented.

Bibliography

Abbate, Janet, *Inventing the Internet*, Cambridge, Mass.: MIT Press, 1999.

Adelman, Kenneth, and Gabrielle Adelman, "Image 8245," California Coastal Records Project, copyright 2002. As of February 25, 2008:
http://www.californiacoastline.org/cgi-bin/image.cgi?image=8245&mode=big&lastmode=sequential&flags=0&year=2002

Allen, William, email to Willis Ware, May 2006.

Anderson, J., Richard L. Bisbey, Denise Hollingworth, and K. Uncapher, *Computer Security Experiment*, Santa Monica, Calif.: RAND Corporation, 1971. Not reviewed for public release.

Anderson, James P., *Computer Security Technology Planning Study*, Bedford, Mass.: Hanscom Field, ESD-TR-73-51, October 1972.

Anderson, Lynn, and C. L. Batten, *The RAND Editor, e: Version 19*, Santa Monica, Calif.: RAND Corporation, N-2239-1-RCC, 1986. As of February 26, 2008:
http://www.rand.org/pubs/notes/N2239-1/

Anderson, Lynn, C. L. Batten, Rosalind A. Chambers, and Sue Payne, *Self-Teaching Guide to RAND's Text Processor*, Santa Monica, Calif.: RAND Corporation, N-2056-1-RCC, 1986. As of February 26, 2008:
http://www.rand.org/pubs/notes/N2056-1/

Anderson, Robert H., M. Gallegos, James J. Gillogly, Rita Greenberg, and R. Villanueva, *RITA Reference Manual*, Santa Monica, Calif.: RAND Corporation, R-1808-ARPA, 1977. As of February 19, 2008:
http://www.rand.org/pubs/reports/R1808/

Anderson, Robert H., and James J. Gillogly, *RAND Intelligent Terminal Agent (RITA): Design Philosophy*, Santa Monica, Calif.: RAND Corporation, R-1809-ARPA, 1976. As of February 19, 2008:
http://www.rand.org/pubs/reports/R1809/

Anderson, Robert H., and Norman Shapiro, *Design Considerations for Computer-Based Interactive Map Display Systems*, Santa Monica, Calif.: RAND Corporation, R-2382-ARPA, 1979. As of February 19, 2008:
http://www.rand.org/pubs/reports/R2382/

Armer, Paul, *The Systems Gap*, Santa Monica, Calif.: RAND Corporation, P-3641, 1967. As of February 19, 2008:
http://www.rand.org/pubs/papers/P3641/

Arnold, Commanding General H. H., Army Air Force, undated report to the secretary of war.

Augenstein, Bruno, *A Brief History of RAND's Mathematics Department and Some of Its Accomplishments*, Santa Monica, Calif.: RAND Corporation, DRU-218-RC, 1993. As of April 25, 2008:
http://www.rand.org/pubs/drafts/DRU218/

Baker, Charles L., "The PACT I Coding System for the IBM Type 701," *Journal of the ACM*, Vol. 3, No. 4, October 1956, pp. 272–278.

———, *JOSS: Introduction to a Helpful Assistant*, Santa Monica, Calif.: RAND Corporation, RM-5058-PR, 1966. As of February 19, 2008:
http://www.rand.org/pubs/research_memoranda/RM5058/

Baran, Paul, *On Distributed Communications*, Vol. I: *Introduction to Distributed Communications Network*, Santa Monica, Calif.: RAND Corporation, RM-3420-PR, 1964a. As of February 19, 2008: http://www.rand.org/pubs/research_memoranda/RM3420/

———, *On Distributed Communications*, Vol. IV: *Priority, Precedence, and Overload*, Santa Monica, Calif.: RAND Corporation, RM-3638, 1964b. As of February 19, 2008: http://www.rand.org/pubs/research_memoranda/RM3638/

———, *On Distributed Communications*, Vol. V: *History, Alternative Approaches, and Comparisons*, Santa Monica, Calif.: RAND Corporation, RM-3097-PR, 1964c. As of February 19, 2008: http://www.rand.org/pubs/research_memoranda/RM3097/

———, *On Distributed Communications*, Vol. VI: *Mini-Cost Microwave*, Santa Monica, Calif.: RAND Corporation, RM-3762, 1964d. As of February 19, 2008: http://www.rand.org/pubs/research_memoranda/RM3762/

———, "The Beginnings of Packet Switching: Some Underlying Concepts," *IEEE Communications Magazine*, Vol. 40, No. 7, July 2002, pp. 42–48.

Baran, Paul, and Sharla P. Boehm, *On Distributed Communications*, Vol. II: *Digital Simulation of Hot-Potato Routing in a Broadband Distributed Communications Network*, Santa Monica, Calif.: RAND Corporation, RM-3103-PR, 1964. As of February 19, 2008: http://www.rand.org/pubs/research_memoranda/RM3103/

Baum, Claude, *The System Builders: The Story of SDC*, Santa Monica, Calif.: System Development Corp., July 1981.

Bellman, Richard Ernest, and Robert E. Kalaba, *Dynamic Programming and Adaptive Processes*, Vol. I: *Mathematical Foundation*, Santa Monica, Calif.: RAND Corporation, P-1416, 1959. As of February 19, 2008: http://www.rand.org/pubs/papers/P1416/

Bellman, Richard Ernest, Robert E. Kalaba, and L. A. Zader [sic: Zadeh], *Abstraction and Pattern Classification*, Santa Monica, Calif.: RAND Corporation, RM-4307-PR, 1964. As of April 21, 2008: http://www.rand.org/pubs/research_memoranda/RM4307/

Bernstein, Mort, Paul Armer, Willis Ware, and Bill Gunning, "The JOHNNIAC," presentation at the Computer History Museum, Mountain View, Calif., September 15, 1998. As of April 25, 2008: http://www.computerhistory.org/events/lectures/johnniac_09151998/

Bilofsky, Walter, *The CRT Text Editor NED—Introduction and Reference Manual*, Santa Monica, Calif.: RAND Corporation, R-2176-ARPA, 1977. As of February 19, 2008: http://www.rand.org/pubs/reports/R2176/

Bishop, Matt, "Computer Security Archives Project," undated Web page. As of February 19, 2008: http://seclab.cs.ucdavis.edu/projects/history

Bobrow, Daniel Gureasko, and Bertram Raphael, *A Comparison of List-Processing Computer Languages*, Santa Monica, Calif.: RAND Corporation, RM-3842-PR, 1963. As of February 19, 2008: http://www.rand.org/pubs/research_memoranda/RM3842/

Boehm, Barry W., *Software and Its Impact: A Quantitative Assessment*, Santa Monica, Calif.: RAND Corporation, P-4947, 1972. As of February 19, 2008: http://www.rand.org/pubs/papers/P4947/

Borden, Bruce, email to Willis H. Ware, April 2006.

Bornet, Vaughn Davis, *L. R. "Dick" Mockbee on "Life with Douglas and Project RAND, 1946–1948*, Santa Monica, Calif.: RAND Corporation, June 29, 1962.

———, *John Williams: A Personal Reminiscence*, Santa Monica, Calif.: RAND Corporation, 1969. For RAND use only.

Brown, Bernice B., *Some Tests on the Randomness of a Million Digits*, Santa Monica, Calif.: RAND Corporation, P-44, 1948a. As of February 19, 2008: http://www.rand.org/pubs/papers/P44/

———, *Tests of the Randomness of Digits*, Santa Monica, Calif.: RAND Corporation, RM-38, 1948b. As of February 19, 2008:
http://www.rand.org/pubs/research_memoranda/RM38/

Brown, George W., *History of RAND's Random Digits: Summary*, Santa Monica, Calif.: RAND Corporation, P-113, 1949. As of February 19, 2008:
http://www.rand.org/pubs/papers/P113/

Bryan, Edward, email to Willis Ware, May 2006.

Buchanan, Bruce G., and Edward Hance Shortliffe, eds., *Rule Based Expert Systems: The MYCIN Experiments of the Stanford Heuristic Programming Project*, Reading, Mass.: Addison-Wesley, 1984.

Bush, Vannevar, *Pieces of the Action*, New York: Morrow, 1970.

Callero, Monti D., D. A. Waterman, and James R. Kipps, *TATR, A Prototype Expert System for Tactical Air Targeting*, Santa Monica, Calif.: RAND Corporation, R-3096-ARPA, 1984. As of February 19, 2008:
http://www.rand.org/pubs/reports/R3096/

Campbell, Virginia, "How RAND Invented the Postwar World," *American Heritage Invention and Technology*, Vol. 20, Part 1, Summer 2004, pp. 50–61. As of February 25, 2008:
http://www.americanheritage.com/articles/magazine/it/2004/1/2004_1_50.shtml

Chapman, Robert, *Description of the Air-Defense Experiments—III: Data Collection and Processing*, Santa Monica, Calif.: RAND Corporation, P-658, 1955. As of April 21, 2008:
http://www.rand.org/pubs/papers/P658/

Chapman, Robert, and Milton G. Weiner, *Cogwheel: A Film Story of Systems Research Laboratory's Activities*, Santa Monica, Calif.: RAND Corporation, P-753, 1955. As of April 21, 2008:
http://www.rand.org/pubs/papers/P753/

Clark, R. L., and Gabriel F. Groner, *The BIOMOD System Implementation*, Santa Monica, Calif.: RAND Corporation, R-747-NIH, 1971. As of February 19, 2008:
http://www.rand.org/pubs/reports/R0747/

Clark, R. L., Gabriel F. Groner, and R. A. Berman, *The BIOMOD User's Reference Manual*, Santa Monica, Calif.: RAND Corporation, R-746-NIH, 1971. As of February 19, 2008:
http://www.rand.org/pubs/reports/R0746/

Clauser, P. H., *Preliminary Design of an Experimental World-Circling Spaceship*, Santa Monica, Calif.: Douglas Aircraft Company, Engineering Division, SM-11827, May 2, 1946. As of February 19, 2008:
http://www.rand.org/pubs/special_memoranda/SM11827/

Clewett, Ray, "Some Memories of the 'Old' RAND," *RAND Alumni Bulletin*, Vol. 28, Spring 2002, p. 4.

Collbohm, Frank, "Show Stealing," memorandum to numerical-analysis staff, February 19, 1953.

Collins, Martin J., *Cold War Laboratory: RAND, the Air Force, and the American State, 1945–1950*, Washington, D.C.: Smithsonian Institution Press, 2002.

Collins, Martin J., and Joseph Tatarewicz, interview with Frank Collbohm as part of the Smithsonian Institution's RAND History Project, July 28, 1987. Summary and catalog information available, as of February 22, 2008:
http://www.nasm.si.edu/research/dsh/rhpi-p1.html

Computer Security Center, *Department of Defense Trusted Computer System Evaluation Criteria*, Fort George G. Meade, Md.: DoD Computer Security Center, August 15, 1983.

Costa, J., "RADC Develops Logic Design for Emergency Broadcasting," *Electronic News*, January 10, 1966, p. 32.

Crocker, David, email to Willis Ware, April 2006.

Culbertson, James T., *Hypothetical Robots and the Problem of Neuroeconomy*, Santa Monica, Calif.: RAND Corporation, P-296, 1952.

Dantzig, George Bernard, *Notes on Linear Programming*, Part III: *Computational Algorithm of the Revised Simplex Method*, Santa Monica, Calif.: RAND Corporation, RM-1266, 1953. As of February 19, 2008: http://www.rand.org/pubs/research_memoranda/RM1266/

———, *Notes on Linear Programming*, Part VII: *The Dual Simplex Algorithm*, Santa Monica, Calif.: RAND Corporation, RM-1270, 1954a. As of February 19, 2008: http://www.rand.org/pubs/research_memoranda/RM1270/

———, *Notes on Linear Programming*, Part XI: *Composite Simplex–Dual Simplex Algorithm—I*, Santa Monica, Calif.: RAND Corporation, RM-1274, 1954b. As of February 19, 2008: http://www.rand.org/pubs/research_memoranda/RM1274/

———, *Notes on Linear Programming*, Part XVIII: *Status of Solution of Large-Scale Linear-Programming Problems*, Santa Monica, Calif.: RAND Corporation, RM-1375, 1954c. As of February 19, 2008: http://www.rand.org/pubs/research_memoranda/RM1375/

———, *Notes on Linear Programming*, Parts VIII, IX, and X: *Upper Bounds, Secondary Constraints, and Block Triangularity in Linear Programming*, Santa Monica, Calif.: RAND Corporation, RM-1367, 1954d. As of February 19, 2008: http://www.rand.org/pubs/research_memoranda/RM1367/

———, *Notes on Linear Programming*, Part XXII: *Recent Advances in Linear Programming*, Santa Monica, Calif.: RAND Corporation, RM-1475, 1955. As of February 19, 2008: http://www.rand.org/pubs/research_memoranda/RM1475/

———, *Notes on Linear Programming*, Part XXXV: *Discrete-Variable Extremum Problems*, Santa Monica, Calif.: RAND Corporation, RM-1832, 1956. As of February 19, 2008: http://www.rand.org/pubs/research_memoranda/RM1832/

———, *Notes on Linear Programming*, Part XLVII: *Solving Linear Programs in Integers*, Santa Monica, Calif.: RAND Corporation, RM-2209, 1958. As of February 19, 2008: http://www.rand.org/pubs/research_memoranda/RM2209/

———, *Linear Programming and Extensions*, Santa Monica, Calif.: RAND Corporation, R-366-PR, 1963. As of February 19, 2008: http://www.rand.org/pubs/reports/R366/

Dantzig, George Bernard, L. R. Ford, and D. R. Fulkerson, *Notes on Linear Programming*, Part XXXI: *A Primal-Dual Algorithm*, Santa Monica, Calif.: RAND Corporation, RM-1709, 1956. As of February 19, 2008: http://www.rand.org/pubs/research_memoranda/RM1709/

Dantzig, George Bernard, and D. R. Fulkerson, *Notes on Linear Programming*, Part XV: *Minimizing the Number of Carriers to Meet a Fixed Schedule*, Santa Monica, Calif.: RAND Corporation, RM-1328, 1954. As of February 19, 2008: http://www.rand.org/pubs/research_memoranda/RM1328/

Dantzig, George Bernard, W. Orchard-Hays, and G. Waters, *Notes on Linear Programming*, Part V: *A Product-Form Tableau for Revised Simplex Method: Computing Appendix for RM-1268*, Santa Monica, Calif.: RAND Corporation, RM-1268/1, 1954. As of February 19, 2008: http://www.rand.org/pubs/research_memoranda/RM1268.1/

Dantzig, George Bernard, and Alex Orden, *Notes on Linear Programming*, Part II: *Duality Theorems*, Santa Monica, Calif.: RAND Corporation, RM-1265, 1953. As of February 19, 2008: http://www.rand.org/pubs/research_memoranda/RM1265/

Dantzig, George Bernard, Alex Orden, and Philip S. Wolfe, *Notes on Linear Programming*, Part I: *The Generalized Simplex Method for Minimizing a Linear Form Under Linear Inequality Restraints*, Santa Monica, Calif.: RAND Corporation, RM-1264, 1954. As of February 19, 2008: http://www.rand.org/pubs/research_memoranda/RM1264/

Davies, D. W., "An Historical Study of the Beginnings of Packet Switching," *Computer Journal*, Vol. 44, No. 3, 2001, pp. 152–162.

Davies, Merton E., and William R. Harris, *RAND's Role in the Evolution of Balloon and Satellite Observation Systems and Related U.S. Space Technology*, Santa Monica, Calif.: RAND Corporation, R-3692-RC, 1988. As of February 19, 2008:
http://www.rand.org/pubs/reports/R3692/

Davis, Malcolm, and T. O. Ellis, *The RAND Tablet: A Man-Machine Graphical Communications Device*, Santa Monica, Calif.: RAND Corporation, RM-4122-ARPA, 1964. As of February 19, 2008:
http://www.rand.org/pubs/research_memoranda/RM4122/

Davis, Paul K., and James A. Winnefeld, *The RAND Strategy Assessment Center: An Overview and Interim Conclusions About Utility and Development Options*, Santa Monica, Calif.: RAND Corporation, R-2945-DNA, 1983. As of February 19, 2008:
http://www.rand.org/pubs/reports/R2945/

Digby, James, *Early RAND: Personalities and Projects as Recalled in the Alumni Bulletin*, Santa Monica, Calif.: RAND Corporation, P-8055, 2001. As of February 19, 2008:
http://www.rand.org/pubs/papers/P8055/

———, "RAND People of Note," *RAND Alumni Bulletin*, Vol. 39, Winter 2005, p. 2.

DoD—*see* U.S. Department of Defense.

Dreyfus, Hubert L., *Alchemy and Artificial Intelligence*, Santa Monica, Calif.: RAND Corporation, P-3244, 1965. As of February 19, 2008:
http://www.rand.org/pubs/papers/P3244/

Drezner, Steve, Hyman L. Shulman, and Willis H. Ware, *The Computer Resource Management Study: Executive Summary*, Santa Monica, Calif.: RAND Corporation, R-1855-PR, 1975. As of February 19, 2008:
http://www.rand.org/pubs/reports/R1855/

Drezner, Steve, Hyman L. Shulman, Willis H. Ware, Giles K. Smith, M. Davis, Robert N. Reinstedt, and Rein Turn, *The Computer Resources Management Study*, Santa Monica, Calif.: RAND Corporation, R-1855/1-PR, 1976. As of February 19, 2008:
http://www.rand.org/pubs/reports/R1855.1/

Electronic Privacy Information Center, undated homepage. As of February 26, 2008:
http://epic.org/

———, "EPIC Online Guide to Privacy Resources," last updated May 6, 2002. As of February 26, 2008:
http://epic.org/privacy/privacy_resources_faq.html

Ellis, T. O., J. F. Heafner, and W. L. Sibley, *The GRAIL Language and Operations*, Santa Monica, Calif.: RAND Corporation, RM-6001-ARPA, 1969a. As of February 19, 2008:
http://www.rand.org/pubs/research_memoranda/RM6001/

———, *The GRAIL Project: An Experiment in Man-Machine Communications*, RM-5999-ARPA, Santa Monica, Calif.: RAND Corporation, RM-5999-ARPA, 1969b. As of February 19, 2008:
http://www.rand.org/pubs/research_memoranda/RM5999/

———, *The GRAIL System Implementation*, Santa Monica, Calif.: RAND Corporation, RM-6002-ARPA, 1969c. As of February 19, 2008:
http://www.rand.org/pubs/research_memoranda/RM6002/

EPIC—*see* Electronic Privacy Information Center.

"F. R. Collbohm, 83, Ex-Head of RAND, Dies," *New York Times*, February 14, 1990, p. B5.

Faught, William S., D. A. Waterman, Philip Klahr, Stanley J. Rosenschein, Daniel Gorlin, and S. J. Tepper, *EP-2: An Exemplary Programming System*, Santa Monica, Calif.: RAND Corporation, R-2411-ARPA, 1980. As of February 19, 2008:
http://www.rand.org/pubs/reports/R2411/

Feigenbaum, Edward A., *An Information Processing Theory of Verbal Learning*, Santa Monica, Calif.: RAND Corporation, P-1817, 1959.

———, *The Simulation of Verbal Learning Behavior*, Santa Monica, Calif.: RAND Corporation, P-2235, 1961.

————, *Computer Simulation of Human Behavior*, Santa Monica, Calif.: RAND Corporation, P-2905, 1964.

Feigenbaum, Edward A., and Julian Feldman, eds., *Computers and Thought*, New York: McGraw-Hill, 1963.

Feigenbaum, Edward A., and Herbert Alexander Simon, *Forgetting in an Association Memory*, Santa Monica, Calif.: RAND Corporation, P-2311, May 1961a.

————, *Performance of a Reading Task by an Elementary Perceiving and Memorizing Program*, Santa Monica, Calif.: RAND Corporation, P-2358, July 1961b.

————, *A Theory of the Serial Position Effect*, Santa Monica, Calif.: RAND Corporation, P-2375, July 1961c.

————, *Generalization of an Elementary Perceiving and Memorizing Machine*, Santa Monica, Calif.: RAND Corporation, P-2555, 1962. As of February 19, 2008:
http://www.rand.org/pubs/papers/P2555/

Finkle, Ivan L., and L. Scantlin, *NOSY: A Core-Saving Operating System*, Santa Monica, Calif.: RAND Corporation, P-3168, 1965. As of February 19, 2008:
http://www.rand.org/pubs/papers/P3168/

Ford, L. R., and D. R. Fulkerson, *Notes on Linear Programming*, Part XX: *Maximal Flow Through a Network*, Santa Monica, Calif.: RAND Corporation, RM-1400, 1954. As of February 19, 2008:
http://www.rand.org/pubs/research_memoranda/RM1400/

————, *Notes on Linear Programming*, Part XXIX: *A Simple Algorithm for Finding Maximal Network Flows and an Application to the Hitchcock Problem*, Santa Monica, Calif.: RAND Corporation, RM-1604, 1955. As of February 19, 2008:
http://www.rand.org/pubs/research_memoranda/RM1604/

————, *Notes on Linear Programming*, Part XXXII: *Solving the Transportation Problem*, Santa Monica, Calif.: RAND Corporation, RM-1736, 1956a. As of February 19, 2008:
http://www.rand.org/pubs/research_memoranda/RM1736/

————, *Notes on Linear Programming*, Part XXXIV: *A Primal-Dual Algorithm for the Capacitated Hitchcock Problem*, Santa Monica, Calif.: RAND Corporation, RM-1798, 1956b. As of February 19, 2008:
http://www.rand.org/pubs/research_memoranda/RM1798/

————, *Notes on Linear Programming*, Part XLI: *Constructing Maximal Dynamic Flows from Static Flows*, Santa Monica, Calif.: RAND Corporation, RM-1981, 1957. As of February 19, 2008:
http://www.rand.org/pubs/research_memoranda/RM1981/

————, *Flows in Networks*, Santa Monica, Calif.: RAND Corporation, R-375-PR, 1962. As of February 19, 2008:
http://www.rand.org/pubs/reports/R375/

Freie Universität Berlin, "About Us," last updated March 20, 2007. As of April 21, 2008:
http://www.fu-berlin.de/en/tour/galerie_neu/luftaufnahme/index.html

Fulkerson, D. R., *Notes on Linear Programming*, Part XLV: *A Network-Flow Feasibility Theorem and Combinatorial Applications*, Santa Monica, Calif.: RAND Corporation, RM-2159, 1958. As of February 19, 2008:
http://www.rand.org/pubs/research_memoranda/RM2159/

Gaines, R. Stockton, and Norman Zalmon Shapiro, "The Next Message System," memorandum to Robert H. Anderson, undated.

Gritton, Eugene C., William King, I. E. Sutherland, R. Stockton Gaines, Carl Gazley, C. E. Grosch, M. L. Juncosa, and H. E. Petersen, *Feasibility of a Special-Purpose Computer to Solve the Navier-Stokes Equations*, Santa Monica, Calif.: RAND Corporation, R-2183-RC, 1977. As of February 27, 2008:
http://www.rand.org/pubs/reports/R2183/

Groner, Gabriel F., *Real-Time Recognition of Handprinted Text*, Santa Monica, Calif.: RAND Corporation, RM-5016-ARPA, 1966. As of February 19, 2008:
http://www.rand.org/pubs/research_memoranda/RM5016/

Groner, Gabriel F., W. R. Baker Jr., Toni G. Christopher, M. D. Hopwood, Norman A. Palley, W. L. Sibley, and H. K. Thompson, *The Design and Evaluation of a Prototype Data Management and Analysis System for Clinical Investigators*, Santa Monica, Calif.: RAND Corporation, P-5746, 1976. As of February 19, 2008:
http://www.rand.org/pubs/papers/P5746/

Groner, Gabriel F., R. L. Clark, R. A. Berman, and Edward Charles DeLand, *BIOMOD: An Interactive Computer Graphics System for Modeling*, Santa Monica, Calif.: RAND Corporation, R-617-NIH, 1971. As of February 19, 2008:
http://www.rand.org/pubs/reports/R0617/

Groner, Gabriel F., J. F. Heafner, and Thomas W. Robinson, *On-Line Computer Classification of Handprinted Chinese Characters as a Translation Aid*, Santa Monica, Calif.: RAND Corporation, P-3568, 1967. As of February 19, 2008:
http://www.rand.org/pubs/papers/P3568/

Gruenberger, Fred Joseph, *The History of the JOHNNIAC*, Santa Monica, Calif.: RAND Corporation, RM-5654-PR, 1968. As of February 19, 2008:
http://www.rand.org/pubs/research_memoranda/RM5654/

Gunning, W. F., and A. S. Mengel, *Summary of REAC Experience*, Santa Monica, Calif.: RAND Corporation, RM-236, 1949. As of February 19, 2008:
http://www.rand.org/pubs/research_memoranda/RM236/

Hafner, Katie, "A Paternity Dispute Divides Net Pioneers," *New York Times*, November 8, 2001.

Hafner, Katie, and Matthew Lyon, *Where Wizards Stay Up Late: The Origins of the Internet*, New York: Simon and Schuster, 1996.

Hall, H. E., Mark LaCasse, Robert H. Anderson, and Norman Shapiro, *The RAND-ABEL Programming Language: History, Rationale, and Design*, Santa Monica, Calif.: RAND Corporation, R-3274-NA, 1985. As of February 26, 2008:
http://www.rand.org/pubs/reports/R3274/

Hastings, Cecil, *Approximations for Digital Computers*, Princeton, N.J.: Princeton University Press, 1955.

———, letter, January 1994.

Hayes-Roth, Frederick, Philip Klahr, and David J. Mostow, *Advice-Taking and Knowledge Refinement: An Iterative View of Skill Acquisition*, Santa Monica, Calif.: RAND Corporation, P-6517, 1980. As of February 19, 2008:
http://www.rand.org/pubs/papers/P6517/

Hays, David G., *Introduction to Computational Linguistics*, New York: American Elsevier Pub. Co., 1967.

Hays, David G., Bozena Henisz-Dostert, and Marjorie L. Rapp, *Annotated Bibliography of Rand Publications in Computational Linguistics*, Santa Monica, Calif.: RAND Corporation, RM-3894-3, 1967. As of February 19, 2008:
http://www.rand.org/pubs/research_memoranda/RM3894-3/

HEW—*see* U.S. Department of Health, Education, and Welfare.

Holland, Wade, *Soviet Cybernetics Review*, Vol. 1, No. 1, Santa Monica, Calif.: RAND Corporation, R-700/1-PR, 1971. As of April 30, 2008:
http://www.rand.org/pubs/reports/R0700.1/

Hounshell, David A., *The Cold War, RAND, and the Generation of Knowledge, 1946–1962*, Santa Monica, Calif.: RAND Corporation, RP-729, 1998. Originally published in *Historical Studies in the Physical and Biological Sciences*, Vol. 27, No. 2, 1997, pp. 237–267. As of February 19, 2008:
http://www.rand.org/pubs/reprints/RP729/

Householder, Alston Scott, *Neural Nets for "Toad TI,"* Santa Monica, Calif.: RAND Corporation, RM-671, 1951a. As of February 19, 2008:
http://www.rand.org/pubs/research_memoranda/RM671/

———, *Some Notes for Simple Pavlovian Learning*, Santa Monica, Calif.: RAND Corporation, RM-678, 1951b. As of February 19, 2008:
http://www.rand.org/pubs/research_memoranda/RM678/

Jackson, Victor G., *National Defense Research Institute, A Documentary History*, Santa Monica, Calif.: RAND Corporation, February 1989a.

———, *National Security Research Division: Research Highlights*, Santa Monica, Calif.: RAND Corporation, February 1989b.

———, *National Security Research Division: Organizational Antecedents, Officers, Research Programs, and Program Directors*, Santa Monica, Calif.: RAND Corporation, February 1989c.

———, *National Security Research Division: A Chronology of Administrative and Organizational Events*, Santa Monica, Calif.: RAND Corporation, February 1989d.

Jardini, David R., *Out of the Blue Yonder: Diversification into Social Welfare Research, 1946–1968*, Santa Monica, Calif.: RAND Corporation, 1996. For RAND use only.

John Williams—A Memoriam, Santa Monica, Calif.: RAND Corporation, 1964.

Jones, William M., M. F. Shapiro, and Norman Zalmon Shapiro, *The Flight Operations Planner*, Santa Monica, Calif.: RAND Corporation, RM-2415-PR, 1959.

Kahn, Herman, *Use of Different Monte Carlo Sampling Techniques*, Santa Monica, Calif.: RAND Corporation, P-766, 1955. As of February 19, 2008:
http://www.rand.org/pubs/papers/P766/

Kaplan, Fred M., *The Wizards of Armageddon*, Stanford, Calif.: Stanford University Press, 1991.

Kaplan, Robert M., *The MIND System: A Grammar-Rule Language*, Santa Monica, Calif.: RAND Corporation, RM-6265/1-PR, 1970.

———, *Augmented Transition Networks as Psychological Models of Sentence Comprehension*, Santa Monica, Calif.: RAND Corporation, P-4742, 1971. As of February 19, 2008:
http://www.rand.org/pubs/papers/P4742/

Kay, Martin, *Experiments with a Powerful Parser*, Santa Monica, Calif.: RAND Corporation, RM-5452-PR, 1967. As of February 19, 2008:
http://www.rand.org/pubs/research_memoranda/RM5452/

Kay, Martin, and G. R. Martins, *The MIND System: The Morphological-Analysis Program*, Santa Monica, Calif.: RAND Corporation, RM-6265/2-PR, 1970.

Kay, Martin, and S. Y. W. Su, *The MIND System: The Structure of the Semantic File*, Santa Monica, Calif.: RAND Corporation, RM-6265/3-PR, 1970.

Kelly, James E., *A Guide to NED: A New On-Line Computer Editor*, Santa Monica, Calif.: RAND Corporation, R-2000-ARPA, 1977. As of February 19, 2008:
http://www.rand.org/pubs/reports/R2000/

Kennedy, John L., and Robert Chapman, *The Background and Implications of the Systems Research Laboratory Studies*, Santa Monica, Calif.: RAND Corporation, P-740, 1955. As of April 21, 2008:
http://www.rand.org/pubs/papers/P740/

Kiviat, Philip J., R. Villanueva, and Harry Max Markowitz, *The SIMSCRIPT II Programming Language*, Santa Monica, Calif.: RAND Corporation, R-460-PR, 1968. As of February 19, 2008:
http://www.rand.org/pubs/reports/R460/

Klahr, A. M., S. F. Payne, and Lynn Anderson, *The eR Program: Formatting Text on the Text Processor and Personal Computer, Version 4.1*, Santa Monica, Calif.: RAND Corporation, 1987.

Klahr, Philip, John W. Ellis, William Giarla, Sanjai Narain, Edison Cesar, and Susan Turner, *TWIRL: Tactical Warfare in the ROSS Language*, Santa Monica, Calif.: RAND Corporation, R-3158-AF, 1984. As of February 19, 2008:
http://www.rand.org/pubs/reports/R3158/

Klahr, Philip, and D. A. Waterman, *Artificial Intelligence: A RAND Perspective*, Santa Monica, Calif.: RAND Corporation, P-7172, 1986a. As of February 19, 2008:
http://www.rand.org/pubs/papers/P7172/

———, *Expert Systems: Techniques, Tools, and Applications*, Reading, Mass.: Addison-Wesley Pub. Co., 1986b.

Kleene, S. C., *Representation of Events in Nerve Nets and Finite Automata*, Santa Monica, Calif.: RAND Corporation, RM-704, 1951. As of February 19, 2008:
http://www.rand.org/pubs/research_memoranda/RM704/

Kochen, Manfred, Donald MacCrimmon MacKay, M. E. Maron, M. Scriven, and L. Uhr, *Computers and Comprehension*, Santa Monica, Calif.: RAND Corporation, RM-4065-PR, 1964.

Kubo, Michael, *Constructing the Cold War Environment: The Architecture of the RAND Corporation, 1950–2005*, thesis, Cambridge, Mass.: Harvard University Graduate School of Design, 2006.

Kuhns, J. L., *Answering Questions by Computer: A Logical Study*, Santa Monica, Calif.: RAND Corporation, RM-5428, 1967. As of February 19, 2008:
http://www.rand.org/pubs/research_memoranda/RM5428/

———, *Interrogating a Relational Data File: Remarks on the Admissibility of Input Queries*, Santa Monica, Calif.: RAND Corporation, R-511-PR, 1970. As of February 19, 2008:
http://www.rand.org/pubs/reports/R0511/

LeLevier, Robert, "The Physics Department," *RAND Alumni Bulletin*, Vol. 41, 2006, p. 2.

Lenat, Douglas B., Frederick Hayes-Roth, and Philip Klahr, *Cognitive Economy*, Santa Monica, Calif.: RAND Corporation, N-1185-NSF, 1979. As of February 19, 2008:
http://www.rand.org/pubs/notes/N1185/

Levien, Roger Eli, *Relational Data File: Experience with a System for Propositional Data Storage and Inference Execution*, Santa Monica, Calif.: RAND Corporation, RM-5947-PR, 1969. As of February 19, 2008:
http://www.rand.org/pubs/research_memoranda/RM5947/

Levien, Roger Eli, and M. E. Maron, *Relational Data File: A Tool for Mechanized Inference Execution and Data Retrieval*, Santa Monica, Calif.: RAND Corporation, RM-4793-PR, 1965. As of February 19, 2008:
http://www.rand.org/pubs/research_memoranda/RM4793/

———, *A Computer System for Inference Execution and Data Retrieval*, Santa Monica, Calif.: RAND Corporation, RM-5085-PR, 1966. As of February 19, 2008:
http://www.rand.org/pubs/research_memoranda/RM5085/

Licklider, J. C. R., "Man-Computer Symbiosis," in J. C. R. Licklider and R. W. Taylor, eds., *In Memoriam: J. C. R. Licklider, 1915–1990*, Palo Alto, Calif.: Digital, Systems Research Center, August 7, 1990.

Light, Jennifer S., *From Warfare to Welfare: Defense Intellectuals and Urban Problems in Cold War America*, Baltimore, Md.: Johns Hopkins University Press, 2003.

Lincoln, T. L., J. Aroesty, G. Meier, and J. F. Gross, "Computer Simulation in the Service of Chemotherapy," *Biomedicine*, Vol. 20, 1974, pp. 9–16.

Lincoln, T. L., G. F. Groner, J. J. Quinn, and R. J. Lukes, "The Analysis of Functional Studies in Acute Lymphocytic Leukemia Using CLINFO—a Small Computer Information and Analysis System for Clinical Investigators," *Medical Informatics*, Vol. 1, No. 2, June 1976, pp. 95–103.

Lincoln, T. L., G. F. Groner, A. K. Williams, and R. J. Lukes, "The Use of CLINFO—a Small Computer Information Analysis System—to Collect and Analyze a Leukemia Lymphoma Data Base," 11th International Conference on Medical and Biological Engineering, Ottawa, Can., August 1976, pp. 356–357.

Liston, Max D., C. E. Quinn, W. E. Sargeant, and G. G. Scott, "A Contact Modulated Amplifier to Replace Sensitive Suspension Galvanometers," *Review of Scientific Instruments*, Vol. 17, No. 5, May 1946, pp. 194–198.

Marks, Shirley, "JOHNNIAC, 1953–1966," press release, February 18, 1966.

May, Andrew David, *The RAND Corporation and Dynamics of American Strategic Thought, 1946–1962*, Santa Monica, Calif.: RAND Corporation, 1998. For RAND use only.

McArthur, David J., Philip Klahr, and Sanjai Narain, *ROSS: An Object-Oriented Language for Constructing Simulations*, Santa Monica, Calif.: RAND Corporation, R-3160-AF, 1984. As of February 26, 2008: http://www.rand.org/pubs/reports/R3160/

———, *The ROSS Language Manual*, Santa Monica, Calif.: RAND Corporation, N-1854-1-AF, 1985. As of February 26, 2008: http://www.rand.org/pubs/notes/N1854-1/

Melahn, Wesley S., "A Description of a Cooperative Venture in the Production of an Automatic Coding System," *Journal of the ACM*, Vol. 3, No. 4, October 1956, pp. 266–271.

Mengel, Arthur Stifel, "Analogue Computer," memorandum to Edwin W. Paxson, September 22, 1947.

Mengel, A. S., and W. S. Melahn, *RAND REAC Manual*, Santa Monica, Calif.: RAND Corporation, RM-525, 1950. As of February 25, 2008: http://www.rand.org/pubs/research_memoranda/RM525/

Nash, Robert, Willis H. Ware, and John Donald Madden, "Open House," memorandum to numerical-analysis department, February 19, 1953.

"New Monument to Take Flight," *Santa Monica Daily Press*, Vol. 3, No. 185, June 6, 2004.

Newell, Allen, ed., *IPL-V Programmers' Reference Manual*, Santa Monica, Calif.: RAND Corporation, RM-3739-RC, 1963. As of February 26, 2008: http://www.rand.org/pubs/research_memoranda/RM3739/

Newell, V. A., and F. M. Tonge, *An Introduction to Information Processing Language*, Santa Monica, Calif.: RAND Corporation, P-1929, 1960. As of February 26, 2008: http://www.rand.org/pubs/papers/P1929/

Norberg, Arthur L., Judy E. O'Neill, and Kerry J. Freedman, *Transforming Computer Technology: Information Processing for the Pentagon, 1962–1986*, Baltimore, Md.: Johns Hopkins University Press, 1996.

Oliver, Myrna, "Franklin Collbohm Dies, Founder of RAND Corp.," *Los Angeles Times*, February 14, 1990, p. A3.

Paxson, Edwin W., *Hand Calculator Programs for Staff Officers*, Santa Monica, Calif.: RAND Corporation, R-2280-RC, 1978. As of February 22, 2008: http://www.rand.org/pubs/reports/R2280/

Payne, Sue, *MH5: Electronic Mail*, Santa Monica, Calif.: RAND Corporation, N-2281-RCC, 1985. As of February 26, 2008: http://www.rand.org/pubs/notes/N2281/

Peek, Jerry D., Bill Wohler, and Brent B. Welch, *MH and xmh: Email for Users and Programmers*, 3rd ed., Sebastopol, Calif.: O'Reilly and Associates, 1996. As of May 9, 2008: http://www.oreilly.com/openbook/mh/tocs/jump.htm

Petersen, H. E., and Rein Turn, *System Implications of Information Privacy*, Santa Monica, Calif.: RAND Corporation, P-3504, 1967. As of February 26, 2008: http://www.rand.org/pubs/papers/P3504/

Pfleeger, Charles P., and Shari Lawrence Pfleeger, *Security in Computing*, 4th ed., Upper Saddle River, N.J.: Prentice Hall, 2006.

PPSC—*see* Privacy Protection Study Commission.

Privacy Protection Study Commission, *Personal Privacy in an Information Society: The Report of the Privacy Protection Study Commission*, Washington, D.C., 1977.

Public Law 93-495, Fair Credit Billing Act, October 28, 1974.

Public Law 93-579, Privacy Act, December 1974.

RAND Corporation, *Second Annual Report*, Santa Monica, Calif., RA-15075, 1948a.

———, articles of incorporation, May 14, 1948b.

———, *RANDom News*, Vol. 2, No. 6, March 18, 1949.

———, *RAND 25th Anniversary Volume*, Santa Monica, Calif., 1973.

———, *Project AIR FORCE 50th, 1946–1996*, Santa Monica, Calif., 1996.

———, *A Million Random Digits and 100,000 Normal Deviates*, Santa Monica, Calif., MR-1418-RC, 2001. As of February 19, 2008:
http://www.rand.org/pubs/monograph_reports/MR1418/

———, *RAND Alumni Bulletin*, Vol. 42, Winter 2006.

———, "Document Information: Design Considerations for Computer-Based Interactive Map Display Systems," Web page, last modified December 7, 2007a. As of May 8, 2008:
http://www.rand.org/pubs/reports/R2382/

———, "Document Information: The GRAIL Language and Operations," Web page, last modified December 7, 2007b. As of May 8, 2008:
http://www.rand.org/pubs/research_memoranda/RM6001/

———, "Document Information: The RAND Video Graphic System: An Approach to a General User-Computer Graphic Communication System," Web page, last modified December 7, 2007c. As of May 8, 2008:
http://www.rand.org/pubs/reports/R0753/

———, "Document Information: Real-Time Recognition of Handprinted Text," Web page, last modified December 7, 2007d. As of May 8, 2008:
http://www.rand.org/pubs/research_memoranda/RM5016/

———, "Browse by Author," last modified December 13, 2007e. As of June 17, 2008:
http://www.rand.org/pubs/authors/

———, "History and Mission," last updated February 18, 2008a. As of February 21, 2008:
http://www.rand.org/about/history/

———, "Document Information: On-Line Computer Classification of Handprinted Chinese Characters as a Translation Aid," Web page, last modified April 21, 2008b. As of May 8, 2008:
http://www.rand.org/pubs/papers/P3568/

Reinstedt, Robert N., email to Willis Ware, May 2006.

Reinstedt, Robert N., and R. Berger, *Certification: A Suggested Approach to Acceptance*, Santa Monica, Calif.: RAND Corporation, P-5023, 1973. As of February 26, 2008:
http://www.rand.org/pubs/papers/P5023/

Robinson, Jane J., and Shirley Marks, *Parse: A System for Automatic Syntactic Analysis of English Text: Part I*, Santa Monica, Calif.: RAND Corporation, RM-4654-PR, 1965a.

———, *Parse: A System for Automatic Syntactic Analysis of English Text: Part II*, Santa Monica, Calif.: RAND Corporation, RM-4654/1-PR, 1965b.

Rumford, D. Tracy, email to Willis Ware, May 2006.

Selover, E. E., "HF Survivable Communications System," *Proceedings of the IEEE Mohawk Valley Communications Symposium (NATCOM)*, October 1965, pp. 35–40.

Serrell, Robert, *Determination of Minimal Component Accuracy for Simulator Systems*, report to Radio Corporation of America, February 1948.

Shapiro, Norm, email to Willis Ware, May 2006.

Shapiro, S. C., *The MIND System: A Data Structure for Semantic Information Processing*, Santa Monica, Calif.: RAND Corporation, R-837-PR, 1971.

Shapley, Lloyd S., *Notes on the n-Person Game*, I: *Characteristic-Point Solutions of the Four-Person Game*, Santa Monica, Calif.: RAND Corporation, RM-0656-PR, 1951a. As of February 26, 2008:
http://www.rand.org/pubs/research_memoranda/RM0656/

———, *Notes on the n-Person Game*, Part II: *The Value of an n-Person Game*, Santa Monica, Calif.: RAND Corporation, RM-0670-PR, 1951b. As of February 26, 2008:
http://www.rand.org/pubs/research_memoranda/RM0670/

———, *Notes on the n-Person Game*, Part III: *Some Variants of the von Neumann–Morgenstern Definition of Solution*, Santa Monica, Calif.: RAND Corporation, RM-817, 1952a. As of February 26, 2008:
http://www.rand.org/pubs/research_memoranda/RM817/

———, *Notes on the n-Person Game*, Part VI: *A Theorem on C-Stable Sets*, Santa Monica, Calif.: RAND Corporation, RM-881, 1952b. As of February 26, 2008:
http://www.rand.org/pubs/research_memoranda/RM881/

Shaw, John Clifford, *JOSS: A Designer's View of an Experimental On-Line System*, Santa Monica, Calif.: RAND Corporation, P-2922, 1964. As of February 25, 2008:
http://www.rand.org/pubs/papers/P2922/

Shortliffe, Edward Hance, *Computer-Based Medical Consultations, MYCIN*, New York: Elsevier, 1976.

Shukiar, Herbert, email to Willis Ware, May 2006.

Simon, Herbert Alexander, and Edward A. Feigenbaum, *Studies in Information Processing Theory: Similarity and Familiarity in Verbal Learning*, Santa Monica, Calif.: RAND Corporation, RM-3979-PR, 1964. As of February 26, 2008:
http://www.rand.org/pubs/research_memoranda/RM3979/

Simon, Herbert A., and Allen Newell, "Heuristic Problem Solving: The Next Advance in Operations Research," *Operations Research*, Vol. 6, No. 1, January 1958, pp. 1–10.

Smith, Bruce L. R., *The RAND Corporation: Case Study of a Nonprofit Advisory Corporation*, Cambridge, Mass.: Harvard University Press, 1966.

Smith, J. W., *On Distributed Communications*, Vol. III: *Determination of Path-Lengths in a Distributed Network*, Santa Monica, Calif.: RAND Corporation, RM-3578-PR, 1964. As of February 19, 2008:
http://www.rand.org/pubs/research_memoranda/RM3578/

Stewart, Irvin, *Organizing Scientific Research for War: The Administrative History of the Office of Scientific Research and Development*, Boston: Little, Brown, 1948.

Sutherland, I. E., *Computerized Commerce*, Santa Monica, Calif.: RAND Corporation, P-5515, 1975. As of February 27, 2008:
http://www.rand.org/pubs/papers/P5515/

Sutherland, I. E., C. A. Mead, and Thomas E. Everhart, *Basic Limitations in Microcircuit Fabrication Technology*, Santa Monica, Calif.: RAND Corporation, R-1956-ARPA, 1976. As of February 27, 2008:
http://www.rand.org/pubs/reports/R1956/

Swain, Craig A., biography of Frank Collbohm, undated.

Tarski, Alfred, *A Decision Method for Elementary Algebra and Geometry: Prepared for Publication with the Assistance of J. C. C. McKinsey*, Santa Monica, Calif.: RAND Corporation, R-109, 1951. As of February 26, 2008:
http://www.rand.org/pubs/reports/R109/

Thorndyke, Perry W., David McArthur, and Stephanie Cammarata, *AUTOPILOT: A Distributed Planner for Air Fleet Control*, Santa Monica, Calif.: RAND Corporation, N-1731-ARPA, July 1981.

Tonge, F. M., *Summary of a Heuristic Line Balancing Procedure*, Santa Monica, Calif.: RAND Corporation, 1959.

————, *A Heuristic Program for Assembly-Line Balancing*, Santa Monica, Calif.: RAND Corporation, P-1993, 1960. As of February 26, 2008:
http://www.rand.org/pubs/papers/P1993/

Trachtenberg, Marc, *History and Strategy*, Princeton, N.J.: Princeton University Press, 1991.

Turn, Rein, and Willis H. Ware, *Privacy and Security Issues in Information Systems*, Santa Monica, Calif.: RAND Corporation, P-5684, 1976. As of February 26, 2008:
http://www.rand.org/pubs/papers/P5684/

Uncapher, K., *The RAND Video Graphic System: An Approach to a General User-Computer Graphic Communication System*, Santa Monica, Calif.: RAND Corporation, R-753-ARPA, 1971. As of February 25, 2008:
http://www.rand.org/pubs/reports/R0753/

U.S. Department of Defense, Department of Defense Computer Institute (DODCI), DoD directive 5160.49, February 12, 1976.

U.S. Department of Health, Education, and Welfare, Secretary's Advisory Committee on Automated Personal Data Systems, *Records, Computers, and the Rights of Citizens: Report*, Cambridge, Mass.: MIT Press, 1973.

U.S. Privacy Protection Study Commission, *Personal Privacy in an Information Society: Report of the Privacy Protection Study Commission*, Washington, D.C., 1977.

Ware, Willis H., *Soviet Computer Technology: 1959*, Santa Monica, Calif.: RAND Corporation, RM-2541, March 1960.

————, *JOHNNIAC Eulogy*, Santa Monica, Calif.: RAND Corporation, P-3313, 1966.

————, *The Computer in Your Future*, Santa Monica, Calif.: RAND Corporation, P-3626, 1967a. As of February 26, 2008:
http://www.rand.org/pubs/papers/P3626/

————, *Security and Privacy in Computer Systems*, Santa Monica, Calif.: RAND Corporation, P-3544, 1967b. As of February 21, 2008:
http://www.rand.org/pubs/papers/P3544/

————, *Project RAND and Air Force Decisionmaking*, Santa Monica, Calif.: RAND Corporation, P-5737, 1976. As of February 21, 2008:
http://www.rand.org/pubs/papers/P5737/

————, *Security Controls for Computer Systems: Report of Defense Science Board Task Force on Computer Security*, Santa Monica, Calif.: RAND Corporation, R-609-1, 1979. As of February 21, 2008:
http://www.rand.org/pubs/reports/R609-1/

————, "Addendum: The Origin of the Phrase 'Code of Fair Information Practices,'" in U.S. Department of Health and Human Services, Task Force on the Privacy of Private-Sector Health Records, *Health Records: Social Needs and Personal Privacy: Washington, D.C., February 11–12, 1993, Omni Shoreham Hotel: Conference Proceedings*, Washington, D.C., 1993, pp. 50–51. As of February 26, 2008:
http://aspe.hhs.gov/pic/reports/ahrq/4441.pdf

————, *A Retrospective on the Criteria Movement*, Santa Monica, Calif.: RAND Corporation, P-7949, 1995. As of February 21, 2008:
http://www.rand.org/pubs/papers/P7949/

————, *The Cyber-Posture of the National Information Infrastructure*, Santa Monica, Calif.: RAND Corporation, MR-976-OSTP, 1998. As of February 21, 2008:
http://www.rand.org/pubs/monograph_reports/MR976/

————, "Introduction to Davies' Paper," *Computer Journal*, Vol. 44, No. 3, 2001, p. 151.

————, "The 1700 Main Street Building," *RAND Alumni Bulletin*, Vol. 39, Winter 2005, p. 6.

————, "RAND Ambassador Party," *RAND Alumni Bulletin*, Vol. 41, Summer 2006, p. 4.

Ware, Willis, Bill Gunning, Paul Armer, and Mort Bernstein, "Building Computers in 1953: The JOHNNIAC," lecture, Mountain View, Calif.: Computer History Museum, September 15, 1998. As of February 27, 2008, transcript:
http://www.computerhistory.org/events/lectures/johnniac_09151998/

Waterman, D. A., Robert H. Anderson, Frederick Hayes-Roth, Philip Klahr, Michael G. Martinson, and Stanley J. Rosenschein, *Design of a Rule-Oriented System for Implementing Expertise*, Santa Monica, Calif.: RAND Corporation, N-1158-1-ARPA, 1979. As of February 26, 2008:
http://www.rand.org/pubs/notes/N1158-1/

Waterman, D. A., and M. Peterson, "Rule-Based Models of Legal Expertise," *Proceedings of the First Annual National Conference on Artificial Intelligence*, Palo Alto, Calif., 1980, pp. 272–275.

Westbury, Judith, *UNIX Guide for Text Processor Users*, Santa Monica, Calif.: RAND Corporation, 1981.

———, *Formatting Guide for Text Processor Users*, Santa Monica, Calif.: RAND Corporation, 1982.

Williams, John D., "Comments on RAND Building Program," memorandum to RAND staff, December 26, 1950. As of February 25, 2008:
http://www.rand.org/publications/classics/building.html

Index

C